SUMMER OF BLAZE

Summer of Blaze

TANYA BECKWITH

Polar Sky Publishing LLC

| 1 |

Blaze Beaumont

Blaze wanted nothing more than to end her day with a nice warm bath and a glass of red wine. She had been sitting in meetings all day long and needed desperately to escape all the red tape and protocol needed to complete the project she was managing. She had stacks and stacks of research material and had been working late into the night all week long preparing for today's meetings. She found herself daydreaming at least twice, which was an indication that she'd had enough for today. She planned to go back to her office, gather her things, and leave by the back staircase so that she did not run into anyone on the way out. When she finally got back to her office, she practically collapsed in her chair. As she began gathering her things, she realized that she needed to speak to Parks about tomorrow's meeting. It was important for her to make sure his part of the presentation was ready. She buzzed her secretary.

"Diane—get Parks on the phone for me please."

"Sure, thing Blaze," Diane replied. Two minutes later Diane buzzed Blaze.

"Blaze, he's not picking up."

"Okay, thanks! Damn, I really need to see him before I leave. I'll just have to walk over to him," she sighed regretfully. She grabbed her files and began to take the walk over to Parks's office on the other side of the building.

As Blaze passed through the long corridors of the fifteenth floor where her office was located, there was a hub of activity with employees bustling around busy with their daily tasks, some were busy preparing for tomorrow's presentation to the Newman Group. Blaze was the lead executive responsible for acquiring what would be one of the biggest deals for the firm. To say she was as excited about the probable outcome would be an understatement. She walked down the corridor preoccupied with the coming events.

Blaze was an attractive woman who carried herself with pride. She had a natural stride when she walked, which was enhanced by her toned legs that she developed from years of dance training. She glided across the floor as she cordially greeted colleagues and staff along the way. Blaze was well-liked and respected by her co-workers, and she genuinely liked the people that she worked with. Her personality was inviting, but she never lost her professionalism in the office. She was as good as, and sometimes better than, her male counterparts and she worked hard to maintain that status. She was stylish and enjoyed her femininity, which was evident by the way that she dressed. Blaze prided herself on her style and she enjoyed being a woman; her clothes always complimented her shapely figure. She was tall and toned and commanded attention when she walked into a room, always with a confident entrance. Although not large, her breast was full and perky, and her tiny waist gave way to a sumptuous derriere usually appreciated by the opposite sex and envied by every other woman. She was the epitome of black beauty with warm brown skin, auburn colored hair, and full lips that dripped with sensuality. She had a broad nose, but that did not hinder her beauty one bit. On the contrary, it accentuated it. Her mother named her Blaze because she came into the world during a heat wave in June. Her delivery gave her mother quite a tough time as she agonized in labor for over twenty hours before Blaze entered the world. Her name always gave pause to wonder whenever she was introduced. People immediately thought she was an exotic dancer—that is until she opened her mouth revealing her vast knowledge and acute business acumen. It was important to her that she was well versed, so she kept abreast of the current trends in the worlds of marketing and business. She developed a love for reading at an early age and she read anything that she could get into her hands. She was able to quote verses from Faust to Zane and quoted bible verses on demand. Her mother told her that she started to read at eighteen months of age and preferred visits to the library or bookstores over other outings. Blaze never subscribed to what others thought she should be and this, without deliberateness, push her to the forefront of her career.

She carried herself very well in the business community, an attribute that she earned from hard work and long study. She possessed an attitude that commanded respect and exemplified dignity. She could be argumentative when she was challenged but would readily admit when she was wrong—sometimes. It was hard for her to relinquish control to anyone, which proved to be her biggest liability. She never wanted to be put in the position to be taken advantage of and she loathed vulnerability in women.

As Blaze approached the area where Parks's office was located, she became distracted by a commotion on the other side of the room. She quickly turned to see what was going on when suddenly she collided with someone who was turning the corridor at the same time as she. For a moment, everything was a blur. All of Blaze's files went up into the air. She somehow lost her footing and began to feel herself fall when two strong arms seemed to catch her in mid-air picking her up before she hit the floor. Blaze, a little dazed, suddenly found herself in the arms of a very tall and very handsome man who was holding her ever so close to him. She could feel his strong body pressed against her own. He smelled wonderful like the finest sandalwood soap and his warm, lightly minted breath aroused her senses in such a way she became lightheaded.

"Whoa, little lady! Are you alright?" he asked as he balanced her body.

Blaze just stared into his eyes which were bright and smiling with little crinkles at each corner. They were the color of cognac with specks of green and gold reflecting the light from where he stood as they danced. His smile revealed a slight dimple on his cheek. She was clearly caught off guard and at a loss for words. This was not appropriate for someone who needed to always be in control. He was the most handsome man that she had seen in a long, long time. He looked to be in his thirties and had to be at least six feet five inches tall. His smile was infectious, displaying an even row of straight, white teeth. His lips were thick and outlined with a finely trimmed mustache. He had a broad muscular chest that was hidden under a well-tailored and expensive navy-blue suit. Blaze thought that she had died and gone to heaven. He was truly magnificent. Seeing him brought visions to her mind of a fine African prince. Finally, after what seemed an eternity, Blaze collected herself and began to speak. She pulled herself away with a sudden jerk in anger at him as she realized how foolish she must look.

"Let me go, please!" she commanded.

The man just looked at her with a mischievous smile across his face as he watched her free herself from his grasp reluctantly letting her go. Blaze noticed that the room had become relatively quiet as all eyes were upon the two of them as they stood so close together in the middle of the aisle. Blaze turned to the onlookers with fire in her eyes. People began to scurry here and there trying to avoid her gaze. Her pale, pink, silk blouse had become undone during the commotion as her breasts threatened to reveal themselves from beneath a lacy camisole of the same hue. Her hair fell into her eyes. She brushed it away and then focused her attention on her skirt which was tightly hiked to just beneath her buttocks. As she pulled down her skirt and tried to button her blouse, the man continued to stand there smiling at her with delight at the sight she presented to him. Blaze looked at him with fury in her brown eyes. She spoke through clenched teeth.

"I hope you're amused Mr. uhhh?"

He extended his hand to her, smiling.

"Jack," he said, still smiling.

"Well Mr. um Jack," she emphasized Jack. "What are you gawking at?" Blaze asked sharply.

"Why I'm enjoying the view, and what a wonderful view it is," he continued to smile.

Blaze felt flushed at his gaze, which made her that much more uneasy. She did not like being compromised in any way.

"Please, allow me to help you," he suggested playfully.

"You most certainly may not," she said indignantly.

"Don't you think you've done enough for today?" she asked gathering her files.

Blaze seemed to amuse him as he chuckled at her frustration with him.

Holding his hands up and taking a few steps back, he teased her ever so slightly,

"Okay, I'm sorry," he said. "But will you at least let me help you with your things?" he asked bending to pick up what was left on the floor.

As they both attempted to reach down at the same time, they simultaneously stood up butting their heads together. As Blaze placed her hand upon her head, she noticed that once again his gaze was focused on her breasts. Immediately, she felt a tingle of excitement from the way that he looked at her. She put her hand to her throat as if to cover herself and mask her thoughts. As they both rubbed their heads, he reached down to pick up the rest of her things and handed them to her. His hand lingered upon hers longer than necessary.

"Thank you," she said as she abruptly pulled her hand back walking away from him.

"What's your hurry?" he asked leaning with one hand on a nearby table.

"I'm late for a meeting," she said lying not looking back.

"I feel as though I'm at a disadvantage," he shouted tilting his head to the side and admiring her walk. "You know my name, but I don't know yours," he yelled to her, his voice echoing as she went further from his sight.

"Blaze," she replied waving her hand in the air as she hurried away disappearing down and around the corridor.

"Hmm...Blaze...I like that," he mumbled to himself. "Blaze you are," he said smiling as he gathered himself and went on his way.

As Blaze turned the corridor and was sure she was no longer in his sight, she backed up against the wall and exhaled deeply. She needed a moment to collect herself after what just happened. She thought about how embarrassing it all was...falling into a stranger's arms—a handsome stranger at that.

Blaze thought to herself:

Damn, he's fine! The way he grabbed me up into his arms effortlessly as if I were a rag doll or somethin'. Girl, get a grip. I don't even know who he is. How dare he think that he can put his hands on me that way. He's probably used to women swoonin' all over him. Well, this honey is not about to join the brood. He can forget that!

Her hands traveled to her chest. She couldn't get his image out of her mind. She suddenly realized that she was standing in the corridor, alone, talking to herself, thinking of a man that she had never seen before. Blaze straightened herself up, smoothed her skirt, and made sure her blouse was buttoned as she continued her walk to Parks's office. Little did she know this wouldn't be the last she would see of the man she simply knew as Jack.

| 2 |

Parker Johnson

Parker Johnson was an up-and-coming executive at Brickhouse, Becker, and Shuman Inc. He was also the resident dog. Parks, as they called him, had a penchant for women. He managed to have slept with practically every woman in the administrative offices. Womanizing was an art to Parks who prided himself on knowing what women liked. He made it a pastime and he used every trick in the book to ingratiate himself right into their panties.

Parks had a gift for gab and could talk himself "into" and "out of" anything. He was also quite smart, which made him an asset to the firm. He studied hard and knew how to play the corporate game. He had a few underhanded tactics that he would use especially when there was a prize to be won—and he was determined to win at any cost.

Parks was the ultimate lady's man, brown-skinned, thin, and well-dressed. He knew fashion well and wore clothes like he just stepped out of a magazine. He knew what type of clothing complimented his thin frame and he enlisted the services of a stylist to ensure he was right on trend. He was an Alpha in college and his reputation on campus was incorrigible. He maintained that same deplorable behavior in business which earned him the dubious honor of top dog among his friends.

Blaze never liked Parks. To her, he was your typical womanizer, but in the professional arena, he was someone you wanted on your team. He was intelligent, sharp, and possessed an innate propensity for business. When Blaze arrived at his office, Parks was on the phone with one of his many conquests. He beckoned for Blaze to come in as he continued his conversation.

"Look baby, I'm sorry about last night. Things got crazy busy at the office, and I had to stay later than expected." He pointed to a chair suggesting Blaze take a seat.

"You know how much they rely on me here and how important my work is to me," he continued while simultaneously winking at Blaze.

"I promise I'll make it up to you suga'. Now be a good girl and put something sexy on for me. I'll see you later tonight. Yeah, don't I always take care of my baby?" He smiled.

Blaze wanted to barf at the arrogance of this man, but she managed to contain herself before speaking. Parks noticed her impatience as he ended his call. Blaze had taken a chair across from Parks as he watched every move that she made. Finally, he greeted Blaze with a phony welcome.

"Well princess, what brings you to my neck of the woods?"

"That was quite a performance," she said referring to his manner on the phone.

"Now, now, no need for you to be jealous my pretty. What ya got?" he asked abruptly changing the subject. Blaze raised an eyebrow before speaking.

"Just wanted to make sure that we have the final figures for the presentation tomorrow," Blaze replied.

"Yeah, I got them about an hour ago. Let me see what you have so we can compare them."

Parks and Blaze reviewed the figures. They adjusted the documents as necessary, and after an hour, they finalized the financial portion of the presentation. Blaze stood up and gathered her files.

"I'll get this over to Diane to incorporate with the current slides and have her set up the smart board run-through before tomorrow's meeting."

"Good...you do that, sweetheart." Parks smiled leaning back in his chair.

Blaze smirked at his remark and left his office annoyed by him. He folded his arms behind his head and his smile slowly turned into a sneer. Although he admired Blaze's body as she walked away, he despised the way she treated him. He shook his head and began talking aloud.

"There goes the high and mighty Ms. Blaze Beaumont. Seems to me she needs to be pulled down a peg or two. I guess I'll just have to see what I can do about making that happen."

| 3 |

Clayton Randolph Smith III

Since college, Blaze had been in a serious relationship with Clayton Randolph Smith III, Clay for short. He and Blaze met during their junior year. Clay was quite driven. He was a socially conscious and outspoken brother. They both attended the University of Maryland at the Eastern Shore during their undergraduate study where Clay was an activist and belonged to the African American Student Union. He was highly active in campus politics and initially met Blaze during a debate. He was also a Que and extremely popular on campus. The ladies said he was the epitome of tall, dark, and handsome.

Although he dated multiple women during his first two years of college, once he met Blaze all bets were off. He genuinely loved her from the start. Clay found her to be smart, opinionated, and extremely beautiful. He affectionately called her his rib because she was more like him than any other woman he had known. After graduation, they decided to live together while they both struggled with work and graduate school. In the beginning, it was heaven for them. They were both content with spending all their time with one another.

Blaze had never gone steady with any of the boys she knew in high school. Instead, she chose to spend her time reading books and enjoying her family. When she met Clay, she fell in love. He became the first man with whom she shared intimacy. They were truly into one another but vowed not to make any serious demands on their relationship. Blaze was sure that she was not ready for marriage, but Clay knew that Blaze was what he wanted in every way. When they both completed graduate school, Blaze immediately landed a position at Brickhouse, Becker, and Shuman Inc. She took advantage of a serious argument they had about their future that revealed she wanted her independence, so she got her own apartment. Clay did not like the idea, but he didn't want to lose Blaze completely. He finally accepted her decision and supported her career choices. Although quite independent she liked the benefits of having someone to come home to, so she gave Clay a key to her apartment. She would soon begin to regret that decision.

Blaze wanted to make partner at her firm while Clay was busy starting his own financial services company. He was practical and grounded while Blaze was free-spirited and creative. Clay worked for a mid-sized accounting firm in Philadelphia that often sent him on business trips to meetings with clients across the country. Lately, his trips out of town had become more frequent. Blaze did not mind it as much as he did. She needed that time apart from Clay. She loved Clay, but she was not sure about marrying him. She wanted something more than just being Clayton Randolph Smith III's wife. She was not sure what she was looking for in a lifelong relationship and even the sound of that gave her cause for apprehension. She did not want to hurt Clay, but she was sure about what she did not want to be doing for the rest of her life.

By the time Blaze arrived home from the office, Clay was already there. She walked in to find a wonderful smell coming from the kitchen.

"Hey babe, how was your day?" Clay asked.

"Fantastic," she replied as she leaned in for a kiss. Her face instantly displayed excitement.

"I think we are gonna nail the Newman account."

"Ah babe, that's great news! I know how much you wanted that account." He placed both hands on her shoulders.

"Yeah, and Sam seemed really confident that we're going to get it too," Blaze added.

"As well he should be after you worked so hard to acquire this one." Blaze took off her jacket and kicked off her shoes. She pulled up her skirt and straddled Clay as he sat on the sofa.

"What'd you want to do tonight?" Clay asked as he caressed her body and fondled her breast.

"Clay, stop and be serious," Blaze replied as she tried to move away from his grip. Clay began to kiss her neck and run his tongue along the length of her.

"What ya want to do?" he asked again as he whispered in her ear. She tried to get away again, but this time not as aggressively as she began to succumb to his touch.

"I'm hungry," she added.

Clay grabbed both cheeks of her behind in his hand and with the other unfastened her bra. As her bra fell away from her breast, her nipples were taut and ripe. She arched her back exposing them even more.

"I have something for you—don't you want to see what I got for you?" Clay asked as he whispered in her ear again.

He gently kissed each nipple very aware of the effect this had on her. Blaze began to moan with desire and delight in what he was doing. He was erect against her thigh, and his breath was warm and wet against her skin. He looked up at her and pulled her to him closer as he kissed her mouth which was slightly open. Clay played in her mouth with his tongue, and she licked at his lip with hers. To Clay, Blaze was a fine instrument, and he played her like an impresario. Her skirt was completely up around her waist and her top exposed both breasts completely now. She was so wet that her thong was drenched with the dew from her lust, and she began to gyrate against Clay with a rhythmic motion as she moved her fingers to grasp the shaft of his penis.

"Oh, Clay," she moaned. "I want what you have for me baby—so please give it to me right now." Blaze slid her hands up and down his penis.

Clay flipped Blaze over and began to bite her as he ran his hands up between her legs to her navel and then along the base of her belly until he found that hidden treasure throbbing and swelling waiting for his lips to taste and caress it. Blaze moaned loudly as Clay gently but firmly touched her emitting excitement from her everywhere. He flipped her to her back again and this time as he opened her legs he bent down and placed his warm, wet, thick lips upon her and licked gently sucking at her clit. She was so overcome with emotions, she wanted to explode. She pulled him down closer to her and he entered her. His strong erect penis finding its way to her pleasure point as she wrapped her long, lean legs around him. Their bodies united in a rhythm of ecstasy and pleasure as they made love starting on the sofa, then the floor, and finally, the bed. When they climaxed, they were both exhausted panting and sweating in each other's arms. After some time went by, Clay went to the kitchen to check on dinner. He plated the pasta primavera while Blaze slept. She awoke to candles, wine, and dinner with her handsome and loving man by her side.

"What did I do to deserve you?" she asked Clay as he sat beside her.

"I'm not sure. I just hope you will always feel this way!" Clay smiled and focused his attention on Blaze's eyes.

Blaze smiled back and began to eat her dinner. She knew she was lucky to have a man as committed to her as Clay. They lounged on the bed and talked before Clay disappeared into the shower. Blaze lay on the bed thinking about the events of the day. Slowly an image began to invade her thoughts and she could not help but wonder about Mr. Jack, the man who so abruptly collided into her life without warning, leaving her curious about him and wondering what he was doing at that very moment.

| 4 |

Oh, craps!

The day finally arrived for the meeting with the Newman group and Blaze was anxious about the meeting. She knew she had to be sharp and very well prepared. She also had a particular style of clothing she wanted to wear, so she chose her attire carefully. She wanted to be taken seriously, but she was not about to compromise her femininity to do so. None of that stodgy navy-blue pantsuit and striped shirt look for her—though she previously wore those on various occasions. She decided on a two-piece, silk blend, suit in a soft beige color for the meeting. She added a cream silk shirt and taupe pumps to complete her look. The pencil skirt fit perfectly and was the appropriate length for business hitting her just below the knee. A single strand of pearls adorned her neck which complimented her attire beautifully giving her a feminine, but smart, look. She pinned her hair up and wore just a touch of lip gloss and mascara to accentuate her natural beauty. Blaze knew that feeling good about herself gave her confidence, and that, coupled with her innate sense for business would be the formula she needed to ace the presentation and place the Newman account in her lap. She took one last look of approval and being pleased with what she saw she headed out to the office.

Blaze arrived at the office earlier than usual. She wanted to get a head start on her meeting and go over any last-minute details with Diane and Parks. By eight-thirty everything was in place, the presentation was in the system, and Blaze was ready to go. She was leading the presentation and she was responsible for pitching most of the proposal. This account was her baby as she so protectively claimed it to be. By nine o'clock, all parties were assembled in the conference room and Blaze was working her way around the room talking with co-workers, members of the legal team, and of course, her team members.

The conference room was located on the south side of the building facing the pier where Sam docked the company boat. The room was a mixture of rich tastes with mahogany tables and leather chairs, luxurious Italian leather sofas, and glass tables trimmed in bronze. The walls were decorated very tastefully with African artwork commissioned by a prominent gallery in downtown Philadelphia. One side of the room presented the most beautiful view of the pier and Delaware Riverfront since the windows extended from the ceiling to the floor and across the entire room. Sam purchased and renovated the building a few years ago specifically because he liked being near the water and was in love with the formal ballroom opting to use it for fundraisers and company events.

Groups of people were already seated along the long mahogany table, while others who occupied a more supportive role in the company were seated in the leather chairs that were lined along the chair rail. The conference room was located on the top floor of the building with the focus of the room being a skylight that sat high in the twelve-foot ceiling. During cooler months, the skylight was opened to infuse light that created an ambiance for business meetings and negotiations. At night when the company hosted evening events the room gave way to a glimpse at the moon when full and the sky when it was lit up with stars.

Front desk security informed Blaze when the Newmans arrived. They needed to be processed and given security badges to enter the upper floors of the building. Blaze took her seat at the table so as not to appear too anxious once they reached the conference room. Most of the team from the Newman group was already in place waiting for the principal team to arrive. From the corridor, Blaze could hear Sam talking as they approached the conference room. Blaze was seated with her back to the conference room door entrance. She stood up and turned around to greet the entourage as they entered the room. She extended her hand when introduced to Thaddeus Newman, the CEO of the corporation, complimenting him on his recent acquisition of Ackerman and Smith which was a manufacturing company that designed chassis for the race car industry. The Newmans would make a huge bundle on that acquisition alone. He, too, was familiar with her work and commented on her ability to land some important accounts on the East Coast.

"Well, it's good to finally meet you, Blaze," Thaddeus said. "I've been hearing nothing but great things about your work. I was happy to hear that you were on this team and would be potentially collaborating with us."

"Well thank you, Thaddeus. I'm looking forward to our collaboration," she said with a smile.

"Ms. Beaumont, this is my son Jack. Jack, meet Blaze Beaumont the senior account executive for Brickhouse, Becker, and Shuman Inc."

Blaze was shocked when she realized that she was suddenly face-to-face with the very man that she had collided with the day before. There he was in all his splendor smiling that broad smile showing those straight, white, teeth and extending his hand mischievously.

"Hello, Ms. Beaumont. It's a pleasure to see you again so soon," Jack said as he took Blaze's hand in both of his.

He seemed to be enjoying her discovery and was aware of the discomfort that it placed upon her. He merely held her hand into his own for what seemed to be forever. Blaze felt awkward under his gaze. He was looking at her with that same playful smile he had on his face the day before. Blaze couldn't believe that she didn't put two and two together yesterday after nearly knocking her client down and being rude in the process. When she was finally able to gather herself, she withdrew her hand and tried to focus on regrouping. She needed to regain her resolve and begin the presentation.

Jack was handsome. There was no doubt about that. He was wearing a dark grey suit, a white shirt, and a red, grey, and blue striped tie. His hands were manicured and strong with long thick fingers. His skin was smooth and rich like fine milk chocolate as he stood there confident and playful at the same time. As he walked away to be seated, he greeted several individuals in the room giving each his undivided attention. He lingered over the women when he spoke, and from their expressions, making each one feel special. Finally, he took his seat as Blaze waited for her cue to begin. As she stood to begin the presentation, all eyes were upon her. She tried to avoid the gaze of one.

Jack was mesmerizing to her, and she found herself drawn to him. During the meeting, he asked her many questions maintaining an air of professionalism the whole time. He was wise, educated, and a stickler for detail. The meeting lasted for two and a half hours. When the meeting was about to conclude, both Sam and Thaddeus spoke briefly about the benefits of their collaboration. Blaze stood up to walk around the table shaking hands and speaking with several of those in attendance. Jack, too, was engaged in conversation having his back to Blaze. One by one the members of the meeting left the conference room. Sam and Thaddeus had long since left together promising to meet on the golf course in the next few weeks. Blaze began to walk towards the chair where she had been sitting to gather her things. She noticed that she was the only one left in the room. She sat down for a moment making notes and mentally reviewing the meeting. Just then she heard someone emerge from the restroom. It was Jack Newman.

"So, you're still here?" he asked feigning ignorance.

"As well you are," Blaze returned.

"Good meeting!" Jack complimented.

"Thank you, Mr. Newman. It's good to know you approve."

"Please, call me Jack. Everyone does," he said through a dimpled smile.

"Well Jack," Blaze said as she stood up and extended her hand to leave the room. "It was good to see you again."

"Are you in a hurry, Ms. Beaumont?" Blaze stopped and looked at him.

"Well, I do have to make some calls and get some notes to my assistant."

"Why don't we do lunch?" Jack proposed.

"I'm sorry, but I'm not available Mr. Newman," Blaze answered too quickly.

"I wasn't asking you to elope with me Ms. Beaumont—just a simple business lunch to go over the account and get better acquainted—after all, we may very well be working together."

"I ummm—well, sure I can alter my schedule for lunch today," Blaze said on second thought. She did not want to cause any conflict and jeopardize the account. Jack was the heir to the Newman group, and she needed to have a good working relationship with him.

"Good," Jack said. "Do you know Dominick's on 3rd?"

"Yes, of course, I do know it."

"Good, let's say one?"

"One is fine," Blaze replied.

Jack smiled and then walked out of the room and down the corridor. Blaze stood there for a few minutes more and then she went back to her office. She walked in and picked up her messages from Diane. There was a call from Clay.

Blaze went into her office and closed the door. She immediately called Clay back. He answered the phone immediately.

"Hey, baby! How's my girl?"

"I'm fine. How are you?" she asked propping her feet up on the desk.

"Good, baby. How was the meeting?"

"I think it went well," she said.

"Good! Then we can have a nice lunch together."

"Clay, I can't. I'm meeting some of the board members in a few minutes. This will probably take a few hours."

"Well, you know I'm gonna be out of town for a few days and I thought we could spend the afternoon together before I left." He hesitated for a second and then continued. "Look, baby. I understand." Clay was disappointed, but he was also trying to be understanding.

"I'll make it up to you later," Blaze said playfully.

"Now that's what I'm talkin' bout," Clay said before he hung up. Blaze hung up too feeling guilty that she had lied to Clay.

'Now why didn't I just tell him the truth?' Blaze asked herself.

Blaze sat in her chair smiling at her exchange with Clay. She adored him and they had so much fun together. If only he didn't want to be so serious and enjoyed their relationship as it was. He would never understand her attraction to Jack, but of course, few men would understand their woman finding another man interesting.

Blaze looked at her gold Cartier watch which was a gift from Clay for her last birthday. It was nearly noon, and she had a few things to do before leaving for lunch. It was an unusually warm and beautiful day in May, and the pier was busy with people coming and going. Some were just idling away the hours by the water. She decided to walk to Dominick's which was not that far from the office. She took her time enjoying the sights and doing some window shopping along the way. When she arrived at Dominick's, Jack was waiting there for her. His tie was loosened as he stood there so proudly talking with the bartender. He leaned against the bar with his jacket open as he shared a joke with the bartender. They were having a good laugh about something, seemingly very funny to them both. Jack's smile was infectious. He was so damn fine it was breathtaking. Blaze stood there watching him as he was being himself—the carefree bachelor so unaware of his magnetism. After a few moments, he noticed Blaze at the door and immediately walked toward her. He began smiling and greeted her enthusiastically.

"So, you made it?" he asked as if surprised.

"I did. I decide to walk a bit and window shop along the way."

"You didn't buy anything?"

"No, but I was tempted," she smiled.

"Come on, we're seated out on the patio. Bobby, could you send our drinks out?" he asked the bartender.

"What would you like?" he asked Blaze as an afterthought.

"McCallum twenty-five with a twist please."

"Wow! A woman with a distinctive taste, I like that," Jack stated as he led her out to the patio.

Dominick's was a small 1960's style café with twenty tables inside and ten on the patio. The patio was shaded with beautiful foliage. It had brick walkways, small intimate tables with white tablecloths, and a mixture of classical music played over hidden speakers. Jack pulled a chair out for Blaze to sit in and then he sat down himself. The warm sun playfully streamed in and out onto the patio area between the green and white awnings that shaded the diners enjoying their meals. A waiter walked over to their table. Jack stood up to give him a warm greeting.

"Dom, how are you, man?" Jack asked as he shook the man's hand and patted him on the back.

"I'm good, Jack—where you a been? Not seen you for some time now."

"I know. They have been keeping me busy, so I haven't been in town much lately."

"Well, it's good to see you. How is ya papa? Tell him I said he owes me a game real soon," Dominick chuckled.

"I'll tell him for sure, Dom. He'll be anxious to call you on that."

"Dom this is Blaze Beaumont. Blaze this is Dominick Taliaferro."

"Pleasure to meet you, Dom," Blaze said extending her hand. "I love your restaurant."

Dominick took her hand in his and kissed it.

"Choi Bella," Dom said. "She's beautiful, Jack!" Blaze blushed as Jack looked at her smiling as he answered Dom.

"Well although I had nothing to do with it, yes, she is beautiful."

Dominick and Jack talked for a few minutes more and then Dominick disappeared in the back promising to make them something delightful for lunch.

"So how do you know Dominick?" Blaze asked Jack curiously.

"My father met Dominick when he was stationed overseas. They became exceptionally good friends. When my dad came back to the states, he helped Dominick and his family to come to America. When he got here, dad and Dominick worked together on a construction project, and years later my dad started his company and Dom opened his first restaurant. We practically grew up eating at

Dom's house or restaurant as much as we did at home. Our families remained friends through the years. He was best man at my dad's wedding."

"Wow, what a history!" Blaze was astonished.

"So, Blaze what about you?" Jack asked interestedly.

Blaze was taken off-guard by the question, "What do you mean?"

"I mean, tell me something about yourself that doesn't have to do with work."

"Well, I'm the youngest of four kids; there's my brother Kush and two sisters, Sydney and Peyton. My mother is a single parent and has been one since my father died when she was carrying me. I did my undergrad at the University of Maryland Eastern Shore and attended graduate school at the University of Pennsylvania. Music is my passion. I mostly enjoy jazz and anything to do with the arts. You know, dance, music concerts, and things like that."

"I'm a big music fan myself," Jack replied.

"Any particular artists come to mind?" Blaze was really curious. She continued, "I enjoy anything from the black experience in music days; you know Black Birds, War, Mandrill, Lonnie Liston Smith that sort of thing."

"Oh, then you'll really enjoy my collection since I have everything from that era."

"Get out!" Blaze blurted in shock.

Jack laughed at her surprise that he would have an interest in the same music as she did. After she finished her cocktail, Blaze began to relax a bit more around Jack. He was entertaining and knowledgeable about everything from sports to post-modern art. Blaze found herself laughing and enjoying his stories. His smile was so warm and inviting and she could not help thinking that he was so damn sexy. His tie was now completely removed, and his shirt was slightly opened at the neck revealing a bit of his chest. When he moved his muscles flexed beneath the stark white of his shirt promising a well-honed physique. They talked entirely through their meal and lingered over the dessert that they shared of cheesecake drizzled with dark chocolate. It was half past three and they were still talking. Blaze excused herself to go to the restroom as Jack stood up in a gentlemanly fashion. When she got to the restroom, she looked at herself in the mirror as she applied a fresh coat of lip-gloss while thinking about Jack. She began to speak softly to herself:

"What are you doing girl? You're supposed to be sealing the deal with Newman, but instead, you're flirting with and enjoying the youngest son as if you're on a date. Get a grip and get back out there and get the deal sealed."

When Blaze returned to the table Jack had ordered another round of drinks for them.

"Oh, I really shouldn't drink anything else," Blaze said as she sat down. Jack just looked at her as if he already knew the deal. He sat back in his chair, hands at his side looking at Blaze.

"So, you leave me for a minute, and I lose you."

"What do you mean, lose me?" Blaze asked becoming uneasy at his words.

"Well, you left here Blaze, the woman, and came back Ms. Beaumont the shark."

"Well, isn't that the purpose of this meeting?" Blaze asked sarcastically.

Jack paused and thought for a moment. *So, she wants to play games, does she? Well, let's see how well Miss all business can keep up.*

"Yes, you're absolutely right. So why don't we get down to business," Jack replied.

This time there was no smile, but a stern look and body language that confirmed he was not pleased. His jaw was tight as he clenched his teeth and a wrinkle formed across his brow.

"When do you propose to deliver a final draft to me for the campaign?" Jack asked.

"Well, I can have it in your office by next Friday."

"I need it by the end of this week," Jack said flatly. "Is that feasible, Ms. Beaumont?"

"I would need a little more time than that, Jack. Next Wednesday by close of business would be better," Blaze stated matter-of-factly.

"Good. Next Wednesday I'll expect a copy in my office. Bobby, can you bring me the check?" Jack asked abruptly.

Jack was clearly annoyed that Blaze could turn herself off and on with him so easily. Blaze could see her error in judgment in dealing with him. She wanted to salvage the day, but she did not know how to go about it. She thought about something that Jack had said earlier and it struck a chord in her. Jack was signing the bill while Blaze contemplated her next move.

"Craps!"

Jack looked up from the table with a quizzical expression, "What?" Jack asked suddenly amused at her language.

"I'm really very good at Craps," Blaze replied. Jack looked at Blaze and a smile slowly appeared across his face.

"You shoot Craps?"

"That's right," Blaze answered confidently. Jack let out a huge laugh and Blaze could not help but laugh too.

"What's so funny? You don't think I can play."

"No, I don't!"

"Well, I can…and I bet I can beat you."

"Beat me? Girl, do you know who you talkin' to?"

"No! Who?" she asked flippantly.

"Girl, I practically financed my education shooting craps."

"Oh yeah? Like I'm really convinced of that," Blaze said sarcastically.

"Look, I know how to remedy this situation."

"Oh yeah? How?"

"Come with me to Atlantic City!" Jack propositioned.

"What?"

"Come to A.C. with me and then we'll see who beats who."

"I'm not going to A.C. with you."

"Why not...what's wrong with me?" Jack asked with a juvenile expression on his face. He also opened his jacket and displayed himself to her.

Chuckling, Blaze replied, "Nothing's wrong with you—I'm just not going to A.C. with you."

"You chicken?" Jack asked.

"No, but tell me why I should go anywhere with you?"

"Cause it'll be fun, and I think you need to back up your words. Tell you what...you come to A.C. with me, and I'll extend the deadline for you to submit your proposal until next Friday."

"You're gonna wager our business relationship on a game of craps?"

"Well not exactly...but it will give you time if you win." Blaze quickly thought about Jack's proposal.

"You're on!" Blaze was not one to turn down a challenge.

"Thursday night, I'll pick you up at six."

"Great!" Blaze gladly accepted the challenge. She grabbed her jacket and briefcase following Jack to the door. "Thank you for lunch Jack. It was a great afternoon." Blaze extended her hand.

"For me too," Jack smiled and returned the gesture happily shaking Blaze's hand.

"See ya Thursday, Ace," she said flippantly as she walked down the street. Jack watched her walk away and smiled.

He thought to himself, *'This is going to be very interesting; very interesting indeed!'*

| 5 |

Jack Newman

Jack Newman was the heir apparent to a multimillion-dollar empire. He was the youngest of the Newman clan and the most promising of all the siblings. The Newman children were a spoiled and brazen bunch, but their parents made sure they were raised to be good, productive individuals. Thaddeus wanted his kids to have the best of everything denying them very little. He was raised in an orphanage, never knowing his own parents, so family was of the greatest importance to him. He married a socialite, Kathryn "Kate" Flemington, whom he met while teaching tennis at a well-known tennis camp in 1970. He was floored by her beauty and charm, and he instantly fell in love with her. They married in a lavish ceremony in 1971 and started their family right away. Rumor has it that Kate was pregnant, and Thaddeus did not have much of a choice but to marry her. Her father would not have it any other way. He raised his daughter to be treated like a princess and expected her to marry well. When she brought Thaddeus home, James was disappointed in her choice. But Kate would have her way and Thaddeus would win him over so, James took Thaddeus under his wing and showed him everything about running the family business. Thaddeus was a natural, and soon he began acquiring small companies, restructuring them, and then selling them for ten times the price that he invested in them. Thaddeus was always careful to retain as much of the original staff as possible emphasizing the importance of family and community. This made James proud and Thaddeus an extraordinarily rich man. Their firstborn was named James after Kate's father. Then three more children followed each year after that, Michael, Elizabeth, and finally Jack.

Jackson Ellis Newman was a born athlete. He could throw a football by the time he was two. His father coached him right through grade school until he made All-City Champion in high school. Jack was active in sports throughout all his years in school and received a football scholarship to Stanford University. He majored in finance and marketing in college and received his MBA from Wharton in 2000. Jack had an All-American kind of look. He was tall, dark, and handsome. He had big brown eyes... the color of cognac with flecks of gold that seemed to sparkle when he smiled...a strong jawline and a dimple that showed up on his left cheek. His skin was smooth, and his hair was thick and cut close to his head. He had broad shoulders and a strong, muscular chest which tapered to a lean waist and six-packed abs. Jack was quite popular, especially with the ladies. He always had an entourage of women competing for his attention but was never serious about any of them.

Thaddeus stayed on his sons about securing a first-rate education that would guarantee them a choice lifestyle and substantial earning potential. His philosophy to his children was to get the finest education and let nothing supersede their dedication to being successful. While Thaddeus tended to the children's material needs, Kate nurtured their spiritual side raising them in the church and preparing them for life through a Christian upbringing. Jack's mother, however, wanted her sons to be married properly and to the right pedigree. Those were the words she used to describe how she felt about her children and marriage. On numerous occasions, she tried to pair Jack with one of her debutante choices, but Jack would have none of it. He adored his mother and because he was the baby of the family, Kate doted on him allowing his exception. Her other children were defiant and sometimes wild, but Jack was more considerate and had a special place in her heart. He was always courteous to his mother and maintained a well-mannered, although fun-loving character that everyone seemed to love. He had his share of incidents—some costing the Newman's a pretty penny—but he matured into a well-established person, after all.

Jack was having too much fun with no thoughts of settling down. He was, however, serious about his role as Vice President of Operations at Newman, and he made considerable contributions to the corporation's equity. Of all the areas under the Newman umbrella, Jack was most accomplished with mergers and acquisitions and had acquired numerous holdings complimenting his portfolio. He loved the chase and the final conquest, so falling in love or getting married was the furthest thing from his mind. Jack had not thought much about any of the women he dated; he just liked having fun. He was not the type to hang out at the clubs, but he went out with his boys on occasion. He was usually the one the women gravitated toward. Sometimes he would leave with someone, but most times he just enjoyed himself and ended up going home alone. He liked it that way. He hadn't spent much time thinking about any woman; that is until he met Blaze Beaumont. She was like no one he had ever met...a bonified challenge in his eyes. He liked her drive, her enthusiasm, and her dedication to detail. He enjoyed toying with her, but there was something more there that he had not seen in the others. He found himself thinking about her after they parted from having lunch. She was talented and extremely beautiful, not to mention, downright sexy. Their next meeting would be interesting. Jack was looking forward to it.

| 6 |

Heads up!

Blaze woke up the next morning and ran her usual three miles before heading to work. She arrived at seven as usual. While walking into her office, she became startled when she suddenly heard a voice bellowing at her.

"Blaze, that you? Come on in here for a minute," was the command. Blaze recognized Sam's voice immediately and started her way to his office.

"Good morning! You're here early," Blaze said as she entered the room.

"Sit down, I want to talk to you," Sam said.

"Sounds serious, what's up?"

"I want to make sure that you are on point with everything regarding the Newman account. You know that Thad thinks you're dynamite, but he won't hesitate to call you on it if you don't give him one hundred percent on this account."

"Sam, I'm on it. This is my baby, and you know how much time I've put into this project. Don't worry boss, I won't let you or Thaddeus Newman down," Blaze emphasized.

"I know that you had lunch with Jack yesterday."

Although it was no secret, Blaze was still a little shocked that Sam knew about the lunch with Jack.

"Watch out for him. He's charming no doubt, but don't underestimate his ability to become a tyrant when it comes to business," Sam commented as he walked to the window and peered down at the docks.

"Now what did you think that the lunch was all about Sam? It was a chance for me to get a better idea about Jack and how his mind works. Believe me, I never lost sight of why I was there. That was the only thing on my mind," Blaze retorted. Blaze thought to herself:

'Oh, if only that were true. It wasn't easy to sit there with him and not fantasize about him. I could not help but notice his hands were so strong and so big. A girl could get lost in hands like that, not to mention the other implications.'

"Blaze, do you agree?" Sam asked as he looked at her funny.

"Uh—oh yes, Sam," Blaze stated as she blushed at her thoughts.

"Are you listening to me? I was just saying that Jack has a reputation for being a lady's man, so don't get caught up in the hype."

"Don't worry about me, Sam. I'll be my usual professional self," Blaze assured him. They talked for a few more minutes before Sam's secretary interrupted them.

"Welp! I gotta get going!" Sam stood up.

"No problem! I'll see you later." Blaze made her way out of Sam's office and down the hall into her own. Sam smiled as she left the room. He had confidence in Blaze, and he had plans for her career. He was already considering her for a promotion that she was unaware of but first came the Newman account.

| 7 |

Xavier Hollander

Xavier Hollander was a Senior Account Manager at Brickhouse, Becker, and Shuman Inc. X, as everyone called him, worked for the company for two years and had extremely ambitious standards and goals for himself. He graduated Suma Cum Laude from a prestigious University, with a degree in marketing and acquired his master's at another well-known and well-respected University. He intended to take his career as far as it would go at Brickhouse, Becker, and Shuman Inc. with designs to acquire a board seat with the prestigious company. He had great ambitions and had no qualms about how to fulfill his goals. He had good taste in almost everything. His style was impeccable, and he loved the finer things in life. His background was from humble beginnings, but he intended to never revisit anything that had to do with his past. X was raised by his mother, a single parent, who worked hard to build a good life for her and her young son. Although times were tough for them, his mother managed to keep a roof over their heads and food on the table. She worked two jobs and went to school at night to acquire a bachelor's degree in science and later nursing school. Betty learned how to attach herself to mentors and kept good relationships with her professors. Through her efforts, she managed to get her license as a registered nurse and then went on to get a Ph.D. She found a lucrative career in writing and developing grants. She soon became the principal investigator on many of the grants she had written, earning her a substantial salary resulting in a good living. Her first grant was worth well over 5 million dollars.

Betty wanted her son to become a doctor, but X did not like that idea. He knew he was creative, and he loved building client relationships and developing top-notch advertising campaigns. He bought several lucrative accounts to Brickhouse, Becker, and Shuman Inc., generating millions for the company. X was downright conceited; he was a legend in his own mind. When he joined the company, he was attracted to Blaze instantly. They hit it off right away. For a brief moment, he was interested in dating her but quickly realized that they had nothing in common romantically and everything in common as friends. X was a high-yellow complexion with black curly hair.

X lived in Olde City Philadelphia in a huge and very posh loft-style apartment, which was both immaculate and stylishly decorated. He enjoyed entertaining friends at home, with his expansive living area and large decked roof. He was notorious for throwing lavish parties where everyone who was anyone would be in attendance. Whatever the holiday, you can bet X was having a party. Blaze was a permanent fixture at all of X's gatherings. She would help him with the themes and often play hostess. If you were invited to an X party, then you could consider yourself on the A list. Women were everywhere at these events. He liked to show off his female friends. Some were former lovers, while others were mere associates; still there remained a few that he called genuine friends—Blaze just happened to be one of them.

At work, X was quite a different person than he was in a social setting. He was clever and ingratiated himself for a perfect position within the firm. He worked with Blaze on the Newman account, helping with the research, and crunching the numbers to develop an outstanding pre-and post-plan of action. He was a hard worker and was not opposed to doing whatever was required to get the job done.

"Hey there sunshine, haven't seen you all day," X said with a big, wide grin as he stood in the doorway of Blaze's office.

"Hey yourself, what are you up to?" she asked.

"Just got in! Wanted to make sure we're straight on the Newman account."

"I am! I went over the final numbers with Parks last night, so I think we're good."

"I thought we might have some time to go over the balance sheets later over a bite to eat or something."

"Can't do it tonight, I promised Jack that I'd have everything over to him by next Friday and most of this has to go to the printers tonight." Blaze pointed to a stack of papers.

"And how is Master Jack?" X asked sarcastically.

"He's okay I guess...why you askin' me like I know what he's up to or something?" Blaze's indignant response sparked off an alarm with X.

"Wow, did I hit a chord? I know you ain't goin' there?"

"What are you talkin' about?"

"You know exactly what I'm talking about? You have been checking out Sir Jack. Just watch yourself. That boy got a rep!"

"Don't worry about me. I've seen how guys like Jack Newman operate. I'm quite professional and know how to handle myself thank you very much!"

X gave Blaze a knowing look like he could read her mind or something.

"Okay, sunshine! Just remember what I said." X replied before leaving Blaze's office.

"Don't you worry, X. I've got this," she said confidently.

What a contradiction since all Blaze could think about was her trip to A.C. with Jack and what she was going to wear.

| 8 |

It's a date!

The next day Blaze worked long and hard to finalize the proposal for review by the team and Sam so she could have everything ready for delivery to Jack's office by the following Friday. It was early Thursday afternoon, and Blaze was finally ready to call it a day and go home to change for her trip to A.C. with Jack. She had been having second thoughts about going with him. She began to get nervous and decided to call him and cancel. As soon as she arrived home, she started to pick up the receiver to call him, but the phone rang instead. Blaze looked at the receiver in her hand as she answered the call.

"Hello?"

"Hey there. I thought I might catch you at home."

It was Jack.

'*Damn,*' Blaze thought to herself.

"So, you did...how are you?" she asked with apprehension.

"Good. Really good, and you?"

"I'm okay," she murmured half-heartedly.

"Then why do I feel like I'm calling at a bad time or that you're not happy to hear from me?" Jack was curious.

"Oh no. Nothing like that." Blaze tried to sound convincing.

"So...are we still on for the shore?"

"Well, I was thinking...I just got home and—"

"Aht Aht! I'm not having any of that. We had a deal, and I won't let you go back on your good word...that is unless you don't think you can win." He knew just what to say to get her going.

"Sounds like you're hoping that I'll back out so you can save face," Blaze said with a challenge. Jack burst into laughter.

"You're something else! I'm gonna keep my eye on you. Slick...very slick." They both began to laugh.

"I'll be there in twenty to pick you up."

"Make it thirty and not a minute sooner," Blaze replied before she hung up the phone not giving Jack a chance to say anything else.

Suddenly, Blaze was excited to go on this outing with Jack. She knew that Clay would be out of town for the next few days, so she took a quick shower and changed into a pair of black pants with a matching crop jacket that showed every curve on her sexy body. She decided on a coral knit top that complimented her skin and hair color and a pair of six-inch strappy black heels. She needed little or no makeup with her smooth clear skin. The only thing she added was a little mascara and a tinted lip gloss. She let her hair fall loosely around her shoulders not caring that it was a bit wild. She grabbed a black and white silk scarf from her drawer tying it to her black handbag. She turned off the lights and locked the door. She started down the hallway and got on the elevator determined to be downstairs before Jack arrived. Looking at herself in the mirrored doors of the elevator, Blaze was pleased with what she saw.

When she got off the elevator and walked out of the door, much to her surprise Jack was waiting for her. There he was tall and handsome smiling that million-dollar smile. He was casually dressed in jeans, a sweater, and a black leather jacket. Smooth jazz softly resonated from the interior of his large Cadillac truck as he leaned against the vehicle in a relaxed posture. His leg was crossed over the other as he smiled while talking into the phone. When he saw Blaze approach the truck, he immediately ended the call. Jack thought to himself as he watched Blaze walk towards him. *'My, my, my...She is one sweet, sexy thing.'*

"Hi Jack," Blaze said as she stood in front of him. "I didn't expect you to be here yet."

Jack didn't say a word. He just looked at her and smiled a mischievous smile.

"What? What is it? Is something wrong," Blaze was genuinely puzzled by Jack's silence.

"Wow...I mean no, nothing's wrong," Jack hunched his shoulders and shook his head in appreciation. "You look fantastic!"

"Why thank you, Jack," Blaze replied playfully.

"I thought my wig was coming off or something," she said patting her hair on the side.

Startled by her comment, Jack's eyes widened in disbelief.

"That's a wig?" he asked surprisedly. Blaze just laughed.

"Yeah, just pull it and see." She grabbed Jack's hand and laid it upon her auburn hair and offered it for Jack to pull. When he frowned in hesitation, she started to laugh again.

"You should see the expression on your face." Blaze continued to laugh. Jack put his fingers through her hair.

"Oh man, I thought you were serious for a minute. If there's anything I can't stand, it's hair weaves," he said relieved.

"What do you have against weaves?" Blaze asked.

"Well, truly nothing in general. I just like running my fingers through the real thing."

"Oh," Blaze replied—her mind wandering as she thought how much she liked having her hair pulled during sex. Her expression was a bit revealing as Jack decided against commenting not wanting to make her uncomfortable. Instead, he opened the door for her to get in the truck.

"Ready to go?" he asked.

"Yes, ready and anxious to win some money," Blaze replied as he closed the door and walked around to the driver's side removing his jacket as he went. Although the windows were down, Blaze reached over to unlock the door for him. Jack smiled as he remembered a scene from a particular film when the young girl opened the car door for the lead character in the movie. Blaze also liked that scene from the movie as well, but she was puzzled as to why she did that. She felt a little awkward afterward since she never even did that for Clay.

| 9 |

Amazing Atlantic City

The ride to Atlantic City was so exhilarating. They were completely engaged with one another with not a moment of silence or awkwardness. They listened to jazz, reggae, and even some blues. They talked about many different subjects including some stories about their upbringings. Blaze began to feel comfortable with Jack and her body language confirmed it. He had a cooler installed in the back of his truck. It was filled with water, champagne, and beer. Blaze grabbed a beer and after a few sips became her flirtatious self with him. She took off her jacket and then her shoes, enjoying the luxury of Jack's truck. She debated him when warranted and listened to him intently when he had a serious comment. He studied her every move. She was like some gorgeous feline with her beautiful cleavage, shapely hips, butt, and slender limbs. It took everything in him to control his urge to kiss her. After an hour or so they were crossing the bridge that entered Atlantic City. The town lit up like a Christmas tree. People were everywhere like in New Orleans during the carnival. Although Blaze had been there many times, this time was different. It was more exciting, and she was fascinated by the sights and sounds of the city. Jack enjoyed her reactions.

When they reached the casino, Blaze put on her shoes as Jack waited to help her out of the truck. He held out his arms as she balanced herself by holding onto his shoulders. Jack's hands went firmly around her waist as he hoisted her up and out of the truck. When he let her down, he did so slowly as her body grazed against his own. Shivers of excitement ran through Blazes' body as she tried to maintain her cool. She smiled and played coy to his machinations.

Jack left the keys and a tip with the valet, and they walked into the lobby of the casino and hotel. As they walked in, Jack placed his hand on Blaze's back near her waist to guide her through the crowd. There were people everywhere, so many people. Blaze felt a shiver of excitement go up her spine from his touch, but she remained cool not acknowledging how he affected her. She went to the restroom to freshen up while Jack stopped at the front desk to check on his room. He always called ahead to reserve a room when he went to the shore just in case he wanted to stay overnight. Blaze returned from the restroom, and they began their adventure into the casino. They immediately went to the table and played craps which Blaze won with skill impressing Jack. At first, he thought it was beginner's luck, but she really knew the game. She knew exactly when and how to bet. He could not remember any other female, except for a chick he met in Vegas, who knew how to shoot craps. It was intriguing to see such a sophisticated and beautiful woman play so skillfully as if she learned the game from the streets; just one more thing about her that surprised him. Next was Blackjack and then roulette. Jack was a good roulette player and he showed Blaze the fundamentals of the game. He was a very patient teacher which gave Blaze cause to believe that he may be patient in other ways as well. Blaze could not help but study him; he was fine. When he was cross or made a call that wasn't beneficial, he got a little line across his brow and his dimple stood deep in his cheek. Jack won a few hands and then asked her if she was ready for some dinner, to which Blaze quickly replied that she was. They walked through the casino talking and laughing. Jack unconsciously grabbed her hand as they maneuvered their way through the crowds of people. Blaze did not object to staying close to him until they reached the restaurant.

Jack chose a steakhouse inside the casino and had a table within minutes. Blaze was impressed with his ease at being in control; she was extremely attracted to his power. Once they were seated at their table, Jack ordered a bottle of wine. He seemed more relaxed than when they first broke bread together.

"So Ace, you having a good time?" Jack asked Blaze.

"I am, Jack! This has been a great evening. I think I like beating you at craps the most," Blaze teased.

"Well, I have never met a woman who shoots craps like you. Where'd you learn to play?"

"My brother and his friends used to play all the time. Of course, the street game is different, but the principles are the same. I learned a lot from them."

"I would love to learn how to play Roulette," Blaze said.

"I'll teach you, it's easy once you've played a hand or two."

"You'll teach me? When do you think either of us will have the time to do that?"

"Well...we'll just have to make the time," Jack said matter-of-factly. Blaze looked at Jack as he was smiling at her showing that deep dimple on his cheek. Once they finished dinner, they sat at the table laughing and talking. Blaze could not believe that she was having such a wonderful time with him. Jack was funny, knowledgeable, opinionated, and compassionate all at the same time. She enjoyed his company and he enjoyed hers. They managed to keep their conversation away from business topics. As they were having a great time, Blaze decided to ask Jack a random question.

"Jack...why is it that some girl hasn't snatched you up by now?"

Jack shrugged his shoulders.

"I guess it would have to be a mutual thing and I'm just not ready to settle down with anyone. I work long hours and I like my free-dom, but I do enjoy being out with a beautiful woman from time to time. I'm not a womanizer as some would like to think. Sure, someday I'd like the house with the picket fence, two children with another one on the way, and the Labrador retriever in the backyard —just not right now."

"Having a relationship with someone doesn't mean that you have to marry them or give up things you like doing. If you establish boundaries from the beginning, then you will not realize that you have lost yourself later."

"Sure, Blaze that's true, but in theory only. Women tend to agree on those boundaries in the beginning, but somewhere along the line, they change and want something more."

"Depends on the woman," Blaze replied matter-of-factly.

"Oh really? So, you're saying that you wouldn't have problems with my lifestyle if you were my woman?"

Blaze spoke confidently as she made her point, "What I'm saying is that there are women who have the same boundaries. You just need to find someone like yourself."

"Are you like me?" Jack asked taking Blaze's hand into his own. He held her hand as he gently caressed her fingertips. He looked into her eyes and knew the answer to his question. "I think that you are very much like me. You're tough but I think that's an act that covers up the real you...the vulnerable you." he said still holding her hand.

Blaze began to feel uncomfortable as if she were cornered and did not know how to escape. When Jack noticed how uncomfortable he had made her he let go of her hand and sat up straight in his seat. Blaze never answered Jack. She was feeling something, and she tried to excuse it by blaming it on the wine she was drinking.

"I think we better get started back home." Blaze said.

"Are you running from me?" Jack asked.

"No, what makes you think that?" Her voice was uneasy.

"I think I need to use the restroom," Blaze said abruptly before she got up from the table.

Jack stood up and watched her as she walked away. She had an incredible body and her perfectly round ass moved so well when she walked. Jack was mesmerized by her, but he did not want to be. He knew it was not a good thing to get involved with someone who could potentially work for his company, and the fact remained that if her firm were awarded the account then Blaze would technically be his employee. He sat there trying to think of something that would get them on the right track. When Blaze returned, she asked him very quickly, "Are you ready to go?"

"Yeah—just let me pay the check and we can go," Jack replied. Jack signed for the meal and then helped Blaze out of her chair. They began to walk towards the lobby in silence. All thoughts of staying over were removed from Jack's mind. He was usually smoother than this, but with Blaze, he felt as if he was off his game. He gave his ticket to the valet as Blaze observed the many people who helped to generate excitement in the air. As they waited out-side of the casino for the car, the night air was warm. There were bright lights shining and changing colors on the huge fountain cen-tered on the grounds of the casino. Neither of them said a word. It was as if they were afraid to speak. Finally, the car arrived, and Jack opened the door for Blaze to get in—but this time he didn't help her up into the truck. This time when he walked around to get in the driver's side, Blaze didn't open the door for him. They drove around the winding path that led onto the streets of the city. The traffic was heavy leaving the casino as they waited many minutes for their turn to gain entrance onto the main street. They were both quiet with only the music from the stereo playing in the background. Suddenly Jack made a sharp turn pulling into a small street behind one of the casinos and parked the truck. Blaze was reclining in the passenger seat with her eyes closed. She was startled by this sudden movement as she sat straight up in her seat. When she opened her eyes, Jack had parked the truck and was now leaning over looking at her.

"What's the matter?" she asked a little shaken.

Jack did not say a word but reached over and kissed Blaze with so much passion that she was paralyzed by his movement. For a moment she sat there with her arms at her sides not kissing him back. He stopped and looked into her eyes. She looked back at him as he revealed all the passion that had built up inside of him. She took her hand and brushed his cheek with her fingertips. He grabbed her hand and kissed the inside of it. She pulled his face to hers and this time she kissed him opening her mouth for him to place his tongue. Their kisses became more intense as the foreplay lasted for quite some time. Blaze was so aroused by him that she moaned at his touch. He whispered in her ear as he gently kissed her neck.

"You're so damn beautiful and sexy Blaze. Do you know how much you've tortured me these last hours? I want you right here— right now." he said.

Blaze wanted Jack as much as he wanted her and so she unfastened her pants and pulled them down still seated. She climbed into the back of Jack's truck and lay back on the seat inviting him to join her. Jack got out of the truck looking both ways as he opened the back door on the driver's side and got in. The seats of the truck reclined almost to the floor, so there was plenty of room for Jack's long limbs to stretch out. Blaze untied her top revealing her breast to Jack. They were firm and taut, and her nipples were hard begging to be touched. She took his hand and placed them upon her breast. He caressed them, placing his wet lips upon one breast and then the other delivering such pleasure that Blaze thought she would explode. She unbuttoned his shirt and loosened his belt. She then took her hand and carefully circled his chest, down over his rippled stomach, and into his pants. He was hard and huge, and she wanted to see what he had to offer her. She gripped him and continued until he was exposed to her. She was delighted with his size and erectness, and she wanted more of him opening her legs to accommodate his touch. Her sheer, black thong panties were wet with her dew, and his fingers found their way to the opening of her body that promised such pleasure. He entered her with his finger, and she moaned with an ache that demanded all of him. Blaze laid back fully for Jack to have complete access to her body. He got pleasure from the sight of her half-naked body in the dim light of the car. He touched her all over taking time to enjoy each part of her. He wanted to savor her as if she was a prized possession to be admired and cherished. Blaze wanted Jack to take her and ravish her completely.

Half moaning—half whispering Blaze spoke to Jack, "Please Jack, don't make me wait, please don't make me wait any longer," she pleaded.

"Hold on baby. Just hold on and let me look at you," he whispered.

Not being able to wait any longer, Blaze reached up to Jack and pulled him down upon her. She opened her legs to allow space for his strong body as she stroked his erect penis with her hand. She felt the massiveness of him and her desire for him mounted as she took him inside of her. She moaned as he entered her gasping at the girth of him. Her body quickly learned his rhythm as she adapted to his body's demands. His stroke grew with each thrust, and she met him completely as he held her body maneuvering their movements to accommodate his need. He lifted her body up to him cupping her cheeks to gain better, deeper access to her. He thrust deeper thoroughly exploring the valley within her until he reached her pleasure point as he stroked the place that ignited her to an explosion of sheer, wild, abandoned pleasure. She became wild, like some untamed creature in his grip as she held onto him deliberately meeting his every movement. Blaze wrapped her arms around Jack's neck holding on to meet his desire. They kissed each other ravenously and together they reach their ascent into a passionate and strong rhythm that climaxed into oblivion.

Blaze lay there spent with her hair wildly thrown against the back of the seat and the moonlight shining upon her face. Trickles of sweat lay glistening between her breast and her bottom was wet and sticky. Jack was on top of her trying to hold his body up so as not to crush her. He rolled over to lay next to her his arm across his face with his eyes closed exhausted from their tryst. Blaze turned towards him admiring his sleek, muscular body.

"Do you have a blanket in here?" she asked him. He sat up on his arm looking at her.

"You cold?" he asked.

"Yes, cold and very wet," she replied. Jack reached up and pressed a few buttons, one of which would begin to warm the seats.

"Is that a little better?" he asked her.

"Yes, it's getting there," she said with a smile.

"You look so sexy right now," Jack said running his finger along her cleavage. Blaze smiled as she stroked his bare leg traveling to his manhood.

"Keep that up and we'll be here all night," Jack joked.

"Where are we anyway, and how long have we been here?" Blaze asked.

"Well, we're in the back of the casino and we've probably been parked here for about forty-five minutes or so."

"Um...seems longer than that."

"Well, that's because you tried to screw my brains out," Jack added teasingly.

"Seems to me I had a little help," Blaze retorted.

"Yeah...I guess you could say that." Jack laughed.

"So...what now?" Blaze asked.

"What do you want to do?

"Well, I'd like to freshen up, but I guess I have to wait until I get home."

"We can go freshen up if you'd like. I have a room at the hotel."

Suddenly Blaze was taken aback by his answer. It made her think twice about what had just happened between them. *Did he plan for this to happen? He's got a room reserved so he must have thought he would get me to have sex with him. But why here in the car, why not in the room?'* she thought.

"When did you reserve a room?" Blaze asked, her mood clearly changed.

"I keep a room at the hotel for times when I'm down here and I don't want to drive back home."

"So, you assumed that we would be staying over?"

"No, it wasn't like that at all," Jack defended himself. "If that was going to happen then we wouldn't have to be concerned about reserving a room is all. Is that so terrible for me to think it would be possible for us to be like this?" he asked. Blaze sat up and began to look for her clothing.

"What are you looking for?" Jack asked.

"I'm looking for my panties and top," she answered, clearly irritated. Jack reached over and picked up Blaze's clothing from the floor in the front of the truck and gave them to her.

"Here!" he said pushing them into her lap. Blaze took her clothing and began getting dressed.

"What's the matter with you?" he asked her.

"What's the matter with me?" she threw back at him.

"I feel as though you've taken advantage of me."

"Hey lady! If I remember correctly, no one twisted your arm." Jack also began to get dressed.

"Hey lady!?" Blaze asked rhetorically. Now definitely feeling manipulated, Blaze sat straight up in the seat. "I'm ready to leave."

"No problem, Slick!"

"Don't call me Slick!" Blaze yelled.

"Well, Ms. Beaumont, ma'am," Jack scoffed at her with anger in his voice. Jack finished dressing and got out of the car, slammed the door, and got into the driver's seat. Blaze got out too and sat in the front passenger seat. Jack was furious and Blaze was steaming. They both had bad tempers, and both thought they were right. The tension in the truck could have ignited a flame. Jack halfway buttoned his shirt and sat at the wheel looking straight ahead. Finally, he turned on the ignition and began to pull out of the parking space. He had never felt such an array of emotions so quickly. He suddenly turned off the ignition and turned to Blaze. He grabbed her and kissed her aggressively. At first, she tried to free herself from his grip, and push him away. Her strength was no match to Jack's. She relented and began kissing him back as they began to make out all over again.

"You are so damn hot girl," Jack said.

"Let's go to the room," Blaze said hoarsely as she placed her hands on Jack's crotch.

This time when Jack pulled out of the parking lot, Blaze was practically sitting on his lap. She was kissing him and taunting him so much that he almost lost control of the truck. He pulled the truck up to the valet and threw the attendant the keys. Blaze jumped out of the truck as Jack came around and grabbed her hand. Walking hard and fast Jack led her through the lobby, nearly dragging her through the crowds of people like a steamroller with Blaze practically running to keep up. They finally reached the elevator and when they got on Jack pushed the button closing the door before anyone else could get on. When the doors closed behind him, he grabbed Blaze and backed her up against the wall of the elevator, running his hand up between her legs while lifting her from the floor. He kissed her grinding against her body as she lay open to whatever he demanded. When the doors opened, they were pinned against the wall in a wild embrace. Jack was aroused and hid himself using his jacket. They got off the elevator and Jack grabbed Blaze's hand again and dragged her through the corridor. They came to room 2040 as he took out the room key, swiping it as the door opened. He switched on the lights as Blaze walked into the room behind him. The suite was massive, with a huge living room, wall-to-wall bar, and floor-to-ceiling mirrors throughout. He led her into the bedroom that housed a huge king-size bed. He threw her upon the bed as he stripped off his clothing. She lay there looking at him with passion and lust. The heat between them rose and he straddled her as he removed her clothing. She played with him licking his navel and rippled stomach. She lay there completely naked as he straddled her running his fingers the length of her body. He grabbed her ankle and turned her over to reveal her bare buttocks. He smacked her on her behind as he ran his hands over both cheeks. He made circles with his hands on each buttock as he sized her up and admired their firmness. He then lifted her body to meet his as his crotch pressed against her bare behind. She felt his hardness against her as he held her around her waist and grabbed a handful of her hair in his hands. He buried his face into her back smelling her scent which drove him wild. She moaned at his maneuvering of her body, but she enjoyed his power over her. He held her tight to him as he let go of her hair and cupped her breast. He sucked at her neck from behind and she moved against him with rhythm and purpose.

"Do you like this?" he asked her in a husky voice.

"Yes!" she replied breathlessly.

"Show me how much you like it. Tell me what you want," he commanded her.

"I like it very, very much," she replied in a trembling voice.

"Then show me how much," he said.

"This much!"

She leaned forward reaching behind her to grab him. She guided him inside of her. He entered her as he gently bit her on the back sucking at her skin and relishing in the sweetness of it. She begged him to make her cum and he willingly and passionately fulfilled her wish. Every stroke was as demanding as the first and he proudly led her to reach an orgasm she had only ever dreamed of having. He also climaxed with primal lust as they both collapsed upon the bed exhausted and satiated.

| 10 |

A Beautiful Night

Entangled within one another, they lay breathlessly on the bed and drifted into a restful sleep. Time quietly went by with the only noise being the light snoring and breathing of them both. They lost track of time not knowing how long they slept before either of them attempted to move again. When Jack awoke, he found Blaze sleeping at his side. She looked wild like she had been riding bareback through the forest. Her lips were slightly parted as she lay on her back in a deep slumber. He traced his fingers along the line of her shapely body admiring how toned and supple she felt. His touch aroused her, and she awoke with him smiling at her.

"Hi," she said sleepily, yawning and stretching as she did like a cat waking from its nap.

"Hello, sleepy head," Jack teased as he kissed her lips.

"How long have I been asleep?" she asked.

"I don't know—I just woke up myself," Jack replied.

"What time is it?" she asked.

"No time, no questions, just relax and let me enjoy you," Jack said. Blaze smiled as she cuddled up to him. Jack placed a blanket around them both as the air in the room was cold.

"Are you comfortable?" he asked her.

"Very!"

Jack stood up and turned on the stereo as the soft music played adding an ambiance to the room that made them want to stay there and block the whole world out. They lay there motionless facing one another taking in each other as the moments passed. Blaze finally broke the silence with a question.

"Jack, can I ask you something?"

"Sure Ace, ask me anything."

"How do you like running Newman?"

"Wow, I thought you were gonna ask me something difficult."

"I'm just curious as to what it's like to have all that responsibility and maintain your position as a first-class operation."

"My dad taught us to be practical, but knowledgeable. He's a self-made man, so nothing came to him easily. He taught us to work hard, be honest, and treat others with respect and integrity; the rest would take care of itself. My parents are Christians, so it has always been important to them to instill in all of us Christian values and morals. We're all quite close and God is the core of our foundation."

"Wow, I never figured you for someone who felt that way." Blaze was a little surprised.

"Why'd you ask me that?" Jack grew curious.

"Because when I run my own company, and I will someday soon, I'd like to practice the same principles that make other successful companies flourish. Newman is at the top of its game, so your example is important to follow." Jack looked at Blaze and smiled.

"You're very ambitious, aren't you?" Jack asked.

"I am. Does that bother you?"

"Why would it bother me? I find it to be one of your best qualities—but don't you want to settle down someday and have a family?" Jack asked.

"Yeah! I would, but that's years away."

"Really?" Jack asked surprisedly.

Blaze had to pee, so she excused herself and went into the bathroom. When she returned Jack was on the phone talking with room service.

"I ordered some snacks for us and some herbal tea for you."

"That sounds great," Blaze smiled.

Taking control, as usual, Jack walked over to Blaze, took her hand, and headed for the bathroom.

"What are you doing?" she asked stumbling along.

"Come on…let's take a shower together."

He was smiling that boyish smile flashing his pearly whites. He was irresistible and Blaze was enjoying every minute. Jack towered over Blaze even in his bare feet. He was magnificent and she enjoyed his body immensely. She lathered his back with her hands lingering around his buttocks, which were tight and firm. He lathered her too, paying special attention to her breast. They were like two melons, ripe and perky. He kissed her mouth as he lathered her behind. She stood on tiptoe placing both arms around his neck. They kissed one another…playing with each other's tongues and exploring each other's bodies. They made love again and this time it was sweet and savoring as if they had been lovers for a very long time. Blaze was truly exhausted when they finished so Jack picked her up and carried her to the bed. He dried her body and hair with the towel and then wrapped her in a huge terry robe.

There was a knock at the door, so Jack answered it allowing room service to enter. He asked for extra blankets, signed for the delivery, and rolled the table into the bedroom. When the attendant returned with the extra blankets, Jack took them into the bedroom and covered Blaze as she snuggled into the big bed. He rolled the table filled with fresh fruits and cheeses close to the bed. Jack lovingly climbed into bed wrapping Blaze in his arms. They fed one another and spent the rest of the night talking. After some hours, Blaze slumbered in Jack's arms, and he too was overcome by a peaceful and well-deserved sleep.

| 11 |

Getting Lost in the Moment

The next morning the sun shone brightly into the suite that Jack and Blaze shared. They had no intention of getting up and slept in well past eleven. There was no need to rush since Jack had a long-standing reservation when he was in town. Blaze woke up and nudged Jack in his side.

"Wake up Jack!" Blaze whispered.

"Why?" he asked.

"Because it's late and we probably should be getting ready to check out."

"Don't worry about it," he said in a sleep-laden voice.

"We have the room as long as we want it."

Blaze was impressed as she lay there looking around at the suite. She could tell that it was one of the more expensive suites in the hotel. There was a sitting room, an excellent view of the beach, and a fully stocked bar. The bedroom was huge and there was a steam shower and Jacuzzi in the ginormous bathroom. Jack covered his head with a pillow to block out the light. When Blaze attempted to get up, a hand reached out and pulled her back into the bed.

"Where're you going?" Jack asked never lifting his face from beneath the pillow.

"I'm going to the bathroom," she laughed.

"Okay! But be back here in five," he said in a muffled voice.

"Yes sir!" Blaze teased.

Blaze returned from the bathroom to find Jack standing on the balcony of the suite in a robe. He turned when she entered the room. The robe was open, and he was naked, not ashamed to stand in the open air in his birthday suit.

"Unless you want us to be bombarded with females at this door, I think you better come in or cover up," Blaze said sarcastically. Jack smiled and closed the glass doors behind him. He walked over to the bed and jumped back in.

"Come here," he gently commanded. She walked over to him, and he snatched her up and pulled her on top of him, and kissed her.

"Good morning, Ace," he said while smiling and staring into Blaze's eyes.

"Good morning!" Blaze kissed him back.

"What do you want to do today?" he asked.

"Today? Shouldn't we be heading back to town?"

"I don't see why we should. It's Friday and things can take care of themselves for a day don't you think?" he asked.

"Yeah, but...I hadn't planned on staying over. I don't have any of my toiletries with me or a change of clothes."

"That's not a problem. We can order anything you want and go shopping and get something for you to wear tonight."

"Tonight!? What's happening tonight?" Blaze was both dumbfounded and pleasantly surprised at Jack's unannounced plans.

"I'm taking you to a party at the Ocean Club. One of my boys is having a birthday party there tonight. We don't have to stay, but I should make an appearance."

"Why didn't you ask me about this sooner Jack?" Blaze asked.

"Well, I really didn't think that we would be together like this," he said sincerely. Blaze didn't have a rebuttal. She just looked at him squinting with her chinky brown eyes as she agreed to go.

"Okay, but I have to find a salon so I can have my hair done too. My hair got wet and it's all over my head."

"I think you look hot and sexy!" Jack began nibbling at Blaze's ear playfully.

"Jack, be serious."

"Okay...look they have a perfectly good salon downstairs. Make an appointment and charge it to the room. You can get a dress at one of the shops in the casino or we can go shopping on the pier and buy you something to wear. We'll have lunch and make a day of it. How's that sound to you?" Blaze pouted for a second and then agreed to Jack's proposal.

"Great," he said. "Now let's go get some chow and get this thing started."

Blaze and Jack showered, dressed, and went downstairs for brunch. She made an appointment for the salon at five, leaving enough time to shop and spend the afternoon with Jack. They walked on the boardwalk and shopped at some exclusive boutiques until Blaze found the perfect dress. She bought underwear to complete her attire. Jack sat patiently as she tried on several dresses giving his nod of approval when he saw the one he liked. Jack didn't care as long as she was happy. They finished shopping by two o'clock and decided to go back to the room for a nap. Their nap turned into another session of lovemaking and by three-thirty, they were soaking in the Jacuzzi.

Jack told her stories about growing up as Thaddeus Newman's son and some of the many escapades in his life. He traveled quite a bit visiting Spain and Italy and even spent six months in France. As a kid, he spent his summers with his family in Barbados where his father was born. He was close to his mother who was a busy socialite and activist. He promised Blaze that when she met her, she would see that she was nothing like the person that the tabloids made her out to be. That afternoon proved to be the beginning of something special between them that they both were not prepared for or had anticipated. Blaze felt a strange closeness to Jack as if they had known each other forever. She was comfortable with him and he seemed, well, at ease with her. They languished in the Jacuzzi until it was time for Blaze to leave for her appointment at the salon. She really didn't want to leave their love nest, but she promised him that she would attend the party with him. Blaze got up and dried off and began to prepare to leave. She donned a pair of jeans and a tee shirt she found while shopping, and a pair of sneakers she purchased as well. She pulled her hair on top of her head, grabbed her bag, and prepared to leave.

"Hey there, you forgot something," Jack said standing by the bathroom door.

"What? I have everything I need," Blaze said as she examined herself from head to toe.

"Come here," Jack commanded.

Blaze looked at him smiling as she walked toward him. Jack stood there with only a towel thrown over his shoulders. When she got close to him, he reached out and encircled her waist with his arm pulling her close to his chest. He kissed her sweetly upon her lips as she closed her eyes and returned the passion.

Still holding her in his arm he said, "I can't wait for you to get back so I can take you out and show you off." Blaze smiled as he let her down from his embrace. When she turned to walk away, he smacked her behind. Blaze grabbed her tender cheeks.

"Ouch! That hurt!" She squealed. Jack bent down and kissed her round bottom and sent her on her way. Blaze was smiling all the way to the elevator and down to the main floor where the salon was located. An elegantly dressed woman standing behind the reception counter greeted her as she entered the salon. She was having "the works" which included a manicure and pedicure, facial, and of course, her hair styled. She relaxed and thought of nothing and no one other than Jack the entire time she was there. She could not believe how much they connected in just a few short hours, but she enjoyed every minute of being with him. Just as she was ready to have her pedicure, her cell phone rang. It was Clay. Blaze answered the call after a few rings.

"Hello?"

"Hey baby, where have you been? I called you a few times last night but couldn't get through."

"Ah yeah…I had a headache, so I turned my phone off," she said.

"That must have been one hell of a headache because I couldn't get you on your cell either. I tried calling the office, but they said you were out today. You okay?"

"Yeah, I decided to take a mental health day and get some things done. When will you be home?"

"I'm taking a flight out tomorrow morning. I left my car at the airport so I should see you sometime Saturday afternoon." There was a brief pause before Blaze spoke.

"Clay…Clay you're breaking up. I can't hear you." Blaze blurted her words just before she hung up the phone. Blaze sat there for a moment not believing what she had just done. She lied to Clay and then hung up before he could say anything else. All sorts of thoughts were running through Blaze's mind as she was thrown off by Clay's call. It brought her back to reality. She had to tell Jack about Clay. It would only be right if she did.

Jack was so honest with me today. What if this changes things between us?' She thought to herself. From that point on, Blaze couldn't relax and enjoy her afternoon at the spa. She even thought about asking Jack to take her home. She felt uneasy about lying to Clay, and Jack too! She was perplexed as to what she should do. She was done at the salon by seven o'clock and headed back to the suite. When she arrived, Jack wasn't there so she turned on the television trying to distract herself from her thoughts about Clay. When that didn't work, she turned on some music. She dozed off across the bed falling into a light sleep. Jack entered the suite undetected by Blaze, undressed, and quietly laid down beside her. He watched her as she lay there so peacefully. She was so beautiful, and Jack knew that he could easily fall for her. He startled Blaze as he pulled her close and lay behind her. He kissed her on the top of her head as she melted into his strong lean body.

"Hey luscious...you miss me?" he asked teasingly.

"Mm-hmm," she mumbled.

"How was your spa treatment?"

"Good!"

"I thought we might have dinner on the balcony tonight if you like."

"That would be wonderful she said cuddling closer to him."

Half asleep and feeling quite content, Blaze napped in her lover's arms. Jack held her as he caressed her breast and touched her body everywhere enjoying her softness. He, too, dozed off and they slept for a few hours. When they awoke, they snuggled under the covers and began making love again. It wasn't until nine that they emerged from bed satisfied and happy.

| 12 |

Meet the Newmans

Thaddeus Newman spent most of his time working deals and entertaining important clients on the golf course or at his estate in Blue Bell. He was a self-made man with the help of his late father-in-law James Martin Flemington. His wife of thirty-five years Kate was very high maintenance. Every year the Newmans hosted two incredibly special events; the Newman Center Three-Day Charity event for disadvantaged inner-city youth which was the hottest ticket in town, and the annual Newman Christmas Soiree. Kate had a team of people who helped her with organizing both events and attracting the most popular people in business and the arts. This year, the event would be held at the African Museum where many students of the arts, who were sponsored by the Newman foundation would exhibit their talent. The proceeds from the event would benefit Kate's charity, *Les Petites.*

While Kate was busy with her charities and social events, Thaddeus was busy as the head of the Newman Corporation. It was said that he had a mistress and that she was a white prominent lawyer who was married to her career and that Kate knowingly turned her head to the whole idea of an affair. Kate was not about to give up her social standing or placeholder as the wife of Thaddeus Newman. 'So what if he was having a little indiscretion as she coined it to close friends, so be it,' she thought.

Kate was a good mother and loved her children unconditionally. They attended the best prep schools and spent their summers at the beach house with their mother or a few weeks in Barbados where their father was born. Thaddeus would take one month to vacation with the family and make visits once a week when he could. Although the children were privileged and somewhat spoiled, they were accomplished and respectable individuals. They were members of the youth choir and youth outreach program, and they helped at the community shelter during the holidays. Two weeks out of each summer, Kate and the children volunteered time at an inner-city summer camp tutoring and mentoring the children. Kate's charitable organization *"Les Petite"* hosted an end-of-the-summer outing for economically challenged youth and offered scholarships to underwrite the cost of college tuition to deserving high school graduates. She used her connections to solicit donations from major corporations that supported her cause.

Kate was an attractive fifty-seven-year-old woman who maintained her svelte 5'9" figure by practicing yoga and Pilates five times a week. Kate employed a full-time cook to make organic natural food dishes for her family. She was a very stylish woman who shopped at exclusive boutiques or purchased her clothing from private showings, but she was just as comfortable wearing select pieces from well-known popular brands for her more casual attire.

Kate was indeed beautiful, with her short, dark, wavy hair that was styled with one side partially covering her left eye that she would fling back when something was funny to her, or when something grabbed her attention. She wore very little make-up unless going out to one of her fancy charity events when she would have a make-up artist and hairstylist come to her home and assist her. Her stylist, who was always on hand for special occasions, made sure he had his pulse on everything fashion-forward. For Kate, none of these things were more important than being home with her family. She insisted that they all had dinner together as much as possible and that Thaddeus was present even if he had to go back out later. Kate was very particular about all of her children and whom they associated with, but she was extremely picky about the girls that her sons brought home. She wanted her children to marry well, especially her sons to someone whom she considered to have good breeding.

The Newman's only daughter, Elizabeth, married soon after graduating college to a successful architect, Bradley Ellington Williams in a lavish ceremony on the Newman grounds. The Newman's oldest son, James, married Rebecca Barton, a young woman from a well-respected family within the Newman social circle. Rebecca was the youngest daughter of the Barton conglomerate and was an accomplished musician. Michael and Jack were the two Newman children who remained unmarried, and Kate did everything to find the right wife for them both. Truth be told, there was no one good enough for either of them, especially Jack.

| 13 |

Curious Kate

Kate was busy finalizing the plans for her charity event. What began as a small gathering of very close friends at her home some ten years ago, blossomed into a full fledge social affair. Kate decided to work out by the pool since it was such a glorious spring day. With a cell phone in hand and a laptop on the table, Kate was eager to get things finalized.

"Dante, I don't want to worry about the minor details darling, that is why I pay you," Kate said while thumbing through her notes. "Just get as much of them as they have, don't worry about the cost. Call me when it's been confirmed." Kate hung up the phone and called out to her assistant.

"Pierre, can you have Bert serve lunch at 12:30 pm instead of 1:00 pm? I have an errand to run in town and want to get back here in time to nap before dinner."

"Sure, Kate. Do you want me to go to town with you?"

"No, I'll drive myself today. I think I'll put the top back and enjoy this beautiful weather. Has anyone heard from Jack yet?"

"No, he hasn't returned my calls but I'm sure you'll hear from him later today."

"Hmm...not like him to do that—I wonder where he is? Did they say when he was expected back in the office?"

"No. His assistant didn't know."

"Get Thad on the phone for me, Pierre. He should know where Jack is." Pierre made a call into the Newman offices and asked the secretary if he could speak with Thaddeus.

"Mr. Newman is on a conference call. Can I have him call Mrs. Newman when his call is completed?" the secretary asked.

"Yes, please do," Pierre replied. "Mr. Newman is on a call and will call you once he's done," Pierre said to Kate. Kate sat back in her lounge chair in deep thought. Just then, her cell phone rang. Kate quickly answered. It was Thaddeus returning her call.

"Thad, where's Jack?" Kate asked angrily.

"I have no idea. Is this what the big emergency is all about?" Thaddeus asked annoyed.

"Well, he works with you! You mean to tell me you don't know where he is?"

"No...I'm not in the habit of keeping tabs on my Vice President of Operations."

"He's your son before he's your employee, Thaddeus."

"Okay Kate, what's wrong?"

"I've been calling him since last night and he hasn't returned my calls. He isn't in the office, and no one seems to know where he is."

"Well, shouldn't that tell you something?" Thaddeus asked coyly.

"Tell me what...that my son is missing, and no one seems to care but me?"

"Kate, stop worrying. Jack's a big boy. He can take care of himself. He's probably off with some young hot thing enjoying himself. I bet he's held up in some love nest somewhere." Thaddeus edged Kate on.

"Okay, that's enough," Kate said. "Honestly Thad, you're incorrigible."

"Yeah, and that's why you love me. I'll see you later."

"Home for dinner, right?"

"Yes, dear I'll be home for dinner."

Thaddeus hung up the phone and shook his head. He knew his wife and she wasn't going to leave it at that. She was on a mission and when it came to the kids, she was relentless. He sat back in his large, high-back, leather chair and thought to himself.

'I don't know where that boy is, but he must be having a hell of a time if he didn't call Kate back when she summoned him. He's in trouble now!'

Thaddeus chuckled to himself before picking up his phone to make another call and thought, *'Better try to warn Jack before he walks right into the fire.'*

He called Jack's cell, but there was no answer. Then he left Jack a message that his mother was on the rampage to locate him and then he returned to his work. Just as he hung up Jack looked at his cell. Ten missed calls and six of them were from his mother. He put the phone down on the nightstand and looked at his sleeping lover. He had no intention of ruining his evening explaining himself to his mother. He'd cross that bridge tomorrow or the next day if possible. Right now, he was going to enjoy this time without any distractions.

| 14 |

All Mine Tonight

Meanwhile, back in Atlantic City Jack and Blaze woke up from their evening naps and had dinner on the balcony of their suite. It was unusually warm and balmy for a spring night at the shore, as the moon and the stars shined brightly in the sky. The moonlight cast a shimmering glow upon the ocean that created a mystical, magical night for the couple. They feasted on lobster and enjoyed steamed asparagus with Béarnaise sauce. Jack tried to encourage Blaze to eat the raw oysters he ordered as appetizers, but Blaze couldn't get past the sliminess of the creatures. She did manage to down two and left the rest for Jack to enjoy. They shared dessert as they sat on the balcony enjoying their wine and each other.

Blaze could listen to Jack talk about his childhood all night. He talked about his parents and siblings and how much fun he had growing up. Blaze shared a few stories with him as well about her own life growing up with her brother Kush and two sisters Sydney and Peyton.

"We were raised by my mother, Jewels, who is a beautician by trade. She grew up in Philadelphia and met my father, Malcolm, who was a welder from North Carolina. When my mom was seven months pregnant with me, my dad was killed in an accident at the plant where he worked. My mother was devastated by my father's death. The company where he worked was found to be negligent in the incident and Jewels was awarded a considerable amount of money. She opened her first salon when I was two years old and established herself as a first-rate stylist. She worked hard to be successful working by day, going back to school at night, and being a full-time mother always. My mother never missed a play, sports event, or parent-teacher conference for any of us. She managed to raise us to be successful confident adults. That didn't mean that there weren't any bumps along the way. I was quite a rebellious child and got into trouble here and there. My brother Kush was there to help mom nurture us girls and discipline us when we needed it."

"What's does your mother do now?" Jack asked inquisitively.

"She currently owns five salons on the east coast; two in Philly, one in Washington, D.C., one in Baltimore, and one in New York. She spends most of her time at the New York salon since she has several celebrity clients that she personally services in that location."

Jack was intrigued by Blaze's family and the more time that he spent with her, the more he wanted to know about her. Although he could have listened to her talk all night, it was getting late, so Jack suggested that they get ready to head out to his friend's party at the club. Blaze chose a black knit dress with a low-cut top that showed her ample cleavage. She wore the strappy shoes that she brought with her which complimented the dress perfectly. The only jewelry she wore was diamond stud earrings and a single diamond tennis bracelet that was also a gift from Clay. Her hair was styled up high with tendrils falling down her neck. Jack entered the bathroom and watched her as she brushed her hair.

"Ah, perfection," Jack smiled. "I want to show you off to the world." Blaze smiled as she turned towards him.

"I could stay right here with you for the rest of the night." Blaze said.

"I know! I just want to make an appearance and then we can come right back as soon as you're ready to." Jack stated while pulling her to him.

"No, no, no! We have to get outta here before anything else goes down," she said trying to loosen herself from him. Jack kissed her neck and nuzzled his face into her cleavage making a roaring sound at the same time. Blaze started to laugh and broke away from him walking into the other room. Jack finished dressing and was ready to leave by eleven o'clock. He wore a black silk suit and a black silk shirt. Blaze looked at him and couldn't hide what she was thinking.

'Damn, he is so fine. I have to keep my composure because I'm sure he hears that all the time. But what does he want with me when he can have any girl he wants? All I know is tonight he's all mine and I plan to enjoy every moment of it.'

"You ready?" Jack asked startling Blaze back to reality.

"Yes, I'm ready," she replied.

"Okay then...let's rock and roll."

Jack ordered a car to take them to the Ocean Club. It was only a few blocks from the casino and hotel. When they arrived at the club, there was a line of people waiting to get in. Jack knew one of the bouncers who quickly checked his name off the list and ushered them into the club. It was your typical nightclub with flashing lights, loud music, several bars, and a huge dance floor. Jack held Blaze's hand as they walked through the crowd on the dance floor to the VIP section. On the way, Jack was greeted by several guys shaking hands and exchanging quick banter. Many of the women were trying to attract Jack's attention while simultaneously giving Blaze the perusal from head to toe. Little snippets of comments were made and heard, but since Blaze was just stunning, they couldn't say too much that was negative. The guys noticed Blaze immediately; some winking, while others gave knowing glances. Jack noticed that quickly and held on to her hand even tighter to claim his territory. When they finally reach VIP, there were a few guys and a couple of women sitting, talking, and having drinks. One who seemed to be the loudest was standing up with an opened bottle of expensive champagne in his hand. Jack walked over to him and said something in his ear that almost made him spit the champagne out of his mouth. He turned and looked at Jack with a hearty laugh.

"What's up boy?" he asked loudly. "You made it after all. Man, I thought you were gonna stand a brotha up."

"I told you I'd be here," Jack responded. They gave one another the brotha handshake and hug and Jack began to speak to some of the others in attendance. Blaze was standing at the entrance of the VIP section watching the interaction between the two men. Jack turned and walked back grabbing her by the hand.

"Everyone, this is Blaze. Blaze, this is everyone," he introduced her to the group. They all returned welcoming greetings. He then turned to his friend and introduced Blaze to him.

"Blaze this is Manny, the birthday boy." Manny reached over to place a kiss on Blaze's cheek and then gave her a big hug.

"Wow, Jack! I see why we ain't been seeing you. You're gorgeous." he said to Blaze.

"Thank you, Manny! Happy birthday." Blaze said returning his greeting.

"Now we can get this party started," Manny said loudly as everyone chimed in agreement. One of the men in the group stood up to offer Blaze a seat, but she declined to excuse herself to go to the lady's room. Jack whispered in her ear.

"Do you want me to go with you?" he asked smiling, his eyes twinkling with delight.

"No!" Blaze said laughing. "I'll be fine. Go have fun with your friends and I'll be right back." Jack looked at her and kissed her on her ear.

"Bring your pretty butt back here. Don't get lost." Jack possessively, but playfully, demanded. Blaze smiled and began her walk through the crowd to the restroom. Jack watched her until she disappeared. Manny and the crew noticed this and commented.

"Damn Jack, is your nose open, babe?" Manny asked sarcastically.

"Man, shut up and pour me a shot," Jack said leaning against the private bar.

The two men conversed and caught up on what one another had been doing. The music was loud, and the party was in full swing. When Blaze returned, Jack poured her a glass of champagne, and they toasted Manny's birthday. Blaze sat on Jack's lap and listened to the guys talking about old times and one another. They reminisced about the trouble they got into in college and even the girls they used to date. Blaze was hysterical with laughter hearing the quips about Jack and his escapades. Jack's hand caressed Blaze's back and encircled her waist. She enjoyed his touch. She liked being considered Jack's piece and felt giddy and high from his closeness. Blaze and Jack danced to a slow song and got lost in one another.

"You smell fantastic," Jack whispered in Blaze's ear. "Just good enough to eat." He resumed kissing her neck. Blaze was enjoying him, and he was also enjoying her. Jack looked at her with pride in his eyes as well as desire, so everyone knew they were into each other. When they returned to the group Manny caught Jack's attention.

"Hey Jack, she's a winner man," Manny said.

At the time, Blaze saw a group of people she knew and went to speak to them. Jack followed her with his gaze as she walked across the room. He enjoyed watching her as she worked her magic. She had natural charisma, and she knew how to win people over. The guys continued to talk and eat as the night was going by with everyone having a good time. They had been there for a little over two hours when Manny spotted someone he knew walking towards the party. Manny tapped Jack on his shoulder.

"Man...don't look now, but here comes Denise." Jack remained cool and unconcerned at Manny's observation. A tall, thin, model-looking woman stepped up into the VIP section along with two other women. She was light-skinned with long black straight hair that she wore in a ponytail. She had on a gold-sequined mini dress and stiletto heels. Her makeup was very precise, and both her pouty lips and acrylic nails were painted fire red. She was an attractive woman, who was used to attracting attention. She spoke to everyone and gave Manny a birthday kiss on the lips. She then walked over to Jack, putting her arms around his neck, and kissed him fully on the lips before he had time to protest. Jack stepped away from her wiping the kiss from his mouth. He didn't embrace her and did not return her kiss. She didn't like that at all and immediately made a fuss.

"What's wrong with you? Aren't you glad to see me?" she asked with her arm propped on his shoulder.

"Hello Denise," Jack said uninterestedly.

"Hello, Denise? Is that all I get? No how have you been? When did you get back home? How did you get down here? Nothing?" she asked directly in his face. Just then Blazed returned from the other side of the club. As she stepped up into the area, she could see the exchange between Jack and the woman as she walked toward them. When Jack saw her, he excused himself to walk over and assist her. When Denise saw Blaze, she retreated into bitch mode.

"What the fuck is this?" she asked loud enough for all to hear. Jack grabbed Blaze's hand and whispered in her ear.

"You ready to get outta here?" he asked. Blaze noticed the way the woman behaved toward Jack.

"No, let's stay," she said, curious as to who this woman was to Jack. Manny and a few of the other guests tried to ignore Denise by striking up conversations with the women she came with and ignoring her antics. Manny tried to get Denise to dance with him, but she wasn't having it.

"No thanks, Manny. I think I'll just have a drink and mingle," she said sarcastically. Denise walked over to Blaze and introduced herself.

"Hello, I'm Denise, and you are?

"Blaze...Blaze Beaumont." Blaze looked Denise straight in the eyes.

"So, are you here with our boy Jack?" Denise asked.

"Yes, I'm here with Jack," Blaze answered back.

"Nice!" Denise said coyly. Just then, Jack took Blaze's hand and turned her around to face him.

"Would you like another drink?" he asked ignoring Denise.

"By all means," Blaze said in return. Jack took Blaze's hand and they walked onto the dance floor and over to one of the bars. One stool was available, so Jack guided Blaze into the seat as he stood behind her and ordered their drinks. She turned her stool to face him smiling.

"Well Jack, I always heard you were popular with the ladies. I guess I get to see that firsthand." Blaze was clearly being sarcastic. "Who is Denise and what is she to you?" Blaze asked boldly.

"I'll tell you all about that as soon as we get back to the hotel." Jack smiled and took her hand into his. He put her hand to his lips and kissed it.

"You are by far the most beautiful woman here, and I only have eyes for you, Ms. Beaumont." Blaze being a little tipsy, decided to go one better and placed her knee between Jack's legs. She reached up and kissed his lips. Jack obliged her returning her kiss. He knew she was a little buzzed and he liked her aggressiveness.

"I think it's time to take you back to the room," he said smiling.

"I'm ready when you are," Blaze eagerly agreed in anticipation of what was to come.

"Okay then, let's say our goodbyes and then we'll leave," Jack added. They finished their drinks and walked back to VIP.

When they returned to the party, they ignored the cold stares that Denise projected to the pair. Jack shook hands with all the guys making plans to catch up soon, and Blaze extended her hand adding she was happy to have met them all. They both wished Manny a happy birthday as they said their goodnights and disappeared into the crowd. Denise was furious and had no chance to continue her little tirade. She thought to herself as the couple walked away hand in hand.

'So, Jack you've found another little playmate. Well, you know what happened to the last one.'

She continued her conversation with herself out loud.

"I wonder if Kate knows about this. I guess it's up to me to tell her. I think I'll pay her a visit when I get home. I'm sure she'll be interested in hearing about Jack's newest conquest." Manny could see the wheels turning in Denise's head. He cautiously approached her with a drink in hand.

"Why don't you just let it go? Ya know Jack ain't gonna take kindly to ya getting in his business."

"Shut up, Manny! No one asked for your two cents," Denise screeched.

"Before I'm through, Jack will be begging me to come back to him," she evilly stated as she plotted and watched the couple disappear into the crowd.

| 15 |

Oh, what a feeling!

Jack was ready to go back to the hotel, but Blaze wanted to take a walk. The night was warm and soothing, and she was having such a great time she didn't want it to end.

"Jack, let's walk." She pulled him by the hand.

"Whatever you want to do. This is your night," he said pulling her to him and kissing her.

Blaze playfully pulled away from him as they walked hand in hand out to the main street. They didn't speak for a while neither of them wanting to broach the subject of what happened at the club.

"This is such a magical night." Blaze's remark was genuine. Jack watched her intently as she walked along the side of a fountain and balanced herself. Jack sat down on a bench and Blaze finally joined him. She sat on his lap and took his face in her hands and kissed his nose.

"You know, you should have told me about Denise," she said. Jack just looked at her not knowing what to say.

"I would have. I just wasn't expecting to have to do that tonight."

"Well, there's no time like the present," Blaze suggested. The last thing Jack wanted to do was to talk about Denise, but he respected Blaze and thought she deserved to know about them.

"Denise is the daughter of one of my mother's oldest and dearest friends. We've known one another since we were children. Our parents thought that we would be a nice match and they wanted nothing more than to see us married giving them grandchildren. During one of our summer vacations in Barbados, Denise and her family came down for a visit. They stayed for two weeks at which time we developed a relationship. It truly was just a summer romance; we were just kids, and it was fun for a while. That fall, I went back to school, and we stayed in touch seeing one another a weekend here and there. We broke up during the holidays and everything else is just history. Whenever we run into one another, Denise tries to reignite old flames. She isn't really interested in me. I think she just likes to tease me. I must admit her fantasy is fueled by encouragement from our parents; specifically, our mothers, but we both know that nothing will ever happen between us. That little display she put on at the club was just that, her attempt at getting noticed, and that's all to it."

"Wow, that's quite a story," Blaze said. "It seems that you and Denise have quite a history."

"This is true, but you cannot make two people a couple if there's no chemistry or they're not fated to be together," Jack said. Blaze was touched by his earnestness, and she wanted to ensure him that it didn't matter to her anyway what happened in his past. She hadn't been forthcoming with Jack about Clay, and they were currently together as a couple. She didn't know how to open the dialogue about that. She was being selfish and didn't want to spoil their moment together.

"I'm sorry for what happened back there. I never want to put you in a position like that again." Jack said sincerely. Blaze looked at him and couldn't help but adore him. She saw the sincerity in his eyes as he held her around her waist and looked into hers. She melted from his gaze and reached down to kiss him fully on his mouth. He returned her kiss with passion as if to never let her go. It was truly a magical night. She had never felt this way about anyone and never so quickly. She felt like a princess and Jack was her prince charming.

"Let's go back to the hotel," Jack said as he hoisted her up from his lap and took her hand in his. Jack called for a car and they went back to the hotel. They were eager to get back to the room which was evident by their inability to keep their hands off one another. That night they made love as if their very lives depended on it. Blaze was tipsy from the champagne and submitted to Jack's every whim. He enjoyed her body like no one he had been with before and he showed his appreciation from his giving as well as taking during the hours that ensued. He kissed and licked every inch of her body whispering and promising what he would do next. She cooed and purred with the delight of his passion and allowed him liberties with complete submission. They lay upon the bed sweat glistening on their bodies, breathless from their ecstasy. Blaze was panting as if she had run a marathon.

"You're something else," Jack said breathing rather hard too.

"I take your lead," Blaze countered. They laughed as Jack got up to get some water for them.

"Do you want something a little stronger?" he asked.

"No thanks, water's just fine!"

Jack brought Blaze a bottle of water and then walked towards the balcony. He opened the balcony doors letting in a cool breeze. He stood there with the moonlight shining upon his lean, muscular body. Blaze turned onto her side to get a better view of him. She propped herself up on one arm watching Jack as he stood there in all his splendor. He had one hand placed against the molding of the doors, and a bottle of water dangling from the other. His body was still glistening with sweat which only served to make him that much more attractive.

"Man, this is really beautiful!" Jack sounded as if he were discovering the view for the first time.

"What's so beautiful?" Blaze asked.

"The view from here is nice. I never took the time to look at it before tonight. Come here!" He wanted Blaze to see the view as he saw it and enjoy it as he did. Blaze stood up and walked toward Jack. Without looking, he extended his arm reaching for her frame and pulling her body in front of his. His body was warm and hard as Blaze reclined against him for support.

"This is beautiful!" Blaze agreed.

It was a picture of tranquility as the moon shone brightly against the water and the sky was brilliant, filled with a million twinkling stars. Blaze couldn't help but feel as if the night were like some fantasy from a romantic novel. She felt complete in Jack's arms. She couldn't believe that she had fallen so quickly for him. She didn't expect or want this to happen, but she was happy that it did. She wasn't sure how he felt about her. And as if he could read her thoughts, Jack, too, was overwhelmed by their encounter.

"Did you think that the day we collided into each other at your office that we would end up like this?"

"I would have betted against something like this happening between us," Blaze answered.

"Why? Is it so out there that you would be attracted to me?"

"It's not that at all. Well, I guess I just wasn't looking for anything like this so how could I expect that it would happen? Lately, I have been so engrossed in working on the account that I haven't had time to think about anything else."

They both stood there in thought for what seemed like an eternity. Blaze was struggling with telling Jack about Clay. She knew that she would have to tell him eventually, but she didn't want to break this moment between them. Her selfishness was unfair to Jack, and she knew it, but she wanted more time. She reasoned with herself on why she shouldn't tell him.

I'm not even sure if it's necessary to tell Jack about Clay. What if this turns out to be a one-night stand? What if we don't see one another again? We'll go back to our lives as usual, and no one would be the wiser. But is that possible now since we have been seen in public together at the club?'

"What are you thinking?" Jack asked. "Clearly, you're in deep thought about something."

"I was thinking about you and how this all came about."

"Do you regret it?" Jack asked still holding Blaze in his arms. Blaze turned to look into Jack's eyes and saw that same sincerity she had seen when they were out by the fountain.

"Look, Blaze, I don't know where this is going. I don't even know if you really like me. All I know is that you are the most beautiful thing I have ever seen, and I want to be able to see you and spend some time with you again. So, I guess what I'm saying or asking is will I see you again?" Blaze smiled at him and felt as if she wanted to shout it.

"Yes, Jack. I will see you again." Jack kissed Blaze this time picking her up into his arms. They kissed for what seemed like forever and then he put her down.

"You've cast a spell upon me," Jack smelled Blaze's hair and kissed her face. Blaze smiled at his confession and presented her best attempt at a pirate's voice.

"Ah mate, the sirens beckon to you and tempt your very soul as you have no defense against their wailing song."

Jack smiled at her attempt, and they laughed as she stood on tiptoe to kiss his lips again.

"Aren't you tired?" he asked her.

"Tired! Tired you say? Well, I'm just getting started," she teased.

"Well, you better get yourself into bed girl 'cause I'm tired. You wore me out."

Jack smacked her bare behind as she cried out rubbing the stinging spot where his hand landed. He went into the bathroom and emerged again dragging himself into bed. Blaze joined him and they cuddled beneath a warm blanket. Before long they slumbered deeply in each other's arms. Jack was out like a light in no time as Blaze lay next to him peaceful and content. They had a full two days that turned out to be more than either of them could have imagined. Nothing else mattered, only that they found each other. All they knew was that their time together was pure bliss as they enjoyed the peace that they shared. Little did they know that the adventure was just beginning and their lives as they know it would be changed forever.

| 16 |

Honey, I'm home!

Clay arrived in town late Saturday morning. He was glad that he decided to catch an early flight so that he could spend some time with Blaze. He decided to call her and make plans for them to spend the day together and was looking forward to them having a quiet dinner and maybe a movie. The past few weeks had been busy for the both of them and he needed to spend time with his woman. After he came home and showered, Clay unpacked his bags and returned a few phone calls. He decided to call Blaze last since he intended on being with her for the rest of the day. He dialed her number but got her voicemail. He thought it strange that she didn't answer, but figured she decided to spend some time running errands and such. It was well past eleven and she sometimes liked to get out early so that she could have the afternoon to relax. Clay then tried her cell which immediately went to voicemail.

"Now that's odd," he said aloud. "She always has her phone with her. The girl can't function without it."

He decided to make good use of this time that he had, as he tidied up his apartment and sorted clothes for the cleaners. After an hour or so he decided to lie down, and he fell asleep and slept through the entire afternoon. When he woke up, it was well past five.

"Damn, I didn't mean to sleep this long. Why the hell haven't I heard from Blaze?"

He dialed her home number again and once more he got her voicemail. He left a message on her machine.

"Blaze, where are you, baby? Give me a call back!"

Clay sat up on the side of his bed trying to wake up and gather his thoughts. He was still a little groggy from sleep. Once he was fully awake, he tried calling Blaze on her cell phone, and once again it went straight to voicemail. Clay held his phone in his hand and looked at it as if it would speak to him.

"This is beginning to piss me off." Clay was an even-tempered man who didn't let too much get to him. This wasn't normal and so his suspicions peaked. Not being able to get in touch with Blaze made him angry, and so he decided to get dressed and go to her apartment. She lived downtown so it took him about thirty minutes to drive to her place. It was a beautiful sunny day and people were out and about riding bikes, picnicking in the park, and visiting the museums on the Parkway. This didn't help Clay's plight since he could only think how much of the day was wasted waiting on Blaze to show up. He arrived at Blaze's by six-thirty. When he got there, she wasn't at home, and it didn't look like she had been there all day. He opened her windows, made something to eat, and turned on the television. He sat down and watched a movie, but his mind was not on the film. All he could think about was that something wasn't right, and he wasn't leaving until he found out what it was.

| 17 |

Where is Jack?

It was a typical Saturday morning at the Newman home. Thaddeus was preparing to go to the club, and Kate was on the patio preparing a list of things for the staff to complete. Thaddeus stuck his head out to tell her he was leaving when she beckoned for him to come out and join her.

"Have you heard from your son?" she asked.

"Which one?" Thaddeus asked kind of annoyed.

"Well Jack, of course! You know I haven't heard from him since Wednesday night?"

"Well, he had some business to attend to," Thaddeus mentioned trying to cover up for his son.

"Well, what kind of businessman doesn't return phone calls?" Kate asked.

"Kate, what is this about? Jack's a grown man. Leave him to his own life. You're always trying to control something or someone. Some things you just gotta let go." He placed a comforting arm around his wife. Thaddeus adored Kate, but she was a handful. He would tolerate her for so long and oblige her every whim until she pushed him too far; then he would take charge and put his foot down.

"I'll see if I can get in touch with him. Once I do, I'll make sure he calls you. Okay?"

Thaddeus gave Kate a peck on the forehead and headed out to the club for a round of golf. Although she agreed to let Thaddeus handle Jack, she decided she was going to get to the bottom of his little disappearance if it were the last thing she would do.

Miles away, Jack and Blaze were awakened by a knock at the door.

"Housekeeping!" A woman shouted at the door.

"We're fine. Come back later please," Jack yelled from the bed. He turned to look at the clock which display the time as twelve-forty-five.

"Damn, looks like we slept in baby." Jack nudged Blaze who was still sleeping.

"I'm not ready to get up." Blaze replied sleepily.

"You don't have to get up princess. Stay in bed all day if you want and I'll stay right here with you," Jack said kissing her face. Jack got up and went into the bathroom. The room was still dark so there was no indication that it was afternoon. When Jack returned, he walked over to the terrace and pulled the draperies back. The brightness of the sun shone through the window blinding Jack as he shielded his face and closed the drapes back again.

"It looks like it's a beautiful day. Do you want me to order some food?"

"Nothing for me," Blaze mumbled.

Jack jumped back into bed and pulled Blaze close to him. She turned to him nuzzling her face into his chest. Jack kissed her face and held her close. She opened her eyes for the first time since she had been awake, and he was smiling at her.

"What's so funny?" she asked while squinting her eyes.

"You look like a woman that's been having sex all night," he said laughing.

"Well, your assumption would be right," she said sarcastically. "I, sir, have been taken full advantage of. What time is it?" she asked.

"It's almost one."

"What?" She shrieked as she hastily sat up in the bed. She was quite a sight to see with her hair wildly cascading about her. She didn't bother to pull the covers around her body as she revealed her naked breast to the delight of Jack. Jack just smiled admiring the sight before him.

"Baby you look very primal and very sexy," he teased.

"Jack, I should be on my way home by now. I didn't tell anyone where I was going. My family must be frantic."

"Then why don't you call them? Did you check your phone? I didn't hear it ring so they must not be but so worried."

"I turned it off last night." Blaze began looking around for it. "Have you seen my phone?" She started to look around the room.

Jack wasn't remotely interested in finding her phone. He was enjoying her as she rummaged through her handbag to find it. She was bending over the chair looking through her bag and Jack was tempted to take advantage of her vulnerable position. Blaze found her phone and quickly turned it on. She immediately noticed she had five missed calls all from Clay. She immediately went into the bathroom to freshen up. When she saw herself in the mirror, she was horrified by her appearance.

"Wow! I look a mess," she said.

Blaze went to wash her face and brush her teeth. She brushed the tangles from her hair and pulled it back into a ponytail. She returned to the bedroom as Jack was hanging up the phone.

"What's wrong?" he asked.

"Nothing's wrong," she proclaimed.

"Come here!" Jack demanded.

Blaze walked over to the bed and sat down on the edge. Jack placed his hand on the back of her neck and pulled her down so that their faces were a half-inch apart.

"Tell me what's wrong and I'll make it better," he said. Blaze gave Jack a smile and lay down beside him.

"Nothing's wrong. I just didn't expect us to be here this long is all."

"I thought we were having a good time?" Jack asked.

"We are. I mean, I am." Blaze stuttered.

"Then why the long face?"

"I don't know. I guess I'm a bit overwhelmed after last night."

"Are you having second thoughts about us?" Jack asked concernedly.

"No, nothing like that. I guess I don't want the magic to end." Blaze looked deeply into Jack's eyes.

"Baby, you don't ever have to worry about that. We got the magic, and I don't plan to let it go. Do you?" he asked.

Blaze shook her head and held it down until Jack placed a finger under her chin to lift her face. He kissed her lips and enveloped her in his arms. They lay there for a long time not saying a word. Blaze broke the silence as she wrote her name with her fingers on Jack's chest.

"I'm hungry," she confessed.

"You like to eat, don't you?" Jack teased.

"Yes, I do and I ain't ashamed of it." Blaze replied. "So where are we going to get something to eat from? It's too late for breakfast, so what do you want to do?" Blaze asked.

"I don't know. Let's take a shower and then we can take a walk on the boardwalk, grab a bite, do some shopping, and do whatever else you want to do."

"Well let's get going." Blaze said. "Are you gonna lay there all afternoon or are you gonna take a shower with me?"

Jack stood up and ran into the shower with Blaze right on his heels. They made love in the shower emerging from the bathroom an hour later. They got dressed after Blaze dried her hair, and then they went out. The carefree pair had brunch in a cabana right on the beach and spent the afternoon talking and cuddling like lovers do. Blaze was having such a good time she nearly forgot about Clay. She knew she had to somehow get away from Jack for a minute to call him, but she just didn't want to leave his side. He was so damn handsome, not in a pretty boy way. He was masculine and strong. She could just look at him all day and found herself staring when he wasn't looking. She enjoyed talking with him and she also was enamored with his knowledge of so many things. He was opinionated but seemed to value hers and asked for it each time they broached a subject. She found herself listening to his every word. Blaze studied his eyes and the way they crinkled at the corners when he smiled. She loved his smile and the way he licked his lips. She could not help reminiscing about where they had been hours before. She loved the way her hand got lost in his whenever he held it, and she couldn't wait to be alone with him so they could make love again. Blaze wasn't alone in her feelings since Jack was smitten with desire for her. He noticed how the men pass would look at her, and he was proud that she was with him. Without makeup, she was gorgeous. Her skin was smooth as silk, which took on a copper hue from being kissed by the sun. Her laugh was infectious and sexy, and Jack became aroused just by the sound of her voice. She played and toyed with him in the cabana making it hard for him to maintain control. He never felt this way about any woman and never expected to; especially not this soon. He found himself thinking about spending more time with her and the many things he would like to do for her. The sun was beginning to set and the view from the cabana was breathtaking.

"Let's take a walk on the beach!" Blaze begged.

She was like a little child asking her parent permission to take part in some fascinating feat. She pulled at Jack who was enjoying her as she frolicked in front of him barefoot. The sun shone brightly through her lean long legs as her breast threatened to escape when she bent down low in the sand trying to pull Jack up from his seat. He was enjoying her and pretended to not be able to get up so that she would continue her ploy. She bent down and untied Jack's shoes and removed his socks from his feet. She rolled his pants up around his ankles giggling the entire time.

"Aw, Jack please let's walk some," she begged.

Jack reluctantly gave in and decided it best to indulge her than to protest. They walked along the beach near the casinos finally deciding to stop and sit on the warm sand and watch the sunset in the distance upon the splashing waves. Blaze was like a happy child playing in the sand as Jack watched her smiling.

"You really are something else," he said.

Blaze abandoned her play to sit next to Jack as he placed his arm around her. The air was quite warm for a spring evening in May.

"I could sit here all night. This is like a little piece of heaven." Blaze looked out upon the never-ending ocean. They sat on the beach until the sun made its descent somewhere behind the ocean.

"I don't want this time to end," Blaze suddenly uttered.

"It doesn't have to," Jack replied.

"I wish that were true, but we both know that we have to get back to the reality of life—and soon," Blaze added.

"Yes, but we still have one more night, and I plan to make the most of it," Jack said. "Shall we go and make this a night to remember?" he asked as he held out his hand for Blaze to take.

She stood up smiling at him as he enveloped her in his arms and kissed her sweetly. She returned his kiss ardently, as they embraced one another standing on the beach as if there was no one else in the world but the two of them. They slowly walked back to the cabana.

Jack paid the check, and they headed back to the hotel. Once inside, they couldn't remove their clothes fast enough as they made love from the doorway to the balcony. They didn't go back out of the hotel room that evening. Jack ordered dinner from room service, and they spent the rest of the evening in bed. He tried to teach Blaze how to play chess and Blaze tried showing Jack some new dance moves. As accomplished as he was, he didn't possess much rhythm. Blaze on the other hand loved to dance and did so very well. Jack was impressed with the way she moved although it wasn't hard to believe since she moved equally as well in bed. They laughed and joked as if they had been together forever. When they finally decided to call it a night, Blaze cuddled next to Jack as they watched a sappy movie. Before long they were both asleep feeling extremely comfortable for two people having just met. Blaze never called Clay and Jack never called his mother or his service for messages. They decided to let tomorrow take care of itself as they made the night their very own.

| 18 |

Concerned Clay

It was well past eight o'clock and Clay had not heard from Blaze. She didn't return any of his phone calls, and he knew she wasn't with her sisters. To say that he was furious would be an understatement. He put in a call to her mother, but Jewels was none the wiser to her whereabouts. Clay made one final attempt to locate Blaze and called her best friend Misha, the one person whom he didn't get along with. Misha and Blaze had been friends since grade school. Blaze considered Misha her best and dearest friend.

It would have been logical to call Misha from the beginning, but Clay and Misha had a tumultuous history. Clay never liked her and for a brief time before he went out with Blaze Misha had a crush on him. When he began seeing Blaze it made matters worse. Misha was opposed to Clay and Blaze from the start. She hated the fact that they were so in love and tried on various occasions to plant a wedge between them. Misha was jealous and resented Clay for dating her best friend. At first, Blaze was reluctant to date Clay, but as time went on, she began to like him more and more and she finally consented to a date with him. From that point on, there was nothing that Misha could say to Blaze to deter her from seeing him. After a few months, Misha backed off and Clay and Blaze became an item, but Misha never forgot and harbored ill feelings for Clay. If Clay and Blaze had an argument, Misha was all about Blaze hanging out with her and meeting some new guys. When Blaze and Clay would make up, as they always did, Misha would become furious and not talk to Blaze for days. Blaze finally caught on to Misha's behavior and learned to not engage her in conversations regarding Clay. Unfortunately, she was the last resort for Clay, but he was worried and broke down to call Misha. He dialed Misha's number which rang several times before she answered.

"Hello."

"Hi, Misha."

There were a few seconds of silence before Misha responded.

"Clay, why you calling me?"

"Look Misha, sorry to bother you but have you seen or talked to Blaze today?"

"Why?" she asked.

"What do ya mean why? Just answer the damn question, Misha."

"Now you wait one minute. Don't speak to me in that tone of voice. Who do you think you are!?" Misha quickly became annoyed.

"Okay, my fault. I was out of line," Clay said reluctantly. "I just need to know if you've heard from Blaze is all?"

Although most of the time she didn't seem to be, Misha was smart, and she knew if Clay was calling her then something must be up between the two love birds. She thought quickly before speaking again.

"She had a seminar today and then they were having dinner afterward. She probably didn't call you since you can't have your cell phone on during those kinds of events."

For the first time all day, Clay felt some relief.

"You're probably right, but I know they get a break or something."

"Well, maybe she left her phone in the room or somethin' since she wouldn't be able to use it. You know she isn't glued to you Clay," Misha stated. Clay was not interested in entertaining the conversation any further and so he opted to not answer her remark.

"Well thanks, Misha. I appreciate it," Clay did not know what else to say.

"Yeah, yeah. You're welcome," she said before hanging up.

Misha immediately called Blaze's cell, but her voicemail came on immediately. She left Blaze a message of caution.

"Blaze, this is Mish. Clay called looking for you. I told him you had a seminar to go to and after you were having dinner with the group. He's really upset you haven't called. You better call me first before you call him so we can get our stories straight. Call me!" Misha hung up the phone and smiled. She was enjoying hearing the concern in Clay's voice and the fact that he hadn't heard from Blaze all day was priceless.

'Guess the lovers had a little spat. Wonder what happened. Had to be somethin' for Blaze to disappear for all them hours. Whew wee, can't wait to talk to her.' Misha smiled as she went back to watching her chick flick.

Clay felt a little better since talking to Misha. At least now he had an idea where Blaze might be. He decided to go out and meet the guys for a game of pool. Since Blaze was probably out having dinner with her colleagues, there was no sense in him spending Saturday night in with nothing to do. He made a phone call to one of his boys and they decide to meet up at a bar and shoot some pool. He thought to himself:

I'll give her a call a little later. By the time she gets back, she'll be tired, and I'll just come by and spend the night here.'

Clay grabbed his phone and keys and headed out for downtown. It was nearly nine o'clock and the evening was just starting for most, while for others it was ending on a more intimate note. When Clay met up with his boys at the bar, they had some dinner and plenty of drinks. It was 2:00 am when they decided to call it a night. Clay had a little too much to drink, so one of his boys drove him home. When he reached his apartment, he took off his clothes and got right into bed. He slept through the night and well into the next day. He didn't wake up until late afternoon being tired from traveling and having more than his share of drinks. Just as he was about to call Blaze, his phone rang. He was pleasantly surprised to hear her voice.

| 19 |

Misha's got it covered

When Blaze and Jack finally decide to get out of bed, they had breakfast together on the balcony of the hotel room. Blaze was wearing a white tee shirt and jeans with no makeup and her hair pulled high upon her head. They talked as they ate and before long it was time to check out. Jack had the hotel staff take the bags down to the lobby and retrieve his truck. When they got in the truck, Blaze chose the music for the trip back. Jack loved old classics, so Blaze was in her element playing the music they both liked.

"I can't believe we have the same taste in music. You like all my favorites. This is so awesome!" Blaze was extremely giddy and full of joy. Jack just smiled as he looked at her face so lit up with enthusiasm. When she wasn't singing and chair dancing, she was cuddling up to Jack like a little girl. He liked that about her. She could transform herself from a bold, sexy, confident woman to a childlike whimsical creature. Jack took the scenic route back home to spend as much time with Blaze as possible.

Once they crossed the bridge into Philly, they both knew that their fantasy weekend was history. When Jack pulled up in front of Blaze's building, they both sat there looking at one another not saying a word. Blaze finally broke the ice not wanting to seem as if she was expecting any promises of future commitments.

"Well, this was really fun Jack." She held out her hand to him as if to shake it. Jack smiled and pulled her to him.

"Remember what I said," he said authoritatively.

He kissed her, and she kissed him back. When he let her go, he got out of the truck and opened the trunk to get her bag. She climbed out and stood next to him taking the packages from him.

"Do you want me to help you take these things in?" he asked.

"No," she replied smiling. "I think I can handle it."

"Well, okay then Ace. I'll see ya!" She walked up the steps into her building. Jack watched her get in, and then he got into his truck and drove away.

Blaze stood in the foyer of her building watching Jack as he drove off. Unexplainable feelings ran through her body. There was longing, sadness, and aching for him that she hadn't felt before with anyone. She climbed up the two flights of stairs to her apartment and let herself inside. The moment she walked in, she sensed that Clay was there.

"Clay?" she called out.

There was no answer and she looked about the huge apartment.

"Thank God," she said. "I'm not ready to face him."

It was past three o'clock and Blaze went about unpacking and putting her things away. She prepared herself for a nice, long, hot, bath. She checked her messages and found that she had several from Clay. She had already checked her cell phone when she was in A.C. with some eight or more messages left by him. She also received a message from Misha telling her to call her before she called Clay. She dialed Misha's number.

"This Misha," she answered.

"Mish, it's me," Blaze replied.

"Girl, where you been?"

"It's a long story," Blaze said.

"Well get to telling me 'cause Clay called here for you and you know he don't be calling me for nothin'," she said all in one breath.

"What'd he say?" Blaze asked.

"He asked if I heard from you. I knew something was up so I told him that you were probably at a seminar and couldn't call him. Then I said you probably went to dinner with the group or something and for him not to worry. I said you more than likely left your phone in the room, cause phones ain't allowed in seminars."

"Gee Mish, you thought of everything."

"Girl, you know I'm experienced with these kinds of things."

Blaze laughed.

"Well, how many times did he call you?"

"He only called once around six or so."

"Okay, I guess I better call him."

"Oh no, not so fast! Where you been?" Misha asked.

"I went to A.C. for a few days is all."

"Wit who?

"No one! There was a marketing seminar at Board Walk Hall."

"Oh! Why didn't you tell Clay about it?"

"Cause, he was in Colorado, and I decide to go at the last minute. Why you askin' so many questions, Mish?"

"Nothing just asking! Why you on the defensive?"

"I'm not...just tired. I'm sorry. Thanks for looking out girl."

"No problem. Call me!"

| 20 |

Let it go, Mom

The Newman home was always a bustle of activity on Sunday afternoons. Kate insisted that her children and grandchildren join her and Thaddeus for brunch to catch up on their weekly activities and spend some quality time with the family. Kate and Thaddeus were members of the United Presbyterian Church of Greater Northwest Philadelphia where Kate was very active on the women's committees. After church, they always returned home to a sumptuous brunch buffet for the family, and often close friends. During the summer months, the clan would gather by the pool, swim, play tennis or scrabble, and enjoy their time together. This Sunday was no different except for one minor detail; Jack was not present. Kate promised Thaddeus that she would not bring up the subject of Jack being absent, but she couldn't put it out of her mind. Jack was such a source of comfort for her that she missed him when he was away from home. Out of all their children, he was the one she had the hardest time letting go. He was the one who usually played scrabble with her when the family was all together. Kate was by no means a humble bumbling housewife; on the contrary, she was an accomplished woman in her own right and had a reputation for being difficult. But when it came to her family, especially her children, she was loving and caring. Just as she was about to give up on seeing Jack, she heard a commotion in the family room leading out to the patio. Elizabeth was running through the house screaming and someone was right on her heels chasing her outside.

"What in the world is going on? Lizzy, what has gotten—"

"Jack, I should've known! You're incorrigible," Kate yelled. Jack came over to his mother and planted a juicy wet kiss on her cheek picking her up at the same time.

"Jack, stop it! Put me down," she protested laughing. Lizzy could not resist laughing at Jack's display of affection for his mother. Soon, Thaddeus and James joined the group while Michael and the children swam over to get out of the pool.

"Where have you been? I've been trying to reach you since Thursday afternoon," Kate began scowling at Jack.

"I went to the shore for a couple of days," Jack answered picking up a croissant from the buffet.

"The shore? With whom?" Kate asked curiously.

"Manny had a birthday party at the club and all the guys went down for a few days."

"Well, why didn't you call me? I called your mobile phone a few times."

"Make that a thousand times," Thaddeus added peering over his horn-rimmed glasses.

"Hey Pop! How ya doing?" Jack hugged his father.

"I'm good, son. You had your mother in a frantic not being able to reach you."

"Well, I'm here now, so what's up?" Jack turned his direction toward his mother.

"Well, I need to know who your guest will be for the charity event next month," Kate responded.

"Why?" Jack asked taking a seat at the umbrella table.

"Well, I need to add the name to the guest list and also determine if lodging is needed or not."

"Mom, can't you just put guest and leave it at that? You just need a headcount, right?"

"That's right, but it would be nice to know who your guest will be."

"I haven't thought much about that mother."

Jack's voice remained unenthusiastic.

"Well, I hear Denise is home for a visit. Why not ask her?"

There was suddenly silence on the patio as Thaddeus and each one of the children looked on as if an elephant suddenly walked into the room.

"Mom, you don't want to go there."

Jack was very obviously annoyed.

"Well, what's wrong with asking her to the party? You know her parents are coming, so she'll be coming anyway. It would just be a nice gesture if you invited her is all."

"Mother, enough! I will not be inviting Denise, so if you plan on inviting her then do so, but don't expect me to play host."

Jack got up and walked into the house. Although he had his own apartment in the city, he still had a room at home. He went upstairs to shower and change his clothes. He had been on a high for the last four days and now in one moment, his mother managed to get under his skin. All he wanted to do the rest of the day was sleep. Jack decided to take a drive instead. Before he was able to escape, he was cornered again, but this time by Thaddeus.

"Going out, son?" Thaddeus asked.

"Yeah, I'm gonna take a drive...clear my head," Jack replied.

"Got a minute to talk to your ole man?" Thaddeus asked Jack.

"Sure, Pop. What's up?" They walked into Thaddeus's study and closed the door.

"Look, I know your mother can be a pain. Lord knows I've been with her long enough to know how much she can seem to be intruding upon your life, but she means well. She has your best interest at heart."

"Pop, I know that, but I have to live my own life. When is she gonna let up on trying to control that?"

"Probably never, son!"

"Well, I'm not having it, Pop! She knows that me and Denise were over before it really began. Denise in my life is some fantasy in Mom's mind. It ain't gonna happen!"

"Okay, I understand! Just be careful son. It's not easy to mix business and pleasure. You gotta have some boundaries."

"I know pop. I'll be alright," Jack said hugging his father before leaving.

Jack decided to take his convertible. He put the top down and turned his music up. It was a beautiful afternoon with blue skies and white clouds cascading around the sun. He drove through an area that was mostly farmland listening to his music and thinking about the past four days. He smiled when he thought of Blaze and her wild side. She was so smart and so accomplished, and he liked that about her. More importantly, she was beautiful and sexy as hell, and he liked that more. He knew he was playing a dangerous game by getting involved with her. After all, she was practically his employee. It wasn't ethical for them to become sexually involved, but ethics went out of the window when he first kissed her. She was as passionate a lover as he was, and he enjoyed her tremendously. As he drove through the winding back roads of the farmlands, he smiled remembering their time together and how much he enjoyed every minute.

Jack didn't even know how long he had been driving, but he was headed toward his parent's home. He felt a sense of melancholy come over him, but he didn't really understand why. It seemed as if something was missing, and then he realized what it was.

"Aw hell! What man in his right mind could give that up?" he asked himself. He thought of calling Blaze but decided not to do so. He didn't like the indecisiveness that he was experiencing. After a few moments, he decided against calling her and turned onto the highway headed for Blue Bell.

| 21 |

Welcome to my home!

It was now Sunday evening and Blaze still had not called Clay. She knew he would want to come over, and she wasn't up to seeing him. She finally called and he picked up on the third ring.

"Hey, baby—where you been? I been calling you," Clay asked.

"I know. I'm sorry, Clay," she said grimacing.

"Why didn't you return my calls?"

"I didn't get in until a few minutes ago. I went to a seminar at the last minute," she said.

"Oh yeah? I don't remember you mentioning anything about a seminar."

"I didn't want to go, but Sam suggested that I go and catch up with the team."

"Oh. So where was it?"

"In Atlantic City," Blaze stated.

"Really! That must've been nice."

"Although I was only there overnight, it was long, and everyone crashed after dinner."

"I can't believe that." Clay said. "Being in such an exciting town as A.C.," he added.

"So how was your trip?" she asked.

"It was profitable. But I can tell you all about it when I get there."

"Clay, can we do this another night? I'm beat and I just want to take a bath and go to sleep."

"How bout I come over and make us some dinner before your bath? Then you can relax.

"Clay I just want to go to bed is all." Clay's demeanor changed abruptly.

"You know I haven't seen you since last Tuesday. You would think that you missed me just a little," Clay said disappointed.

"I do miss you, Clay. I'm exhausted, and I have a full day tomorrow. Sorry but I just can't tonight. Please try and understand," Blaze pleaded.

"Okay then. If you're not up to seeing me, that's that! I'll see ya later," Clay said before hanging up.

Blaze hung up the phone and sat in the middle of her bed. She didn't like lying to Clay. She felt bad having to do that, but she just couldn't pretend to want to be with him tonight. Clay could be very needy at times, and she just wasn't able to fulfill those needs tonight. Blaze laid back on her bed and closed her eyes. All she could see was Jack. She opened her eyes and tried to focus on something else.

"I can't get involved with him. What happened was by chance and I just can't let it happen again. Get that into your head Blaze," she told herself.

Blaze got up from her bed, and took a towel, shampoo, and bubble bath from her linen closet. She ran a bath and then removed her clothes. The water was a little hot, so she added some cold to it. She stepped into the tub and immersed herself in the bubbly water. It was soothing and warm and she closed her eyes as she laid her head against the back of the tub. She had been relaxing there for about fifteen minutes when she heard her cell phone ring. The sound was coming from somewhere in the bathroom and she realized she left the phone in her jeans pocket.

"Damn! Who could this be?"

She reached over the tub and took the phone out of her pants pocket. She recognized the number immediately and began to smile from ear to ear.

"Hello?" She smiled at the phone.

"Hey, beautiful! Jack Newman here." Blaze's smile widened.

"I know who it is," she said. "This is a nice surprise!"

"Is it? I wasn't sure if I should call you so soon," Jack said.

"You can call me anytime, Mr. Newman."

"So now it's Mr. Newman now that you've screwed my brains out, spent some time with me, and gotten to know me a little better," he teased.

Blaze laughed.

"Have I?" she asked.

"Yes, of course, you have and very quickly I might add."

"Where are you?" she asked. "Sounds like you're driving?"

"I am. I decide to take a drive through the county since it's such a beautiful day."

"Wow, I admire your stamina."

"You do, huh? What are you doing?" he asked.

"I'm taking a bath."

"Oh, I didn't mean to disturb you."

"You're not disturbing me. I'm just soaking, and relaxing is all."

"Do you need someone to scrub your back?"

"I think I can handle it," Blaze laughed.

"Was everything alright when you got home?" Jack asked.

"Sure... uh yes, why do you ask?" Blaze asked nervously.

"Just asking?"

There was silence and then they both began to talk at the same time. Blaze laughed and Jack followed with a chuckle.

"I can't believe this," Jack stated.

"Believe what?" Blaze asked.

"Believe how you affect me. You make me feel like a schoolboy."

"There is nothing remotely similar to a schoolboy about you Jack."

"Hey what does that mean? I'm a nice guy."

Blaze burst into laughter again at his interpretation of a nice guy. Jack's tone changed abruptly.

"I want to see you again," he said. Blaze was taken off guard by his statement.

"Are you sure, Jack?"

"No, I'm not sure, but I would like to give it a try."

"Jack, we should talk about this."

"Okay. Invite me over and we can talk."

"Tonight?" Blaze asked.

"The sooner the better," Jack added.

"Why don't I come to you?" Blaze asked.

"Okay, that's not a problem."

"Where do you live, Jack?"

"I live on South 2nd Street. It's an old, refurbished warehouse. I have the 10th floor."

"Okay! I'll be there in about an hour." Blaze concluded.

When they hung up the phone, Blaze was astonished at the energy that she acquired. She bathed and began to groom herself. She wanted to look and smell beautiful for Jack and so she applied body cream and parfum to every intimate part of her body. Blaze loved anything black, so she decided to wear black slacks and a black silk button-down shirt. She added a simple pair of hooped earrings and a pair of black pumps. She brushed her hair from her face and added a thin headband. She was stunning even in this simple attire. She grabbed her purse and keys and headed out of the door down to the garage where her car was parked. She drove ten blocks from her apartment to the warehouse district where Jack lived. Parking was always difficult in the city, but luckily there was a lot across the street from his apartment. The neighborhood was part construction and part warehouse buildings in a historic section of the city. Acquiring property in this part of town was a sure bet that the person who owned it was successful. This was a desired location for the up-and-coming young professional. Blaze paid the parking attendant and began to walk toward Jack's building. A few people were out walking their dogs or strolling through the area. The neighborhood had plenty of restaurants, shops, clubs, and museums within walking distance.

She found the building and began to walk up the steps to ring the bell. There were only three occupants in the building each owning one of the loft-style apartments, but Jack lived on the 10th floor. The remaining floors contained offices with an entrance to them on the other side of the building. Blaze was buzzed in and took the private elevator up to the 10th floor. When she arrived, the doors opened directly into Jack's apartment and into a room reminiscent of a layout in Architectural Digest. Cherry wood floors were adorned with several burgundy and tan Tibetan carpets thrown about as she walked into the main room. It didn't look like an apartment at all but more like a house within a flat. The floor plan was open and airy, providing the right amount of light and ambiance. One side of the room from the ceiling to the floor was all exposed brick adorned with various types of African masks and paintings by African American artists. Shelves lined part of the wall which housed thousands of vinyl albums from jazz to classical music. The other side of the room contained large windows extending the length of the apartment with a magnificent view of the city. The ceilings were high, and the lighting was recessed and warm. There was a fireplace in the living room area directly in front of a distressed, burnished-colored, leather sofa almost the length of the room. The only other piece of furniture was a huge mahogany wood cocktail table. The kitchen was complete with another fireplace and a professional-grade stainless steel range and convection oven. In the center of the room, the island housed numerous shelves for cookbooks and a dozen drawers for utensils and supplies. Overhead was an array of pots and pans of all types.

From the living room area, Blaze could see the spacious bedroom with two large floors to ceiling windows that were bare, with the exception of burgundy taffeta silk curtains that cascaded along the hardwood floor. A magnificent four-poster king-size bed sat upon a platform commanding attention as the focal point of the room. Two oversized wooden night tables adorned each side of the bed with overhead ensconced lighting set in brass fixtures. A wooden chest sat at the foot of the bed with richly colored brocade comforters of different hues of burnt orange, plum, and burgundy stacked upon it. A clay-colored leather chair was planted by one window with a mink throw haphazardly thrown upon it. It was definitely a man's apartment, but it had character and style.

Jack emerged from the bedroom wearing a pair of jeans and a black tee shirt, his muscular frame threatening to burst the seams of his shirt. He walked towards Blaze with a huge smile on his face and kissed both her cheeks.

"Welcome to my home," he said as he took her hand.

"It's fantastic, Jack…and the view is breathtaking."

"I'm glad you like it. The building is being renovated and once it's completed, I plan to sell it."

"You own the entire building?" Blaze was astonished.

"You seem surprised," Jack responded.

"No, I just didn't think that it was yours," she said feeling a little silly.

"When the city made plans to demolish the buildings in this area to begin gentrification, my dad decided to purchase several of them. We knew that once they started to renovate this area the properties would be worth a fortune. My father gave this to me as a gift when I finished grad school. It was nothing but a shell at that time. I've been overseeing the renovations since then." Blaze was intrigued by Jack's many talents.

"Make yourself at home and pour yourself a glass of wine while I finish dinner."

"Okay!" Blaze said needing the libation.

Jack returned from the kitchen and sat down as Blaze walked through the apartment admiring the artwork and the wall of albums that Jack had collected. He watched her intently as she moved about the room.

"I can't believe this collection, Jack. You have everything from Miles and Charlie Parker to the days of the Black Experience in Music and beyond."

"Yeah, there's some Jay-Z and Tupac mixed in as well. A lot of that stuff was my dad's, but my mother threatened to throw it out, so I took most of his collection. He comes here a lot to just sit, play the music, and chill."

"That's nice. You seem to have a good relationship with your father."

"Oh yeah! We get along well. It's not bad being the youngest son of Thaddeus Newman, but I am the only one that works with him."

"Really? That's interesting." Blaze's curiosity peaked. "Why are your brothers and sisters not involved in the business as well?"

"Well, they are in a way. They all own stock in the company, but they're not physically involved in the day-to-day operation."

"Enough about me. Come here and talk to me." Jack patted the sofa gesturing for Blaze to come and sit with him. Blaze walked over to the sofa and sat down beside Jack. She was trying to avoid being so close to him for fear of what might happen. She was nervous being in his apartment. Jack touched her hair and then her face.

"What's the matter? You seem nervous," Jack asked.

"I guess I am a little nervous," she replied.

Jack chuckled.

"Why? We spent three whole nights together. How can you be nervous now?"

"It was different then. We were in a hotel, so it was sort of like mutual ground. Now we are in your home, and I guess I feel vulnerable."

"Okay. What can I do to make you feel comfortable in my home?"

"Just give me a few minutes and I'll be okay."

Jack got up and walked into the kitchen to check on the chili he was making.

"Do you like chili?" he asked.

"Yes!"

"Good cause it's almost ready."

"Do you make it really hot?" she asked.

"Not too hot. Just wait until you try it."

Blaze walked over to the stereo and tried to understand how to work the very sophisticated and complicated system. Jack noticed that she was struggling with getting it to work, so he showed her how to change the music as she placed an old record on the stereo. Both Blaze and Jack had a great appreciation for older music. She had taken her shoes off when she entered Jack's apartment and she was now sitting Indian-style on the floor flipping through the albums. Jack watched her from the kitchen area as he put the finishing touches on dinner. He was no longer hungry but had other things on his mind. Blaze chose Grover Washington Jr. as she sipped her wine. She began to unwind and felt more comfortable as the warm libation trickled down her throat. She was humming the melody of *Sausalito* as the music echoed throughout the apartment.

She walked towards the kitchen to pour herself another glass of wine. Jack watched her as she sauntered over towards him smiling. She put her glass down and stood in front of him with her hands placed on her hips.

"I love this track," she said swaying to the rhythm.

"You do, huh?" Jack asked surreptitiously.

"Dance with me Jack," she commanded pulling him towards her. She took both his hands and placed them around her waist. She then put her arms around his neck and began to move seductively with the rhythm of the music. Jack stood still his feet planted firmly on the ground. He reached down and kissed her lips as she parted them for his tongue to enter her mouth. They kissed one another with passion as Jack picked Blaze up lifting her so her feet no longer touched the floor.

"I promised myself that I'd be cool." Jack's tone was hushed. "But I decided that I don't want to."

"Why would you make such a promise to yourself?" Blaze teased as she kissed his neck and face. Jack walked her into the bedroom her legs now wrapped around his waist. He laid her down on his bed and joined her there. He ran his hands over her body while removing her clothing. He opened her blouse and nuzzled his face into her breast kissing and licking her. Blaze couldn't resist him as she noticed the mirror on the ceiling. It startled her at first as she watched them in their embrace.

"Jack, you have mirrors on your ceiling!" she stated, pointing out the obvious.

"Mmhmm," he uttered without losing stride.

"Now, I know how freaky you really are." She began to unbutton his jeans.

Jack gave her a knowing glance as he stated matter-of-factly, "You have to be a freak to know a freak." He kicked off his pants. Blaze had already removed her clothing and now only wore her black lace underwear.

"Where are those shoes you had on when you came in?" Jack asked her.

"They're in the living room by the door," she replied.

Jack got up from the bed and walked into the living room returning with shoes in hand.

Blaze watched him walk away admiring the strength in his muscular, lean body and the way his buttocks moved when he walked. She was more delighted when he returned having a frontal view that took her breath away.

"Here, put these on." Jack handed her the shoes and sat in his chair. Blaze did as she was told as Jack watched her intently. She got up and walked towards Jack with a slow and purposeful swing in her hips. She stood in front of him so he could get a full view of her. Jack gazed at her from head to toe taking in every curve, every valley, and every mountain which was Blaze. He grasped her around her waist as he buried his face into her belly. She bent down to him lifting his face and kissed him passionately. Jack was aroused by her fragrant body and the touch of her soft skin next to his own. He ran his hands along her long, lean legs lingering at her ankles. He then stood up as she took in a full view of his erectness. Jack picked her up and took her back to his bed. She lay on her back and watched him as he kneeled on the bed to better view her body. She wrapped her legs around his waist and held him close to her. His scent permeated her soul with the fragrance of sandalwood his signature scent. Blaze captured his every move in the ceiling mirror which served to arouse her anticipation of him even more. His muscles rippled at each movement and Blaze took pleasure in the sight of him. Jack was patient with her and spent time enjoying her body. He needed no introduction or guidance to the place he longed to be as he found his way inside of her; first with his fingers finding the pleasure zone that she needed to be touched. When neither could stand it any longer, he took her, and she willingly obliged him.

"Blaze," he whispered her name in her ear. "Aw, baby I can't hold it any longer."

"Yes, Jack," she said in response her desire now peaked. As she reached a plateau of sheer pleasure, she was high from him. Blaze held on to Jack, moaning his name and holding him tighter as she reached a very long and fulfilling climax. He, too, followed like a wild beast tamed by the very essence of her love as they lingered in the moment together. They fell back upon the bed in a release of satisfaction unknown to either of them, at any time, with any other before.

| 22 |

Stay with me tonight

Blaze lay sleeping in Jack's arms exhausted but very happy being so near to him. She wanted to melt into him and never return from that place. Jack gently nudged her to see if she was still hungry.

"Hey beautiful, are you ready to eat?"

Blaze yawned and stretched before answering, "I'm famished."

"Okay then. One bowl of chili coming up." Jack stood up to go to the kitchen.

Blaze slowly got up and went into the bathroom to pee and freshen up. When she entered the bathroom, it was as if she stepped into another realm. The mocha-colored walls were embraced by the white trim of the deep-seated windowsills and stark whiteness of the large face bowl and the deep walk-in tub which was full of water and lots of bubbles. The heated marble floor was warm to the touch of her toes as she tiptoed over to the commode to pee. Candles were everywhere and soft music from the stereo was piped in through hidden speakers. She put her hand in the water which was now cold. She giggled to herself that Jack must have been planning a co-ed bath for them. She smiled as she remembered their shower at the hotel and thought to herself that they never even made it that far this time. Blaze left the door open so when Jack walked in, he found her kneeling by the tub playing in the bubbles.

"The water has to be cold by now," he said startling her.

"It's very cold, but the atmosphere is so nice in here. I love this tub. It's big enough for two."

"If you want, I can run you another bath."

She smiled at him, "Where's my food? Feed me."

"Okay woman. Your food is in here so come on and get it."

"You know you gotta feed a woman," Blaze said jokingly.

"Yes, I do know. If I remember correctly, you like to throw down."

Blaze laughed as she walked back into the bedroom taking a throw from the chair and wrapping herself in it.

"You cold?" Jack asked.

"A little," she said. "Nights are still a little chilly."

"Well come into the living room. I think it's warmer in there.

Blaze followed Jack as he took the tray of food and placed it on the coffee table. The fire roared in the fireplace making the room nice and toasty.

"Oh Jack, this is wonderful!" she exclaimed.

Jack grabbed another cover from his sofa and laid it on the rug in front of the fire. He then placed the bottle of wine and the tray of food on the floor as well. Blaze sat on the floor in front of the fire wrapped in the fur coverlet. When Jack joined her, she opened the blanket sharing her warmth with him, and they ate and talked in front of the fire. The reflection of the light cast a warm glow all about the room. It was nearly midnight, but neither Jack nor Blaze cared that they were expected to show up for work the next morning. As Blaze attempted to act out some story she was telling Jack, the cover fell away from her revealing her naked body for Jack to admire. Jack enjoyed watching her as she had no inhibitions and spoke her mind freely. They laughed as each shared their stories with the other. Blaze was on her knees in front of Jack just talking away when he reached up and pulled her down upon him. He kissed her lips with urgency, and she returned his ardor with her own. Jack looked into her eyes with a serious expression as his hands playfully ran through her hair.

"Stay with me tonight," he commanded.

Blaze was stunned at his request.

"Jack, I can't stay. I have to be in the office early and I don't have a change of clothes or my briefcase…nothing," she admitted.

"I don't care," he said. "We'll get up early and get your things before work. Just stay with me tonight," Jack reiterated his request.

"But my car is parked in the lot."

"Don't worry. It's a twenty-four-hour lot."

Blaze looked at him and saw the look in his eyes and realized she couldn't resist him. She answered his question by placing her mouth fully upon his and pushing him back against the sofa. She straddled his lap and wrapped her arms around his neck. Jack enveloped her waist kissing her neck and breast and then her lips again. They made love again and when they were finished Jack pulled the blanket around them.

"Are you okay?" Jack asked.

"I'm fine!" Blaze answered.

"I told you…I know you're fine…but the question is are you alright?"

Blaze chuckled at his reference to her and turned around to face him as they lay on the floor.

"Jack, I have to know something."

"Sure, what does my baby want to know?"

"What happens now?"

"What do you mean?" Jack asked.

"Well, today we get back to reality...you at Newman and me at Brickhouse, Becker, and Shuman Inc."

"Blaze, if you're asking me will this change anything between us the answer is no!"

"But Jack, I may work for you. Well, I mean I work for Newman."

"You were right the first time," he teased, "You work for me!"

"Jack, be serious!"

"I am being serious. I'm your boss and you are my most favored employee." Jack pulled her close to him.

Blaze broke free from him and sat up on her side.

"Jack, I don't want to compromise the campaign by sleeping with you."

"Well, it's a little too late for that don't you think? Oh—I see—so is this all there is to you?" Jack asked. "Are we just sleeping together and when we get back to work it's business as usual? How cold is that?"

"I didn't mean it that way." Blaze was trying to be diplomatic.

Jack, clearly annoyed, sat up as well.

"Look, Blaze...I like you—a lot. I wouldn't have spent all this time with you just to get laid. I could have done that with any number of women."

"Oh, is that so?" the tone in her voice changed.

"I only meant that you mean more to me than just an easy lay. I enjoy your company. I think that you're a great mixture of intelligence and beauty, not to mention a little minx in bed. I thought that these few days clued you in on who I am. I see that I must have assumed too much."

"Jack, that's not where I was going with this. Shit, this is coming out oh so wrong." Blaze placed her hands in her hair, clearly feeling challenged. She tried again to explain how she felt.

"My work is important to me, and I don't want my staff or colleagues to think that I'm on this account because I slept my way into it."

"Blaze, you're smart and respected. I doubt if anyone would assume that."

"But we are sleeping together," Blaze added.

Jack looked at her and knew that she was serious. He took her hands into his and kissed them both. Then he looked at her before he spoke.

"Blaze, if you're trying to tell me that you don't want to continue to see me, then I can respect that. But don't use our working relationship as a scapegoat to justify that."

"I'm doing no such thing, Jack. I cannot risk compromising my position with the firm let alone your company."

"You won't. I promise not to let that happen."

"What if it gets out of hand and out of your control?"

"Not gonna happen," Jack said with confidence.

As Blaze looked at him a smile slowly formed across his mouth. Blaze started smiling too.

"That's my girl," Jack said enveloping her in his arms.

"Now what do you say we get some sleep? We gotta get up pretty early to get you on your way," he said before kissing her.

"Okay, but let me help you clear the dishes and put things away."

"No! I have someone to come and do that for me in the morning."

"Is she pretty?" Blaze asked.

"Why? Are you jealous my sweet?"

"Not at all," Blaze lied, "but she better know her boundaries around here is all I gotta say!"

"Check you out! Now I'm seeing the real Blaze Beaumont come out," Jack teased.

He laughed holding his hand out his hand to her. Together, they walked into the bedroom.

Jack and Blaze lay in each other's arms until they both fell asleep. Within a few hours the morning was dawning, and Blaze got up, showered, and dressed. She was quiet not to wake Jack from his sound sleep. She gathered her things and tiptoed over to Jack placing a kiss on his lips. He mumbled something and smiled as Blaze quietly stepped onto the elevator for her journey back home. Although spring was well on its way out and summer was ready to begin, the air was brisk and cool as Blaze enjoyed her drive back home. She thought about her time with Jack. She couldn't believe how much she enjoyed being with him nor that he was interested in her. There had to be a catch. There was always a catch when it came to matters of the heart, she thought. She pulled into her parking garage and took the elevator up to her apartment. She changed her clothes, styled her hair, and had just enough time to get a container of yogurt and her briefcase for work. She knew that it would be difficult getting back into the routine after her time away, but she was determined to be ready for the next steps of the Newman campaign. She arrived at the office a little after eight and went right into work mode for most of the morning. She had a meeting with Sam and a lunch appointment with Z. Her day was set. All she had to do was stay focused and keep her mind off Jack. She smiled as she thought how impossible that was going to be.

| 23 |

Back at the Newmans

Kate didn't appreciate that Jack ran off, going who knows where after just arriving back home from a long weekend. It wasn't like her son to be so secretive. This somehow had all the subtle details of a woman's involvement. She knew how these things worked, and up until now, she had been successful in keeping the wrong type away from her son. She was hell-bent on making sure that all her children had the right upbringing, and that they chose the proper spouses to maintain the right lineage for their future generations. She couldn't remember another time when Jack disappeared without notice for days only to come home and leave out right away. She immediately became suspicious but wanted to confirm her thoughts. When Jack left to go for his drive, Kate left her family on the patio and went into the house. She made a phone call to her confidante Edward Thompson. Ed and Kate had been friends for years. They dated in high school, and most of college, and spent their summers together at her father's house at the shore. Ed was her escort for her debutante coming out party and he was her boyfriend while she attended college. Kate knew that Ed loved her from the very start, and she realized that he still did, even though he had a family of his own. It nearly broke his heart when she married Thaddeus, but she maintained a friendship with him despite it all. She called Ed's cell phone, which was always the best way to get him. Like always, he picked up right away when he realized it was Kate.

"Kate...to what do I owe this wonderful surprise to hear from you on a beautiful Sunday afternoon?" Ed asked jovially.

"Hello, Ed," she said pompously. "Do you have some time to come out to the house tomorrow for lunch?"

"I'm meeting with a client in the morning Kate, and I don't know how long I'll be engaged in the matter."

"This is very important to me Ed. I'd appreciate it if you could come by when you're done."

"Is something wrong?" he asked.

"Well not directly, but I feel if I don't look into this now, I may regret it later."

"May I ask what this is about?"

"It has to do with Jack, but I'll fill you in tomorrow. I just can't get into it right now with the family here," she said cautiously.

"Okay, I'll get there as soon as I can," Ed obliged.

"Oh good. I'll see you then. Oh, by the way, Ed, thank you." Kate felt relief. She hung up the phone and stood by the ornate telephone table for a minute. She looked at herself in the mirror and smoothed her well-coifed hair in place. She nodded at herself with approval and made her way back out to the patio joining the rest of the family. Thaddeus looked at her over his horn-rimmed glasses quizzically as she approached the blue and white chaise lounge to sit down.

"Where'd you go?" he asked.

"I was giving Bert some instructions for dinner," she lied picking up her magazine.

Thaddeus knew his wife very well and was determined that she was up to something. He looked at her until she looked up at him.

"What?" she asked in a guilty tone realizing he was on to her.

"You know perfectly well what?" Thaddeus said to her in reply.

"Whatever are you going on about Thad?" she replied condescendingly as she opened her magazine. Thaddeus just shook his head and continued to read his paper. Kate put on her sunglasses and lay back in her chair looking like the cat that swallowed the canary.

Monday morning arrived with the usual fanfare at the Newman home. Kate was up early for her morning workout and Thaddeus was in the gym on the treadmill watching the financial news. They both ate a moderate breakfast of fresh fruit and oatmeal and then said their goodbyes until Thad would return home at the end of the day. Once Thaddeus was off to the office, Kate showered and went into the study to look over meal plans and discuss her schedule with her personal assistant, Pierre. Pierre Dubois had been with Kate for two years, which was the longest that she had ever held onto an assistant. She had a reputation for sucking them in and spitting them out. Rumor had it that she once hired and fired two on the same day. Pierre's longevity could be credited to his ability to combine the right amount of kiss ass along with a certain amount of efficiency. He had a certificate of completion from the Fashion Institute of New York, which was a catalyst in Kate's decision to hire him. She liked that he had style, so he doubled as her personal fashion consultant. Pierre would often say, "It is my honor to serve a woman of such elegance and fierceness as Madame Newman."

Pierre was a thirty-five-year-old, fair-complexioned man, tall and thin with dark straight hair cut close to his head. He had tiny little slits for eyes, a keen nose, and small lips. He was always well groomed and wore only designer fashions that he would beg, borrow, or steal from designers. He was at Kate's beck and call day and night. He didn't have a personal life except for a few one-night stands he had while cruising the city nightlife. He lived and breathed fashion and could do very well managing his own image consulting business if he wasn't contracted out to Kate. She paid him handsomely to dominate his life while doubling as her personal assistant. Kate loved Pierre but loved controlling his life more and making him miserable as often as she could. This morning would be no different!

"Pierre, what's on my schedule for today?" she asked.

"Well, you have a meeting with the caterer at ten, the Museum Committee meets at two-thirty, and your manicure appointment is at four. Dinner will be at eight tonight since Mr. Newman has a late meeting, so you may want to use that time before dinner for your fitting."

"Oh no, no, no! I don't want to be rushed into doing that. The last time Nina had me tied up for hours."

"Okay then, would you like to make any changes to the schedule as it stands, or can I confirm everything?"

"Yes, that's fine." Kate did not bother to look at Pierre. "But I want no interruptions during lunch. Mr. Thompson will be stopping by. When he arrives, I don't want to be disturbed. Is that clear?"

"Yes, of course," Pierre agreed immediately.

"That will be all, Pierre." Kate dismissed him from the room.

Pierre disappeared around the corridor and down the hall to the entrance of the server's quarters. Once he entered the back of the house he proceeded to the kitchen, where he relaxed and undid his tie. When Pierre came into the kitchen, Bert, the family cook, was conducting an inventory of the cupboards to ensure she had the proper ingredients for the weekly meal plan as instructed by Kate.

"How is she this morning?" Bert asked.

Ed Thompson arrived at the Newman home around twelve-thirty. He was a husky, dark-skinned man about six feet tall. His head was balding at the top with the remainder of his hair trimmed close around the back and sides. He had a thick mustache that sat upon thick dark lips. His dark-brown eyes were warm and friendly and when he laughed, they disappeared until he stopped. He had a coarse manner about him from working in the criminal justice system as an investigator for the District Attorney's office. After Kate married Thaddeus, two years later Ed married a woman named Abigail Foster. He was on the rebound from Kate whom he never managed to get over. Ed and Abigail had two children, Walter, and Belinda, who everyone called Bee. Ed adored his children which kept him in his marriage. There was also the issue of Abby tolerating Ed's relationship with Kate. Abby despised Kate! She thought of her as a spoiled privileged woman who had no regard for anyone but herself and what she wanted from others, namely her husband's time. Although Abby knew Ed didn't love her, she was devoted to him and vowed to never leave him at any cost.

Kate received Ed on the patio where they dined on cobb salad. She had a bottle of white wine chilled by the time Ed got there. Kate was sitting at a table under the umbrella wearing a black, white, and tan shirt dress and black leather sandals. Her long legs were crossed showing off a tiny gold ankle bracelet that reflected slightly in the sunlight. Three gold bangles adorned her tiny wrist tinkling each time she reached for her glass of iced tea. She smelled of a very expensive parfum, her signature fragrance, which she always wore. She was gorgeous with her stylishly cut dark hair and freckled nose. Ed reached over to peck her on the cheek before he sat down at the table.

"How are you, Kate? You look lovely as ever." Ed admired her beauty.

Turning her cheek to him she replied snobbishly, "I'm wonderful Ed. How is your family?" She only asked as a formality.

"Everyone's good," he said as he draped his napkin upon his lap.

"Did you and Abby receive your invitation for the BBQ?" Kate asked.

"Yes, thank you very much. I believe Abby RSVP'd last week."

"Well, I'm sure that Pierre has her response along with the others."

"Ed, I want to get right to the reason I asked you out here today. I have a favor I need from you.

Looking very sincere, Ed reached over placing his hand on Kate's knee.

"You only need to ask, Kate. I'll do what I can. You know that."

"This is very confidential, and I mean no one can know about this."

"Okay!" Ed was intrigued.

"I want one of your investigators to follow my son."

Ed looked at Kate with a surprised expression.

"Which of your sons?" he asked inquisitively.

"Jack!"

"Jack? May I ask why?"

"I think that he's seeing someone, and I'd like to know about her—who she is, where she lives, her family, you know the usual things."

"Do you have a name or anything?"

"No. I know nothing about her. That's why I called you."

"Kate, are you sure you want to do something like this? If Jack ever found out what you're up to or Thaddeus for that matter, there will be hell to pay."

"You let me worry about that. Just get me the information I need, and I'll take it from there."

"May I ask why you are so concerned about Jack's personal life?" Ed asked.

"I'm his mother Ed, and I want only the best for him. Heaven knows what kind of woman he may have gotten himself involved with. He has never stayed away for the entire weekend with not so much as a call or anything to me. I suspect that he's spending time with someone, and I want to know who she is," Kate was clearly agitated.

"Don't you think you're jumping the gun here Kate? It could be something very innocent." Ed tried to be convincing.

"No. I know my son. He was quite different when he got home yesterday, and he immediately went back out and stayed in the city overnight. I don't call that a passing thing at all. My instincts tell me differently."

Ed sat in his chair arms folded listening to Kate's tirade. She was just as magnificent as she was when they were kids. He still had it bad for her, so he would do anything she asked him to do and she knew it.

"Okay, I'll start working on this right away. As soon as I have anything to report I'll be in touch."

"Thank you, Ed." She placed her hand over his. "This is very important to me."

Ed, very uncomfortable at the Newman home, took his napkin from his lap and wiped his mouth.

"Well alright then. I must get back into the city. I have a meeting in an hour."

"I'll walk you out," Kate stood up from her chair and grabbed Ed's arm. She folded her arm into his and placed her other hand upon his. They walked through the garden casually chatting. When they stopped at the gate, Ed turned toward her and spoke.

"Why don't you come into the city and have dinner with me this week?" he continued to hold her hand.

"Oh Ed—what a lovely thought," she said. "I'm just not sure that I can. I have so much to do with the charity event coming up in less than two months. Ed looked disappointed but smiled anyway.

"Sure, I understand," he said. "I just thought since you canceled Tuesday—"

Kate cut him off before he could finish.

"I know and I promise I'll make it up to you." Ed kissed her hand and turned to walk out of the gate. Kate stood there as he left to get into his car. She waved to him as he drove away. She briefly thought about how different her life would have been if she would have married Ed. She quickly abandoned the thought and went back to continue with her day.

| 24 |

Clay, we need to talk

Clay wanted to do something special for his woman. He thought about what she might like. He was sitting at his desk when it occurred to him that they hadn't been away together anywhere since last year. The summer season was about to begin, and they hadn't made any vacation plans. He thought of where they might go and decided to call a travel agent for some suggestions. The agent sent over some destinations for him to think about and he decided that he would talk to Blaze about it over dinner tonight. He hadn't been with her for nearly a week, and he longed to spend some time making love to her. He thought to himself how lucky he was to have such a beautiful, intelligent woman. His thoughts wandered as he remembered how sexy she could be. He picked up the phone and dialed her number at the office. As usual, Diane answered after the second ring.

"Blaze Beaumont's office! How may I help you?"

"Hey Diane, it's Clay."

"Hello, Clay. How are you?" she asked.

"I'm good, Diane. Is Blaze around?

"Yes, she is but she's in a meeting right now. May I take a message and have her call you back?"

"Yeah, ask her to call me. It's important." Clay was annoyed that she wasn't available yet again.

"Is there anything I can do to help you, Clay?" Diane asked.

"No, thank you, Diane. Just have Blaze call me when she gets back."

"Okay, will do," Diane did not sound unenthusiastic at all.

"Thanks!" Clay hung up.

'This is getting ridiculous.' Clay thought to himself after hanging up the phone. 'I can't even get my woman on the phone or see her at home. This shit has to stop!"

Clay sat in his chair at his desk in deep thought. He couldn't help but feel as though he was being deliberately put off. He got up and walked around his office pacing back and forth. He decided to send Blaze a bouquet of flowers to her office. He called a local florist that he previously used and ordered two dozen Super Star roses. He had the florist write on the car: *You're my shining star. I look forward to seeing you tonight. Love, Clay.* He was assured by the florist that the flowers would be delivered today. He then went back to work on his accounts satisfied that this would get her attention.

Clay couldn't completely concentrate on his project, so he left work early to get a head start on his evening with Blaze. He stopped at home first to shower and change his clothes, and then he planned to be at Blaze's apartment, as he had done many times before when she arrived home. He made reservations at their favorite restaurant and picked up a bottle of wine to chill, so they would have it once they came home from dinner. He wanted to make this a special evening, and most of all, he needed to spend time with her. He arrived at her apartment around four-thirty and relaxed until she arrived home.

Meanwhile, at her office, Blaze finished a meeting with the accountants and had lunch with Z. They chose a popular restaurant on one of the side streets a few blocks from the office. It had been a while since the two had a chance to catch up. Z had been Blaze's confidante on many occasions and always told her the truth when she asked for his opinion. They arrived at the restaurant a little before the mad rush.

"You want to sit outside or in?" Z asked.

"It's such a beautiful day, let's sit outside."

They chose a table with a view of the pier that sat off the beaten path so that they could talk. Z, always the gentleman, held Blaze's chair as she sat down. He loosened his pink tie before sitting down himself.

Blaze looked at him and smiled, "You're the only straight man I know that can pull off a pink tie," she laughed.

"That's cause I got it like that." Z was full of confidence.

"Yeah, yeah! So, what's been happenin'?" she asked.

"You tell me! You're the one that was missing all weekend."

Blaze gave Z an unapproving look after his comment.

"I wasn't missing. I just wasn't letting folks know where I was is all." Blaze's defenses went up.

"Like I said, missing! Well, the weekend is over so spill." Z smiled.

"I went to A.C, for a couple of days."

"With whom?" Z was surprised by her admission.

"With a friend!"

"Aw shit! It's on now. Come on wit it." Z was now more interested than ever.

"Look Z, you're one of my very best friends...and I share a lot with you about my personal life, but you gotta promise to keep this under wraps and I mean do not tell anyone."

"Have I ever betrayed you?"

Blaze didn't need to think hard at all. Z was loyal.

"No!" she blurted out.

"Then I don't plan to start now. Who was he?"

"It was Jack!"

"Jack Newman?" Z almost spit out his drink.

"Yeah, Jack Newman!"

"I knew it!"

"You knew what?"

"I could tell that you were attracted to him. Hell, there ain't very many women who wouldn't be."

"Z, I swear I never meant to get involved with Jack. I mean it just happened so suddenly. We went to lunch and the next thing I know..."

"You landed on his dick, right?"

"You're so damn crude. Now, why do you think that anything like that happened between us?"

Z started laughing, "I couldn't let that one slide." He laughed some more. "Cause ya glowin', that's why...and ya feet haven't touched ground yet. When did this happen?"

"We went to A.C. to shoot craps."

"Shoot craps?"

"Yeah, it was on a dare. He wagered that if I won, he would set the final draft deadline back to the end of this week, so I went for it. One thing led to another and before I knew it, we had been together for three days; the best three days I've had with anyone."

"Well, sunshine that's all well and good, but you forgot one minor detail."

"What?" Blaze asked wide-eyed.

"What the hell you gonna do about Clay?"

"I don't know, Z. I'm so confused. I love Clay. You know that. But Jack, oh Jack!" she sighed.

"Girl, you somethin' else! I'm glad I didn't pursue you like I wanted to. That would be my heart you'd be pickin' up off the floor. How you gonna tell him?"

"Tell him what? Who ya talking bout?'

"Clay, fool! Have you talked to him about this?"

"No, are you crazy? I haven't even seen him since I been back. He wanted to get together last night after I got in, but I told him I was too tired."

"Well, that makes sense. I mean ya done been wit the other boy for three days. You would really be a whoa if ya slept with Clay last night."

"Gee, thanks my friend, for the support."

"I'm sorry, Blaze. I don't mean to make light of the situation. I see you're really torn about this."

"I really am, Z. But the worst part is after I told Clay I was too tired to see him, I went over to Jack's and spent the night with him."

Looking at Blaze…eyes bulging and almost spitting out his drink again, and almost shouting, "Uh uh…I take it back you is a whoa!"

Blaze looked at Z again with a disapproving glance and then burst into laughter at his comment. They were both laughing so hard that other patrons couldn't help but smile too. They finally managed to contain themselves long enough to order their meal. They settled down to talk about the Newman project, finish their lunch, and headed back to the office.

When Blaze arrived in the office, she was surprised to see a bouquet of roses waiting for her to return. She read the card and began to feel guilty about what she had been up to with Jack. Clay loved her—of this she was certain—but she knew for some time now that the feelings she once had for him were not the same or how else would she be able to take up with Jack so easily. Diane told her that Clay called and that he wanted her to call him back. Blaze went into her office and closed the door. She retrieved all her messages from the computer and managed to return a few important calls right away. She then sat in her chair in deep thought.

'How am I going to face Clay tonight? I know he wants to see me, and he probably will be at the apartment when I get home. I can't sleep with him after being with Jack. Even if Jack and I don't ever see one another again, I just can't deceive Clay that way.' Blaze sat back in her chair in deep thought until Diane buzzed her for her next meeting.

After a few hours had passed, Blaze decided to call it day, so she packed her briefcase and headed home. She arrived at her apartment building at five forty-five and noticed that Clay's car was parked on the street. She parked her car and walked up to her floor. She could hear music coming from her apartment as she tried to ready herself for what was to come. She unlocked her door, and there was Clay waiting for her to arrive. She swallowed hard and feigned a smile.

"There's my girl!" he took her bag and closed the door behind her.

She smiled and kissed him quickly.

"What kind of kiss was that for someone who hasn't seen her man for days?"

He turned her around to him and planted a big kiss on her lips pulling her close to him. Blaze forced a smile and kissed him back. Clay could sense that there was something,

"What's wrong?" he asked feeling her hesitation with him.

"Nothing. I'm just a little wiped out today."

"You sure you feeling alright? You were tired when I spoke to you last night too. You're not coming down with something are you?"

"No, Clay! I'm fine! Nothing that a hot bath won't cure," she said.

"Well, you take your bath 'cause I made reservations for dinner."

"Oh, Clay I just want to stay home and relax. I've been on the go for the last couple of days. Besides, I want to talk to you about something."

"Okay sweetness, whatever you wanna do. If it's that important, I'll just cancel our reservations and we can order in."

"Okay!" Blaze felt relieved. "I'm gonna take a bath and I'll be back shortly." She disappeared into her bedroom and closed the door. Clay walked in behind her and put his arms around her waist.

"What's with the closed door? You don't usually shut me out of your bath," he said kissing her neck. Blaze didn't want Clay to be suspicious of her behavior, so she stood there while he continued with his display of affection. She tried to gently pull away from him, but Clay was like a dog in heat. He pulled her closer and began to get a little aggressive with her. He unbuttoned her blouse and pulled up her skirt. Although she was uninterested, she let him.

"Clay! I'm tired," she said to him.

Clay was clearly aroused and continued to kiss her taking off her blouse and then trying to unfasten her bra. Blaze giggled and broke away from him and walked to the other side of the bed. Clay followed her with hunger in his eyes.

"Baby—I want you!" he said his eyes grazing over her. "I haven't tasted that sweet body in days, and I miss it."

This only repulsed Blaze, but she knew she only felt that way because of Jack. She decided to give in to him. She didn't like the idea of being with both men so close together, but she knew that he would be relentless. He kissed her with passion and lust. His hands touched her everywhere exciting and arousing her even though, in her mind, she fought to not have those feelings. He got on his knees, took off her skirt, and ran his hands up her legs and between her thighs. He pulled off her panties and began to kiss her gently biting her inner thigh. She fell upon the bed as his fingers entered her while he kissed her where she could no longer control herself. Clay knew her body and he coaxed and guided her until she submitted to his every whim. When they were done, Clay lay next to Blaze on the bed. They were both half-dressed, and Blaze suddenly felt so ashamed that she succumbed to him so easily.

"I've missed you, baby," Clay stretched. He turned to caress her, but she immediately got up and went into the bathroom, and locked the door.

"What do you want for dinner?" he yelled through the closed door.

"I don't care. Whatever you order is fine with me." Blaze felt awful and she started to cry quietly so Clay wouldn't hear her. She looked at herself in the mirror with disgust.

'Z was right—you are a whoa,' she thought, Tears streamed down her cheeks.

Sitting on the toilet seat with her head in her hands, Blaze sobbed. She ran her bath water so Clay wouldn't hear her crying. Blaze stepped into the tub, sat, and soaked for an hour. She thought about everything involving Clay and Jack and wondered what she was doing with them both. When she was finished with her bath, she dried her body and went into her room to get dressed. Clay was laying on the sofa watching television. He called for her to come out and join him, but she couldn't bring herself to face him. She finally pulled herself together and entered the living room sitting down beside him on the sofa. He immediately pulled her to him and kissed her face.

"I love you, baby. I missed the hell outta you," he said sincerely.

"Clay, we have to talk."

"Okay...about what?" he asked.

"Can you turn the TV off please?" she asked.

Clay looked at her quizzically and using the remote turned the TV off.

"Okay, now you have my complete attention," he said.

Blaze was suddenly frozen and at a loss for words. She didn't know how to begin the dialogue that would ultimately change her relationship with Clay forever. She was suddenly afraid of that change, and she didn't want to lose her best friend. Clay and Blaze had been a constant for a long time and this news would surely change the dynamics of their relationship. The last thing she ever dreamed of doing was hurting Clay, which would be like hurting herself. Clay looked at her and saw the utter terror in her eyes.

"Hey baby, what is it?" he asked now very concerned.

"Clay, you know I love you, don't you?"

"I hope so." Clay had a faint smile.

"And you know that I have never lied to you about anything?" she added.

"Well, for the most part, yeah I agree."

Blaze looked at him sitting next to her so trusting and loving that she couldn't bring herself to say the words. Clay pulled her to him and placed his arms around her holding her tightly. Blaze buried her face in his chest and sobbed. Clay lifted her face and looked into her eyes.

"Baby, what's this about? Just tell me."

Blaze looked at him and gently kissed his lips.

"I love you, Clay. I just wanted you to know that." Those were the only words Blaze could allow to escape her lips.

Clay smiled and spoke softly to her, "I love you too baby so much that I want you to be my wife. Blaze closed her eyes and decided that she couldn't tell Clay about Jack. She didn't say another word but simply lay in Clay's arms as he held her close to him. They sat there for what seemed an eternity until the doorbell buzzed with the food delivery causing them to break their embrace. Clay answered the door and paid for the food while Blaze went to the kitchen to get napkins, plates, and utensils. They ate dinner in the living room and retired to bed early. Clay made love to Blaze again—sweetly this time. He fell asleep shortly after as she lay next to him wide awake. She knew she had to forget about Jack. It was the right thing to do.

She decided to avoid Jack as much as possible except for when she had to see him professionally. She would let Z and her staff handle the day-to-day obligations to Newman while she engaged herself in the other projects in which she was involved. She convinced herself that she was just a passing thing for Jack and that their affair would soon dissolve. Clay was who she was supposed to be with, and she would make good on her promise to marry him someday. Jack was her fantasy, a notion that could never become something real in her life. She convinced herself that she was doing the right thing and so she was satisfied that everything would get back to the way it was between her and Clay. She tried to close her eyes, but all she saw was Jack smiling at her. She drifted off with those same visions in her head while speaking his name softly from her lips.

On the other side of town, Jack Newman thought about Blaze. When Jack left town before the weekend, he left behind a desk full of contracts to sign and messages to return, so Monday was quite a hectic day for him. He spent the morning on conference calls, had lunch with his father to catch up on things, and the remainder of the afternoon in meetings. By seven o'clock in the evening, he was still busy with the accountants in a forecast meeting that had been going on since three o'clock. Jack got up from the conference table and excused himself to take a phone call on his cell. He walked down the corridor and into his office. When he was finished with his call, he sat at his desk looking over a ton of new messages left for him by his assistant, Tommy. After he went through the messages, he sat back in his chair and placed his hands behind his head putting his feet on his desk. He closed his eyes and pondered on a few of the items discussed in the meeting. As he relaxed in his chair his mind began to wander. His focus shifted off of business as he began to envision a beautiful woman, with long slender legs, and a brown curvaceous nude body before him. He smiled as his eyes traveled the length of her, taking in her beauty and sexiness when finally, he met her gaze. Opening his eyes, he smiled as he picked up the phone and dialed out. The phone rang twice before it was answered.

"Becker, Brickhouse, and Shuman—how may I direct your call?"

"Blaze Beaumont's office please," he said as he settled back in his chair.

"I'm sorry, sir. Ms. Beaumont has left for the day. May I take a message and have her return your call?"

"Uhh, no thank you!"

Jack hung up the phone clearly disappointed. He felt let down as if he opened a beautifully wrapped box only to find nothing inside. He sat there for a moment pondering his next move. He thought about calling her at home but decided not to. He realized that she hadn't called him all day and he didn't want to be overbearing. He got up from his chair and walked down the corridor—this time with less of a stride in his walk. He walked the corridor slowly and purposefully putting one foot strategically in front of the other as he prepared himself for the next round of discussions. He entered the conference room and resumed his position at the table. He consumed himself with the details at hand to relieve his feelings of longing for Blaze. He worked very late until he decided to call it a night and go home. By the time he reached his apartment, he was too tired to think of anything besides going to sleep. So, he showered and retired for the night. Once in bed and almost asleep, he reached out more than once touching the pillow where she had only hours ago laid her head only to awake and find her not there. He drifted off to sleep with Blaze haunting his dreams.

| 25 |

Goodbye, Jack

For the next several weeks, Blaze worked to maintain her professionalism with the Newman account. When meetings were scheduled to discuss issues on the campaign, she would send Z or one of the other team members to attend in her place. She remained active with her other accounts, tending to the client's needs, meeting with the team, and scheduling as much travel time as possible. She went to work early, and most times left very late. She spent the remaining time with Clay going to dinner or the shore house when they could get away. Blaze's family had a home in Cape May, so she went down there as often as she could. She loved the beach and looked forward to spending time there. Some weekends she would bring Clay along, but she mostly spent time alone or with her sisters and mother. She was sad for the most part, but by keeping busy she kept her sorrow at bay. Still, she couldn't help but think about Jack and what he was doing or how he was doing. He tried to call her on several occasions, but she wouldn't return his calls. She had Diane field her calls to make sure that they were not related to the account. After about two weeks he stopped calling her. A man like

Jack Newman didn't have to run after any woman. He could have his pick of whomever he wanted. When his calls stopped Blaze knew that he wouldn't pursue her anymore. Blaze did a good job occupying herself with work and being Clay's girl. She tried being the perfect girlfriend and was convinced that she could get over Jack.

It was the weekend of her birthday, and her family planned a little party for her at the beach house. They invited Z and some of the team at the firm including Sam and his family. It was a beautiful day for an outdoor party, with the warm summer breeze floating off the ocean and the sun shining brightly in the sky. The back of the beach house had a view of the ocean where everyone gathered on the deck. Blaze's mother made her famous potato salad to go with the crab legs and corn on the cob, while the caterer grilled steaks, chops, chicken, and vegetables for everyone to enjoy. The champagne was flowing, and the beer was ice cold. Blaze was beginning to feel like her old self again. It was good to see Z and the crew having such a good time as they danced to the sounds the DJ mixed on the turntable.

"This is a great party if I may say so myself," Z commented.

"Thanks, Z! I'm glad that you're here," Blaze responded.

"Haven't seen much of you this summer," Z said taking Blaze's arm.

"Z, the summer has just begun."

"Whatever! All I know is you been making yourself pretty scarce."

"I've been in the office every day!" Blaze defended herself.

"Yeah, but girl you been in hiding."

"No, I haven't."

"What's got you so down lately?" Z asked concernedly.

"What do you mean? I'm happy as a clam," Blaze feigned a fake smile.

"Are you sure?"

"Nothing's wrong," Blaze said walking out to the ocean.

Z followed not giving up.

"Look, Blaze, how long have we known each other?"

"I don't know. Three years maybe."

"Yeah, and I think I know you pretty well by now. You gonna be straight wit ya boy or what?"

Blaze hesitated before speaking.

"I had a wonderful four-day affair with Jack Newman, and I tried to tell Clay about it, but I couldn't hurt him so I ended it with Jack before it even began, and now, I'm miserable because I can't think of anyone but him."

Z thought long and hard before he answered.

"I thought I told you to stay clear of him. I knew that if you got involved wit that brotha that something like this would happen."

"It just happened! One moment we were shooting craps and having dinner. The next moment we were spending the most awesome four days together. I never expected to feel like this about him. I thought I could forget and get things back to normal with Clay, but I just can't as hard as I try."

Z was conflicted about something as he began to speak, "Blaze, there's something you should know before—"

"Blaze! Blaze! Baby, can you come up here please?" Clay yelled from the deck of the house.

"Look, Blaze, promise me you won't do anything hasty?" Z asked.

"What are you talking about?" Blaze asked trying to divide her attention between what Z was trying to say to her and Clay calling for her to come back to the house.

"Blaze, come up here," Jewels yelled down to her.

"Okay. I'm coming. You'd think that they were planning something—oh no!"

Blaze looked at Z with an expression as if she had some sort of revelation while walking up to the house. When she got to the deck, everyone was waiting for her. The DJ had stopped playing the music and everyone had gathered around as if someone was going to make a speech.

"What's up with everyone? Is it time to cut the cake or something?" Everyone laughed.

"Yeah, something like that," Jewels said.

Clay walked over to Blaze and stood in front of her. He took her hand in his and then got down on one knee. He pulled a blue box from his pants pocket and opened it.

"Blaze, I love you with all my heart. Will you marry me?"

In the box was a 3-carat solitaire diamond ring in a platinum setting. It sparkled and shined as the setting sun shone upon the solitaire stone. Clay stayed down on his knee as he and the others waited for Blaze's reply. She was frozen and couldn't speak. Suddenly she looked at Clay and pulled him to his feet.

"Why did you do this now?" she asked him.

Clay looked at her with a puzzled expression before speaking. "I wanted to make this a special day with it being your birthday and all," he replied.

"But couldn't we have talked about this?" she asked. When Jewels realized that the surprise wasn't going as planned, she tried to give the couple some space to talk alone.

"Maybe we should all go inside and let them talk," she said to the guest.

"No mom. You all stay. I'll go."

Blaze ran from the deck and out to the street where her car was parked. Her keys were already in the car, so she jumped in turning on the ignition. Clay came running behind to stop her, but he wasn't fast enough. She pulled out of the driveway and onto the street as she sped away.

"What the hell happened?" Clay asked as the others surrounded him.

"Give her some time, Clay. I'm sure she'll be back soon. She probably just needs to clear her head." Jewels tried to comfort Clay.

"Clear her head about what? I just asked the woman I love to marry me, and she ran out of here like I was trying to kill her." Clay put his hand on his head and walked into the house dumbfounded, embarrassed, and sadder than ever.

"Z, what were you two talking about down there?" Jewels asked.

"Nothing in particular. We were just catching up," he blatantly lied.

Jewels knew her daughter well and she wasn't convinced that Z was telling the truth. She went into the house where a few guests were gathered and collected her children.

"Will you all excuse us for a moment?" she asked. "I need to speak with my children." Sidney and Peyton followed her into the kitchen.

"Where's your brother?" Jewels asked the girls.

"He's still down on the beach playing ball with the guys," Peyton replied.

"Go get him right now. I want to talk to the three of you. It was quite embarrassing. I've never seen her act like that with Clay."

"Mom, you know Blaze. She does exactly what she wants when she wants. I'm not so sure she was expecting that proposal!" Sidney stated.

"Well, that's still no excuse for her to run out on her own party like that. Poor Clay, the guy looks heartbroken."

Jewels was equally as surprised by Blaze's reaction as Clay who sat on the deck staring out at the ocean like he just lost his puppy.

Kush entered the kitchen.

"Hey, guys! What's up?" he asked.

"You're completely oblivious as usual," Peyton remarked. "All hell could have broken loose, and you would be none the wiser."

"That's enough!" Jewels yelled. "And you watch your language." She looked at Peyton.

"What I do?" Kush asked stuffing an hors d'oeuvre in his mouth.

"Your sister just took off speeding down the road and we don't have a clue as to what's wrong with her."

"Why something gotta be wrong with her mom? Maybe she had someplace to be."

"Honestly!" Jewels replied. "You're impossible and absolutely no help."

"I told you he was clueless, mom," Peyton added.

"You shut up?" Kush responded.

"All of you keep quiet," Jewels yelled furiously.

Jewels left the three siblings in the kitchen to hash it out while she tried to salvage the party. Clay decided that he would try and look for Blaze, but Jewels talked him into staying until she returned. They all went back to the party trying to pretend that nothing ever happened and that the guest of honor was not missing.

The sun was beginning to set presenting a glorious picture along the horizon. It had been an hour and Blaze had not returned to the house. The party was in full swing with some new guests arriving surprised that the guest of honor was not there. Blaze left her handbag at the house, but she had her cell phone with her. She took a drive ending up on the Parkway. Before she knew it, she was headed for Atlantic City which wasn't that far of a drive from where she was. She looked at the clock not knowing how long she had been driving. When she entered Atlantic City, she drove around looking at all the summer tourists converging upon the outlet shopping area. She parked her car in a lot not far from Atlantic Avenue and sat there contemplating her next move. She didn't mean to run out on Clay like that, but she felt like she was being smothered by everyone there watching her. She tried to call the house, but no one picked up the phone, so she left a message telling her mother she was alright and for her not to worry. She sat in her car in deep thought.

'Why would Clay do this now? I had no idea he was going to propose. This is a shock, and I wasn't prepared for that. I wish we could have talked about it first. I bet my mother knew what he was going to do and probably even encouraged it. Why didn't Kush or Peyton tell me? I would have expected that from Sydney, but not them.'

Blaze reclined the seat in her car and turned on the radio. She switched stations trying to find something she liked. She was searching for something when she came across a familiar tune. She turned her stereo up and listened as she immediately remembered where she had heard that tune before. It was the first night she and Jack were at the hotel, and they had just made love. She closed her eyes as the melody brought back vivid memories of her night with Jack. She could see his face and his smile exposing his dimple. She could smell his scent and it permeated her senses. She spoke his name, "Jack" as if he were there with her. Tears streamed down her cheeks as she tried to wipe the memory from her mind. She heard Jack ask her, 'What are you doing?' She recalled herself responding to him by saying, 'Making a memory!' She wiped the tears from her face and looked for her phone.

"No messages." She was surprised.

She put the phone down, but immediately picked it back up. She searched through her phone book and found Jack's number. She pressed call and the phone began to ring. Her heart pounded as she anticipated hearing his voice. She was nervous and her throat was dry. She panicked and hung up the phone before there was an answer. She sat there staring into space.

"What is wrong with me?"

Blaze turned on the ignition and drove out of the lot and made her way back to the expressway. Before long she was pulling up to the beach house. It was now after eight o'clock and the party was in full swing. The deck was decorated with lights and the music was pumping with quite a few people dancing. Clay was talking to one of the guests when Blaze walked out on the deck.

"So, you're back!" Jewels said hugging her daughter.

"I'm sorry, mom. I didn't mean to ruin the party. I just wasn't ready for my surprise from Clay."

"Don't worry about the party, but I do think you owe Clay an explanation. Go and talk to him," Jewels said coaxing her daughter on. "He's been worried sick about you."

"Where'd you go?" Kush asked approaching Blaze. "You okay?"

"I'm fine." Blaze hugged her brother.

Blaze left her mother and brother and walked to the end of the yard where Clay was standing with a few of the guests. When he saw her approaching him, he excused himself and began to walk toward her.

"Are you alright?" he asked her.

"I'm fine, Clay. Will you walk with me?" she asked.

Clay took her hand, and they began to walk towards the beach. At first, they didn't say a word to one another. Finally, Blaze broke the silence.

"Clay, I owe you an apology. I don't know what got into me. I think that I was in shock or something. This all kind of took me by surprise," she explained.

"I just wanted this to be a memorable day for you," he said.

"I know—and it was a wonderful surprise. I'm so sorry I ruined it by reacting that way," Blaze admitted.

"Don't you want to get married to me?" Clay asked.

"Yes, of course, I do, but I thought we would wait a while longer before making it official."

"We've been together since college. You've known about my feelings for you since then. Nothing's changed for me."

Blaze knew Clay loved her, and she loved him too, but she felt that something was missing from their relationship. She knew he was a good man, and most women would jump at the chance to be with him. Her logic told her to go for it, but her heart told her differently.

"Clay, will you give me another chance?" Blaze asked.

"Baby, all I want is to make you happy."

Blaze placed her arms around Clay's neck and kissed him.

"You do make me happy," she said.

"Okay, then. What do you say we try this thing again?

"I say, yes!" Blaze replied.

Clay stepped back and took the blue box from his pocket. He took the ring out and Blaze extended her hand.

"Blaze Beaumont...will you marry me?"

"Yes, Clay. I will marry you!"

They kissed one another in a long and sincere embrace and held hands as they walked up the beach toward the house. When they got to the backyard, Blaze asked the DJ to hold the music. Clay took the microphone and began his announcement.

"May I have everyone's attention for a minute? I've asked Blaze to be my wife and she said yes."

Everyone applauded. The happy couple was embraced by each of the guests, one by one. Jewels was so excited and asked the caterer to open a few bottles of champagne for a toast to the newly engaged couple. After the toast, Blaze and Clay danced together eliciting best wishes from everyone. Then, they all joined in to dance with the happy couple. The DJ started the music, and everyone was on the dance floor. They partied until after midnight with everyone having a great time. It was a fitting end to what had been an eventful evening.

When the last guest was gone, the family sat around laughing and talking until the early morning. Finally, everyone retired to their rooms as Clay slept on the pull-out sofa. Jewels was very pleased with the outcome and felt relieved that her daughter made the right decision. When Blaze reached her room that she shared with her sisters, Peyton and Sydney, they were sound asleep. She undressed and put on a tee shirt leaving on her panties. She sat in the middle of her bed looking at the huge diamond ring on her finger. Tears welled up in her eyes as she tried to suppress her cry. She got down on her knees to say her prayers.

"Dear Lord—please help me to be a good wife to Clay and help us to make this work," she prayed. "Bless my family and keep them safe—and Lord please take good care of Jack and please bless him too. Amen."

Blaze climbed into bed and pulled the covers around her. She felt so empty and alone. She knew that what she was feeling had everything to do with missing Jack. She spoke softly into her pillow.

"I have to forget you, Jack," she whispered before she closed her eyes and drifted off to sleep.

| 26 |

How dare he!

The news of Blaze's engagement quickly traveled through the office. There were congratulations and best wishes all around. The news also filtered through to the Newman camp as well. When Jack first learned about the engagement it took him off guard in a way that nothing ever had before. He didn't see this coming and for the first time in his life, he was duped. He was in shock that she had kept the fact that she was involved with someone. He never let on that he was disturbed by the news, but he was quite taken off balance by it. He never understood what happened between them that would make Blaze cut him off so severely. He went over the last hours they were together many times in his mind. There was nothing that he could surmise except that she had decided to just not see him anymore. He became quite angry with the way that she handled things, but he was also surprisingly hurt by it and that wasn't something that he was prepared for. He had never felt for a woman the way he did for Blaze and that made him even angrier at the way she just cut him off. That first week after they had been together, he tried calling her at the office and on her cell, but she would not return his calls. He could have used the account as a way of manipulating her to talk with him, but Jack didn't play games. After trying to reach her on numerous occasions he decided to let it go. He thought about calling and congratulating her on her engagement, but he wouldn't have meant it, and just hearing her voice was too much for him to take. He decided that it was best to cut Blaze out of his thoughts for good.

The following week a conference call was scheduled on Monday morning between the Newman camp and the Becker, Brickhouse, and Shuman Inc. team. When Tommy informed Jack about the meeting, Jack decided to attend. This was an unusual move for Jack who normally didn't attend meetings at this level. To say that his motives were less than professional would be an understatement. The Newman finance team was headed by Marcus Waters who officiated during the conference call. The participants began signing on and by 10:00 am everyone who was invited to participate was accounted for and so Marcus began the discussion.

"Is everyone present that is scheduled to be a part of this call?" he asked. There was a unanimous affirmative heard from both teams.

Parker Johnson was the lead for Brickhouse, Becker, and Shuman Inc. and so he responded to Marcus's question with enthusiasm, "Unfortunately, Ms. Beaumont will not be joining us on this call," Parker announced to the group. "I will be her deputy in her absence," he added pleased with himself. When Jack heard Blaze's name, he immediately chimed in.

"Is there something more pressing that your team leader can't be available for this call?" Jack asked annoyedly.

"Well Jack, Blaze has asked me to sit in on her behalf so we assumed that would be okay with your group," Parks answered coyly.

"Well Parks, it's not acceptable that she isn't a part of the call since this is officially her account, so I suggest that someone find her and get her on the call—we'll wait," Jack said defiantly. Parks put the call on mute. Although he took this as an opportunity for him to shine, he was more pleased that Blaze would be reprimanded.

"Have someone go find Blaze and tell her what Jack said. Get her down here pronto," Parks commanded. One of the assistants called Diane who buzzed into Blaze's office.

Blaze was busy with another account when Diane buzzed her office.

"Diane, I told you no calls right now."

"Blaze, Parks is holding a conference call with Newman, and Jack has asked that you be present for the call."

She sat motionless in her chair. Her radar went up as soon as she heard Jack's name. She wasn't prepared to sit in on the meeting, but she immediately collected herself and went right into survival mode.

"Diane, can you get me the agenda for this meeting and get Parks on the phone right away?" Blaze commanded with authority. After a few minutes, Diane buzzed Blaze again.

"Yes, Diane?"

"Blaze, I have Parks on line one."

Blaze immediately picked up the phone.

"Parks what's going on?" she asked.

"We have the conference call with Newman this morning to discuss the financials and the final copy, and Jack is sitting in on Newman's side. He asked that you be present for the call."

"Damn!" Blaze said under her breath.

"Okay! Which conference room are you in?"

"We're in conference room A."

"I'll be right down."

Blaze walked out to Diane's desk.

"Get me everything we have so far on the Newman account—like yesterday. Bring it to conference room A. I'm on my way down."

Diane gathered the information as Blaze walked down the corridor and over to the east side of the building where the conference room was located. When she arrived, everyone seated at the table was looking quite nervous and uncertain of what would happen next. Parks stood up as Blaze walked in.

"Okay—you continue to lead on this, and I'll chime in when needed," Blaze directed.

Parks took the call off mute and began to speak.

"Jack, you there?" he asked.

"Mr. Parks, I'm stating this for the record I don't like to be kept waiting. Now has

Ms. Beaumont arrived?" Jack asked.

"Yes Jack, I'm here," Blaze answered.

"Well so good of you to join us," Jack said sarcastically.

There were a few chuckles from both groups.

"Sorry Jack, but I didn't think I was needed at this juncture."

"What's the matter, Ms. Beaumont? Is the Newman account not important enough for you to give us an hour of your time for a conference call?" he asked.

"Of course, it is Mr. Newman. Shall we get on with the call?" she asked suppressing her embarrassment.

Parks continued to lead the conversation with Blaze adding comments when appropriate. After an hour, most issues on the agenda were addressed and the Newman group flagged areas that needed further explanation. Before the call ended, Jack spoke.

"Thank you, Parks, for a very productive session. We appreciate your attention to the details we've marked and look forward to you getting back to us with your results by tomorrow." Jack added.

"No problem, Jack. We'll have a copy of the proposal sent to you by tomorrow," Parks replied feeling championed by Jack's comment.

"Oh, by the way, Ms. Beaumont can you stay a minute? I'd like to have a word with you," Jack requested.

Everyone in both rooms tried to hide their knowing looks that Blaze was going to feel the brunt of Jack's anger.

"Sure, Mr. Newman. Give me one second to confer with the team," Blaze replied. Blaze spoke briefly with the team setting up a meeting for later that day to debrief on the results of the call. After everyone left the room, she returned to the call picking up the phone to speak with Jack.

"Hello, Mr. Newman. I'm back now," she said. There was an awkward silence. Jack hesitated before answering, "Is there a problem, Ms. Beaumont?"

"Why, no. There's no problem," Blaze replied.

"Then why do I get a distinct notion that you are trying to avoid me?"

"I'm not avoiding you."

"Then why weren't you at the meeting? I expect one hundred percent from the firms we enlist services from, and your firm is no different." Jack said authoritatively.

"I understand, Mr. Newman," she meekly replied. "I will not make that mistake again." Blaze said calmly.

"Good! Then I can expect that you will personally see that I receive the information requested during the call. And I would prefer that you deliver everything to me in person."

Blaze was shaken by his request. She tried to compose herself before answering him.

"Of course!"

Jack abruptly hung up the phone. Blaze was angry. She was more than angry, she was livid. She marched back to her office not even acknowledging Parks as he tried to get her attention. She went into her office and quietly closed the door. She buzzed Diane and asked that she not be disturbed. Blaze sat at her desk and stared into space. She knew Jack was angry with her—but was it necessary to reprimand her in that way—and in front of her staff? Blaze swiveled around in her chair stopping once she faced the window. She had a view of the pier and would often get her inspiration from the beauty of the waterfront. The water had a calming effect on her. Usually, it inspired her productivity, but not today. Today was different in every way. She was trying to calm herself after Jack's tirade.

'How dare he order me around like some peon. And now he has the gall to request that I deliver the final draft to him in person?' Blaze thought to herself.

She knew that this meant she would have to see Jack, and she didn't want to. She was afraid of what he might see in her eyes. Blaze could handle Jack in business—that wasn't what worried her. But on a personal level, she was no match for him right now. She called Diane into her office and asked her to send out for something to eat.

"It's gonna be a late evening," she said to Diane.

"Do you need me to stay and help you with anything?" Diane asked.

"No, thank you, Diane. I think I need to spend some time perfecting my knowledge on this account. You go home to your family. I'll be fine."

Blaze made sure that no stone was unturned. She read every single line of the presentation, reviewed the storyboards for the commercial, and familiarized herself with the figures. She was ready for anything that Jack had to dish out. By ten thirty, she was exhausted and decided to head home. She called Clay earlier in the evening to let him know that she wasn't going to meet him for dinner and that she would see him tomorrow. She went home, took a bath, and climbed right into bed. Blaze wanted to be sharp when she finally met with Jack. Although exhausted, she didn't fall quickly asleep but instead dreamed of being consumed and ravished by a distant, but not so distant, lover.

| 27 |

Broken

Jack hadn't seen or heard from Blaze in four weeks. He couldn't figure out what went wrong and why she got cold on him. When he found out about her engagement with Clay, he assumed that was the reason for her distant behavior.

"She played me," he said to himself. *'All that time we spent together she never even told me she was seeing someone,'* he thought.

Jack never had occasion to second guess himself when it came to women. He would have fun with them and then after a few weeks the affair would cool off and they would go their separate ways—that is until he met Blaze. He hadn't been able to keep her off his mind. He dated a few women in the last weeks hoping that he would get back into the swing of things and take life a little less seriously, but he was not successful. He hated to admit it, but he took the meeting with Brickhouse, Becker, and Shuman, Inc. just to hear her voice. When he found out she wouldn't be there, he felt anger and he wanted to let her know that. After the meeting, Jack didn't go back to his office. He told his assistant Tommy that he would be leaving early. He got into his Porsche and took a ride along River

Drive. Driving always managed to calm him when he was bothered by something. He ended up back in the city at Dominic's for a bite to eat. The restaurant wasn't far from his loft, so he ate there often. Dominic's was like being home as it gave him feelings of comfort. He had a bowl of pasta, Bolognese style, and a few bottles of beer. Since it was a slow night at the restaurant, Jack talked to Dom for over an hour about things at the company, his father, and women. Dom was very knowledgeable about the female psyche and tried to give Jack some fatherly advice about how to deal with them, patiently. They laughed and shared stories until Jack decided to call it a night. Since he lived close to the restaurant, he parked his car in Dom's lot and decided to walk home. The night air was cool after a very warm day, and the streets were filled with people who were out enjoying an evening in the city. Couples passed by holding hands and they seemed to be sharing some intimate secret as lovers often do. Jack smiled remembering his time with Blaze and the closeness they shared. When he got home, for a second he thought of calling her, but his pride wouldn't let him be that human, so he lay in bed. He tried reading, but that didn't work so he began watching a late-night talk show. Nothing seemed to relax him. It wasn't until after midnight when sleep finally came to Jack's rescue, but his mind was wrought with the vision of a fiery vixen whose image haunted his dreams.

| 28 |

The Delivery

Tuesday morning came quickly as Blaze readied herself to face Jack. She assumed that he'd heard about her engagement by now, and if he hadn't, she would need to tell him. She woke up early, ran three miles, came home, showered, and dressed for work. She changed her clothes five times trying to find the appropriate attire for her meeting.

"Oh, damn," she said. "Why can't I just find something to wear? You would think I was getting dressed for a date. Why should I care so much about the way I look? Jack is my client, and I must maintain a professional demeanor with him. I can't wear anything too provocative, or he'll think that I'm coming on to him."

Blaze decided on a sleeveless red sheath dress and a matching crop jacket. The neckline of the dress was cut low, so she decided to keep her jacket buttoned. The suit fit her body perfectly showing just enough curves to be feminine but tailored enough to be professional. She didn't realize that her color choice matched the fire that blazed within her. The length of the dress showed off her long legs and the tan pumps she chose complimented them nicely. A tiny gold bangle adorned her wrist with the only other piece of jewelry being her engagement ring. She pulled her hair back from her face and up off her neck. Then, she took one last look in the mirror before grabbing her briefcase, keys, and purse, and headed out the door. Blaze was confident that she was properly prepared for the meeting with Jack. She only needed to remain professional and not let her emotions get in the way.

Blaze went right to the office and made some calls. She had a meeting with the creative department, and they went over the storyboards and blue lines for a final look. Z and Parks were present for the meeting too. She wanted everyone involved to be on board with the perusal of the final product. She wanted and needed everything perfect. The quality of the account depended on it and so did her reputation.

It was half past noon when the meeting concluded, and the package was finalized. It was ready to be given to Jack. Blaze suddenly became nervous. She was scheduled to meet with Jack at 1:00 pm, so she traveled across town to Rittenhouse Square. The Newman offices were in The Plaza suites Office Towers, a premier office building. The Newmans occupied the top five floors of the tower. Blaze took the elevator to the 20th floor where the Newman's Executive Offices were located. She arrived fifteen minutes before schedule. When she stepped off the elevator, there was only one large office before her. She walked through double glass doors that led into a large and airy room. A young man was seated behind the desk, and he stood up to greet her as she entered. He was a short and slim young man about twenty-five years old. His nameplate read "Thomas Williams" and he worked as an assistant to Jack. Tommy came to Newman straight out of college with a bachelor's degree in business. He worked at Newman for one year before gaining the position as Jack's assistant. Jack liked him immediately and so he took him under his wing.

"Hello, Ms. Beaumont! It's a pleasure to meet you. I'm Tommy, Mr. Newman's assistant."

"Good afternoon." Blaze extended her hand. "It's nice to meet you as well."

"Mr. Newman will be with you shortly. Please have a seat. May I offer you a beverage?" Tommy sounded well-rehearsed.

"No, thank you! But if you would direct me to the lady's room?"

"Why certainly. It's down the hall and to your right."

"Thank you, Tommy. I'll be right back!"

Blaze walked down the corridor and found the lady's room. She studied herself in the mirror making sure that she was presentable. She hadn't seen Jack in over a month and she was so excited but at the same time, she felt nervous about seeing him again. She examined her clothing and checked her hair. Her engagement ring reflected in the mirror before her shining brilliantly as she touched her lip gloss with her finger. Suddenly her excitement turned to regret.

"Get it together, girl," she told herself. She stood there for another minute to compose herself before she went back to Jack's office.

She walked back to the reception area of Jack's office, which was bright and cheery. The lighting in the room was warm; none of that fluorescent brightness like most offices had. The design of the room was very modern, almost art deco. The artwork was abstract in design and the color scheme incorporated hues of blue, tan, and brown. Suddenly, the door opened, and Jack appeared in the doorway. The mere sight of him startled Blaze. He opened the door so quickly.

"Come on in, Ms. Beaumont. Sorry to keep you waiting." "Did Tommy offer you something to drink?" Jack smiled.

Tommy immediately replied, "Yes sir, I did, but Ms. Beaumont declined."

"Okay, just making sure you're doing your job. Gotta watch this one. He plans to take over my position someday." Jack stood back allowing Blaze to walk into his office. Tommy laughed as he closed the door behind them.

Jack's office was enormous. A sitting area with two brown leather chairs, a sofa, and a black marble coffee table sat strategically on one side of the room. The carpet was a mocha hue and Blaze could feel the plushness as her feet sank when she walked. Floor-to-ceiling windows lined the area behind Jack's desk allowing natural light to flow throughout the entire room. A huge television was on the wall and a stereo system was placed directly beneath it. The built-in bookshelves were filled with books, contracts, and architectural magazines. A work area was covered with blueprints and drawing material, which appeared to be where he spent most of his time.

"Please, sit down," he said never taking his eyes off Blaze.

Blaze sat down in one of the leather chairs sinking into the soft supple comfort of it. Jack walked over and sat down on the sofa.

"How are you?" He genuinely wanted to know.

"I'm fine?" she said before she realized it.

"I know you're fine, Blaze."

Blaze smiled hearing him say the words he said to her when they first met.

"How are you?" she asked with emphasis on you.

"I'm good!" Jack sat back on the sofa. He relaxed in the seat and opened his jacket. He was wearing a blue pin-striped suit and a tailored white shirt. His red tie was hanging on his work area where he had taken it off earlier and left it. His shirt was opened at the neck making him look sexier than any man should ever look. Blaze tried containing herself and began to hand the package with the contracts and presentation over to him.

Jack rubbed his forehead as if he had a headache and sat up to take the huge envelope out of her hands. He looked through the material briefly and then got up and opened the door to his office.

"Tommy—take this down to legal and have Marcus look everything over. Have him call me once he's had a look at it so we can go over the details." Then he closed the door. Jack walked back towards the sofa and sat down.

"So what's this I hear you're engaged?"

Blaze was taken off guard not expecting him to broach the subject so soon.

"Yes, it was something that happened suddenly," she said.

"I'll bet!" Jack replied. "Why didn't you tell me that you were involved with someone?" he asked.

"I was gonna tell you, Jack. Things happened so fast and well…"

"Blaze—we were together for four whole nights. You had plenty of time to tell me."

"Jack, you must believe that I never thought that we were gonna get involved. What happened between us was so fast and—well I was having such a good time with you. I didn't want to spoil it. I did try to tell you a few times, but the timing never seemed right."

Jack sat on the end of the sofa legs spread apart with his hands folded in front of him. He was staring at Blaze taking in her every word. The silence became deafening as Blaze wanted some response from Jack.

"Jack, please say something?" Blaze wanted to curl herself into a ball.

"What do you want me to say? Do you love him?" he asked getting up and walking to the window. She didn't know how to answer him. Jack never turned around but continued to ask the same question.

"Do you love him?" he asked again this time in a deliberate tone. Blaze held her head down not knowing how to answer him. She got up and walked over to Jack standing behind him.

"Will you please hear me out Jack?" she asked.

"Go ahead." He continued to face the window.

"Clay and I have been together since college. He is the only one that I have been with ever...until I met you. When we went to Atlantic City, I never dreamed that I would be with you in that way. I felt things so quickly and I just didn't think that you wanted anything more than just a passing thing. I never thought that a man like you would ever be interested in someone like me."

"What the hell is that supposed to mean?" Jack asked angrily as he turned to face her. "What kind of woman are you that I wouldn't feel something for you?"

"I didn't expect that you could ever be serious about me. I thought it was a fling and so I saved you the trouble of trying to get out of it. That's why I didn't call you back. I also didn't want to hurt Clay. He's a good guy and deserves better than that from me."

"So, you pitied him and said yes to his proposal? What about me? Don't I deserve your pity too?"

Blaze stood there speechless. She couldn't find the right words to say. He was standing there with one hand in his pocket and his foot on the ledge beneath the window. This was exactly the way he looked in the hotel room that night standing by the balcony in the nude.

"I'm sorry, Jack. I know that you can't understand why I wasn't honest with you but believe me I wanted to tell you."

Jack was now facing the window again looking out across the city. He didn't respond to her and so Blaze felt defeated. Blaze walked toward the chair and picked up her purse. She turned to walk out of the office.

"Wait!" Jack commanded her.

He turned around with both hands in his pockets looking at her with contempt in his eyes. He was so fine Blaze thought that she would faint. She was so weak for him when he looked at her that way. Jack walked toward her. He stood in front of her and saw the tears in her eyes. He pulled her to him and looking down upon her like some ancient warrior snatched her close to him.

"I don't want you to go," he murmured.

Blaze reached up and put her arms around his neck. She kissed him as he held her with one arm around her waist. When he didn't return her kiss, she pulled back with a look of confusion as she looked into his eyes. Suddenly, he pushed her against the door and kissed her back with all the passion that had been welled-up inside of him since he last saw her. They kissed one another feverishly. Jack unbuttoned her jacket and took it off of her while locking the door with his other hand. He unzipped her dress letting it fall to the floor. He stood back looking at her body from head to toe. She stood there in her sheer beige bra and panties and wanted to cover herself in shame.

"You are the most beautiful thing that I have ever seen." Jack took the pins from her hair and ran his fingers all through it. His hands touched her along her neck and then traveled down to her breast.

"I missed you, Jack," she said breathlessly.

He placed his arm against the wall above her head looking deeply into her eyes,

"Then why the hell didn't you call me or tell me that? Do you know what you put me through?" he asked. The golden flecks sparkled in his eyes as if they were on fire. He picked her up and took her to the sofa.

"All I could think about was you. I couldn't concentrate on anything else but you. I could smell and taste you and I wanted to drag you out of wherever you were and make love to you right then and

there. I didn't give a shit who was around. You have me like that."
Jack began spreading her legs and kissing her all over her body. He
held his arm around her waist as she arched her back accommodat-
ing him. "I need you, Blaze! You're under my skin like no other
woman has ever been," he admitted.

Blaze sat up on her knees and unfastened his belt and pants, all
the while looking into his eyes. They said nothing but their actions
spoke volumes. She lay back on the sofa removing her panties so
Jack could have her the way they both wanted. Jack entered her
with a force that made her moan in ecstasy. He was relentless in
his stroke and Blaze met him at every thrust. He backed away from
her looking into her eyes with such intensity she could not bear it.
He reached for her body pulling her to him and flipping her onto
her belly. He kissed her neck shoulders and back running his hands
along her body. Blaze moaned at the anticipation of him. He placed
his arm around her waist and pulled her body to him as his hardness
pressed against her buttocks. Blaze begged him to enter her.

"Please Jack, please."

He responded in a husky voice his warm breath against her ear.

"Tell me what you want baby? Don't you realize what you do
to me?" He called out her name in a whispered voice. "Blaze, Blaze,
I want you and I don't want anyone else to have you but me." His
breath became more rapid with each word. She didn't answer but
reached behind and placed him inside of her. She then held onto the
end of the sofa as he rode her until they climaxed together with such
ardor. Jack covered her mouth to mask the sounds of ecstasy that
began to escape her. When they came together, it was like nothing
either had ever experienced, and they lay spent upon the sofa in the
aftermath of their tryst.

Jack and Blaze lost all sense of time as they lay in each other's
arms. Blaze lay on the oversized sofa with Jack against her back. He
encircled her body with his strong arm while leaning on the other.

Blaze was more content being with Jack than she had ever known with anyone before. Jack kissed her back and fondled her breast arousing such desire within her. His hard, lean, muscular body was pressed against her own. She wanted to melt into him. His scent captivated her making her dizzy with delight. They lay in silence for what seemed forever until Blaze turned toward him. She lay there looking into his eyes.

"What you looking at?" he asked smiling and rubbing his eyes.

"I need to take this all in. I want to remember this moment forever," she said.

Jack's smile faded as he looked at her with a serious expression.

"Blaze I'm not gonna let you go that easily."

"I don't want you to let me go," she replied.

"Then, you have to be honest about what you're going to do next. Know this, I will not take a back seat to anyone. If you're to be mine, then be mine, but you must make a decision about what you want. If you decide that it's me, then I'll be right with you every step of the way."

Blaze buried her face in Jack's chest as he caressed her.

"Look at me Blaze!" he commanded.

"No, I can't."

He lifted her chin and firmly pulled her to him.

"I'm not letting you go again. I thought I had lost you for good and it bothered me to know that you were with someone else. That's an emotion that's new to me, so it took me a while to accept. I'm not in the habit of laying it all out about the way I feel about any woman. I'm very particular, and I don't treat sex lightly. Contrary to the rumors, I don't sleep around and have casual sex with just any woman. The time we spent together meant a lot to me. It came as a surprise to me too, but I was glad it happened and thought you were too."

"I was Jack—I mean, I am—that time still replays in my mind. I've been miserable these last few weeks. I wanted to call you and tell you how much I missed you, but I didn't want to be vulnerable. I didn't want to be one of your bitches. I want to be the only one you want."

Jack chuckled, "I don't have no bitches and there's no one else in my life. You're it," he said with sincerity.

Jack kissed her and she kissed him back. Blaze covered Jack's face with kisses. They made love again and stayed in the office until Tommy buzzed Jack's office. He wanted to inform Jack that he had a meeting at four with finance. Jack told Tommy to reschedule with his apologies and for him to take the rest of the day off. By this time, it was after three o'clock and Blaze decided to call Diane to tell her she would be detained and would not be back in the office today. After they rearranged their calendars, Jack returned to Blaze who was now cuddling under his jacket on the sofa. He sat down beside her and placed his arms around her. She immediately settled into his arms.

"Want to get out of here and get some food?" he asked.

"I want to get out of here if you take me to your place," she responded.

"Consider it done." Jack thought about food. "We'll pick up some steaks to grill, maybe some vegetables, and fruit from the terminal. We'll have a healthy feast."

"I don't care what we have as long as you promise me dessert." Blaze said stroking him.

"You're insatiable, Blaze, my little nympho," he teased.

Blaze blushed at his declaration.

"Come on. Get dressed!" Jack said while getting up to look for his clothing. Blaze was especially calm after being with Jack. She was quiet and did whatever he asked. Blaze wasn't a passive person, but she was content and didn't care what was happening in the rest of the world. Right now, she was with Jack and that was all that mattered to her.

Jack drove to the grocery store. They walked through the terminal hand in hand as lovers do. They noticed the glances that they received but neither cared. They whispered in each other's ears, and Blaze cuddled up to him when he was wagering for something he was buying. Jack took her around to some of his favorite vendors buying from some and just talking with others. They finally left the market with their arms filled with groceries.

They went back to Jack's apartment and Blaze immediately took off her clothes and ran a bath. She got in and relaxed in the bubbles while Jack put the steaks on the grill and prepared a plate of veggies, fruits, and cheeses. He opened a bottle of wine and then joined her in the tub. They talked more about what happened between them and promised to never let communication, or the lack thereof, be an issue between them. Jack asked her questions about her relationship with Clay, and she was honest and forthcoming with him about everything.

"Do you love him?" Jack asked.

"I guess I do, but not in the way you may think. Clay has been in my life since college and we've been through a lot together, but I don't feel the same way about him that he does for me."

"Then why agree to marry him?"

Blaze told Jack about the way Clay proposed in front of her family and guests. She told him how she ran off to A.C. and tried to call him. She explained that she thought it was over between them and that Clay was there to pick up the pieces so to speak. She also wanted to please her mother, so she accepted his proposal.

"I know it was wrong to do that," Blaze admitted. "I just couldn't hurt him."

SUMMARY OF BLAZE – 171

Jack exhaled deeply and sunk into the tub surrounded by bubbles and water.

"So, what's next?" he asked.

"Well, I'll have to tell him about us, but it won't be easy."

They were quiet with one another for the rest of their bath. Blaze dried off while Jack plated their dinner. After they finished their meal, Blaze climbed into Jack's bed and fell asleep. Jack went into the living room and made a few calls before he came back into the bedroom. When he got in bed, Blaze was already asleep. He studied her face as she slept. He thought she was so beautiful, even without makeup and her hair all tousled and wet. He gently pulled the covers up around her and she nestled deeper into the bed. Jack put on a pair of sweats and a tee shirt and went to his computer. He returned some emails and made a few calls. He couldn't help but think about Blaze and the effect she had on him. He was also concerned about what they were getting themselves into. They were both driven, strong-willed individuals who worked hard to build their careers. How would they manage to maintain a relationship with the dynamics they had before them? Jack pondered his thoughts for over an hour and then made a few more calls before getting into bed. Although it was still early, they were both exhausted from the stress of the day, so they slept until midnight when Blaze woke Jack up to make love once again. As they held each other closely and whispered endearing sentiments to one another, they were oblivious to the lone figure sitting in the shadows outside of Jack's apartment in a black sedan chain smoking and changing the lens on his camera.

As the ashes from his cigarette fell to his lap, he dialed a number on his cell phone and waited for a response from the one he called.

"I've got the photos!" he said in a less-than-audible voice. "I'm sure your client will be pleased with the results," he added. Without saying a word, the person on the other phone smiled and hung up the receiver. After he ended the call, the anonymous figure turned on the ignition of his car and proceeded to drive off into the night. At that very moment, another figure stepped out from the shadows into the light of the streetlamp across from Jack's apartment. He looked up to Jack's window and after a few moments, he went on his way disappearing into the night.

| 29 |

Off to lunch!

It was three days before the Newman Barbecue and Kate and Pierre were busy with last-minute details for the event. Kate was being her usual difficult self, making everyone's life miserable— especially Pierre's. There was a drainage issue with the ice sculpture which was insane to have in the first place since the temperature hadn't been below 85° degrees in weeks. There did not seem to be an end in sight and the forecast for the day of the barbecue promised to be in the 90s. Kate wanted her way and was assured that the matter would be handled, so an ice sculpture it would be. Pierre had several meetings scheduled for Kate to attend, but she decided to postpone or cancel them all at the last minute. It seemed that something pressing had just come up that needed her immediate attention. Pierre was quite observant and noticed that there seemed to be a lot of secret meetings between Kate and Ed Thompson recently. He knew it had nothing to do with the event, and so it piqued his interest.

"Miss Thing certainly is spending an awful lot of time with Mr. Ed," Pierre said to Bert sarcastically. "I wonder if Mr. Newman knows about this?"

"You should mind your business," Bert said in her most direct and protective manner.

"Oh, hush ole woman!" Pierre said rolling his eyes and sucking his teeth.

Kate entered the kitchen and gave Bert instructions for dinner and handed Pierre the latest rounds of RSVPs for the event. As usual, Kate was self-indulgent never noticing the tension between her two employees.

"I have to take a trip into town, but I should return after four," Kate said as she was leaving. She decided to drive herself today since she didn't want anyone to know where she was headed. Of course, Pierre took note of that little detail and with a sly smile, placed it in his memory banks for safekeeping.

Kate arrived on the street where Ed's office was located a little after one o'clock. She was late, but that didn't matter to Ed. When she arrived, he was waiting patiently. He thought to himself as she emerged from her Mercedes convertible how stunning she looked after all these years. Kate was wearing a black tailored pants suit with an off-white silk blouse. Her tan and black leather loafers completed her classic look as she removed the Chanel scarf from her head tying it to her very expensive handbag. As she got in Ed's car, she shook her raven hair running her fingers through her thick locks. Ed started the car and whisked her away to a little cabin not far from Valley Green. The ride was quiet and peaceful as they listened to Frank Sinatra.

"Ed, I'm so sorry I'm late," Kate said leaning over to offer her cheek to him.

Ed kissed her cheek lingering to take in her scent. She withdrew from him as she positioned herself in the seat to face him. "How are you darling?" she asked concernedly. "You look tired." She touched his cheek with her fingers.

"I'm fine," he answered her patting the other hand in her lap.

"You don't look fine. Is something bothering you?"

Ed looked at her with a plastered smile on his face. "I'm okay. Really, I am. I'm just anxious to see you," he added sincerely. Kate smiled back at him and held onto his hand.

"You have the package?" she asked.

"Yes, here it is." He handed over the rather large manila envelope.

Kate wasted no time in opening the package and looking at the photographs that were inside. There were photos of Blaze and Jack leaving his office walking hand in hand, embracing in the terminal marketplace, arriving at his apartment, and several taken through his window of them kissing one another.

"Who is she?" Kate asked clearly displeased.

"Her name is Blaze Beaumont."

"Blaze—what kind of name is Blaze—sounds like a stripper," Kate interrupted.

"She's no stripper!." Ed objected matter-of-factly! She's an executive at Brickhouse, Becker, and Shuman Inc. who comes highly qualified with impeccable credentials."

"Really, so what is she doing with my son?" Kate asked arrogantly.

"She's the lead executive on the new marketing campaign for Newman. She acquired the contract and has been leading the team on every aspect of the project. She's been seen with Jack twice... one time when they spent three days together in Atlantic City."

"I knew that he was with a woman those days I couldn't reach him. Go on," Kate was fully invested in the conversation. Ed continued, "The interesting thing about Ms. Beaumont is that she's recently engaged to her college sweetheart—Mr. Clayton Randolph Williams III."

"Really?" Kate's eyes lit up from the news. "Does Jack know about this engagement?"

"That, I don't know," Ed said earnestly.

"Well, Ed—isn't that exactly why I'm paying to have them followed, to get me this kind of information?"

"Now hold on, Kate. You know I don't do this for the money. For you, it's a favor to my special friend."

Kate realized perhaps she should be more tactful in dealing with Ed.

"I'm sorry, Ed. Forgive me?" She softened her demeanor. "I'm a bit frustrated with my son's choices in companionship. For the life of me, I don't know what he's thinking—dealing with women with no breeding."

Ed looked at Kate over his glasses with a disapproving scowl.

"You know nothing of her breeding, Kate. They are not pedigree hounds to be mated and sold." Ed was clearly angered by Kate's words. "Is that the way you think of me too?" Ed asked.

"Maybe you should back off and let your son live his own life. He may surprise you and make a good choice."

"These things must not be left to chance. I won't have it! Once I'm done with her, she'll be on the next flight to the moon. I'll have to think about this a bit more."

There was silence for the next few minutes. Kate realized that she should try and redeem herself with Ed.

"You're so quiet today." She touched Ed's hand.

"I'm fine, Kate. Just a little swamped with my cases," he lied.

He looked at her with adoring eyes.

"You're still the most beautiful woman I know," Ed said as he reached over and brushed the hair from Kate's eyes. Kate smiled and moved closer to him as they drove to their destination. Once inside the mid-sized rustic cabin, Kate took off her jacket and shoes as Ed opened a bottle of wine. He sat down next to her on the overstuffed sofa and kissed her forehead as she cuddled next to him.

"How are things going at home?" he asked. "Any trouble getting away this afternoon?"

"No, just so much to do organizing this event. You'll be there won't you?" Kate asked.

"Yes, I'll be there. You know I have to bring Abby."

"I know. What can I do? Forbid you from bringing her?" Kate asked as she looked up at Ed. She reached up, gently grabbed his face, and kissed him with passion letting him know that she desired him.

"I don't have a lot of time today," Kate said as she began taking off her blouse.

Ed got up and took her hand. They walked into the bedroom and shut the door. They were there for over an hour before resurfacing. Kate got dressed, fixed her hair and makeup preparing to leave.

"I won't be able to make it for the next several weeks," she yelled to Ed who was still dressing in the other room.

"Why not?" He stopped to look in the mirror clearly disappointed.

"We leave for the shore house right after the party."

"Oh, when do you return?" Ed asked entering the room.

"We'll be there for a month."

Ed walked toward her and took her hand pulling her up off the sofa and to her feet. He embraced her as he spoke.

"Then I really wish we had more time today." He held her tightly.

"Oh, darling, me too."

Kate placed her arms around his shoulders glancing at her watch. Ed kissed Kate one last time before they left to take her back to her car. When they reached her Mercedes, they said their goodbyes. Ed waited until Kate was safely in her car as she drove away before heading back to his office. He wished that he didn't love Kate, but he looked forward to their weekly meetings. They had been meeting every week for the last fourteen years, and every time she went away, he felt the same way. He had no idea what he would do with himself for the next month.

| 30 |

Thank you for the invitation!

Clay arrived at work early Wednesday morning to resume working on the three projects that were due by the end of the week. Since it was so early in the morning, he put off calling Blaze as he sometimes did before leaving for work. When he arrived in his office, an envelope addressed to him was laying on his desk. Clay wasn't expecting anything urgent, but he began to open the envelope anyway. Inside was a pair of tickets to the Newman charity event which was one of the most sought-after invitations among the business elite. Clay viewed this as an opportunity to network with some of the major players in the business and political community. Every year, the event attracted CEOs, executives, and major stockholders from the top 100 companies in the nation. The Newmans flew important clients and close friends and family into the city for their annual charity event that supported disadvantaged inner-city youth. The event would begin on Friday night with an awards ceremony and cocktail reception honoring achievers from various walks of life. On Saturday, Kate planned the annual Newman barbecue, an all-day event highlighted by a magnificent firework display, and on Sunday, a worship service on the Newman grounds with brunch following, which would conclude the event. Everyone tried to wrangle an invitation to the swarthy affair but only A-listers were invited. Clay wondered if Blaze had something to do with him being invited since she was working on the Newman account. He would have to thank her in a special way for pulling the strings to land him this opportunity.

Blaze called Clay the night before to let him know that she would be working late and then going straight home. She sounded exhausted when he spoke with her, so he didn't press her to come by her apartment. He would be seeing her that night, and after they were married, every night for the rest of their lives. He thought to himself that he had nothing to worry about, and any reservations he may have had were now dispelled with Blaze accepting his proposal. To him, things between them had never been better and Blaze was making every effort to be attentive and loving to him. He had no reason to think anything other than she loved him and would soon be his wife.

Meanwhile, over at Brickhouse, Becker, and Shuman Inc., Blaze couldn't get her night with Jack out of her head. She tried to stay busy all day at the office but found herself daydreaming about him. She had no idea when she went to Jack's office for their meeting that it would end up with her spending the night with him. She'd thought that things between them were over, and she resigned her-self to being married to Clay and making a life with him. Since she wasn't getting much done, she decided to leave work a little early and head home. She wanted to relax and just be alone to think things through. Blaze arrived at her apartment, changed into a tee shirt and sweats, and relaxed on the sofa with a glass of wine. She had just settled down to do some reading when the phone rang. It was Clay and she wasn't prepared to talk with him, but she knew if she didn't answer it, he would continue to call until she did, and since she didn't want him showing up at the apartment, she picked up the phone.

"Hello!" she said.

"Hey, baby! How you doing?" Clay's voice was full of enthusiasm.

"I'm fine, Clay. How are you?"

"Good. Really good!" he answered.

"How was your day?" Blaze asked robotically.

"It was good, mostly routine except for a few meetings. Hey—by the way, thanks for the invitation."

"Invitation? What invitation?" Blaze asked.

"You know the invitation to the Newman barbecue. I know it was you who got me invited."

Blaze nearly dropped the phone.

"Clay, I didn't give your name to anyone at Newman. When did you get the invite?" Blaze sat up trying to compose herself.

"It was delivered to the office today. The interesting thing is that the event is this weekend and there was no card to RSVP. Looks like someone is expecting me to attend." Clay smiled from ear to ear, and although Blaze could not see him, she could feel his excitement.

"I hadn't planned on going," Blaze said lying.

"Why not? Wouldn't that be politically incorrect since you're working on the company's ad campaign?"

"Yeah, but I planned to work all weekend on the account, so I really hadn't thought about going to the event."

"Well, we don't have to go if you don't want," Clay reassured her. "But I think that this is a great opportunity that would help further my career and benefit both of us."

Blaze didn't want to seem selfish, so she reluctantly agreed.

"Okay!"

In her mind, Blaze was preoccupied with who would send Clay an invitation to the Newman event. She was saved from furthering the conversation when Clay told her he had another call and would see her tomorrow.

Once she hung up the phone, Blaze did some serious soul-searching. She was overwhelmed with the task of breaking off her engagement to Clay. She would have to be honest with him and tell him that she loved him, but not enough to marry him. Then there was the issue of telling him she was seeing someone else, and of all people, it was of all people jack Newman.

| 31 |

Late Night Surprise

Blaze made herself a cup of herbal tea to help calm herself so she could think. She sat in the window seat of her bedroom and looked out upon the dark street. She remembered that first night at Jack's apartment when he made her a cup of tea. She smiled when she thought about him and how handsome he was. She knew he was sincere when he said that he cared for her, but she wondered if that was enough to build a relationship. Blaze decided to try and forget everything for the rest of the night. She took off her clothes and slipped into a tee shirt. She roamed around her apartment aimlessly as she was restless and could not stay focused. When she tried to sleep, she could only see visions of Jack which made her want him even more. She fought the desire to call him and began to turn the lights out in her apartment.

It was now 11:30 pm, and the only light left on was the one in her bedroom. Blaze picked up a book she had been reading and propped her pillows up on her bed. She began to read when the phone rang. Blaze immediately looked at the clock.

"It's almost midnight." She looked at her phone and assumed it was Clay since no one else ever called her at that hour. She picked up hesitantly.

"Hello."

"Hey—what are you doing?" the caller asked.

Blaze smiled as she recognized Jack's voice.

"Hey yourself," she said sitting up in the bed. "What a nice surprise!"

"I hoped that you would see it that way," Jack said.

"Of course, how else would I see it?" she asked puzzled.

"Well considering the hour, you may think that this is a booty call."

Blaze burst into laughter.

"Is this what this is?" Blaze asked.

"I don't know." Jack smiled.

"Well, now that you mentioned it, sounds like a booty call to me."

"Now, I feel self-conscious for just wanting to call my woman and see how she's doing."

"Your woman, huh?" Blaze repeated taken off guard by his statement.

"Well, I would be honored if you would be my woman, but if you're not then I'm prepared to do what I can to make that happen."

"Really? So, you think I'm just that easy huh?" Blaze teased.

"No, I just know that we're right for each other and I want only to do the right thing."

They both laughed as Blaze made herself comfortable on the bed.

"What are you doing?" Jack asked.

"Reading," Blaze quickly replied.

"I see. Is it a romantic novel or some boring research material?"

"It's a novel, but not romantic."

"I want to see you," Jack said abruptly spewed out.

"I want to see you too."

"Okay, then it's settled," Jack stated matter-of-factly. "Open the door!"

"What?" Blaze was shocked. She jumped up. "Where are you?"

"Open your door and see."

Blaze walked into the living room with the phone still against her ear. She peered through the peephole, but she couldn't see anything. She unlocked the door and opened it to see Jack standing there. His head was down, and he was holding the wall with one hand and in the other, he held the phone to his ear. He was wearing a white shirt hanging loosely outside of his jeans and a blue blazer. His tall handsome frame fit so well in his attire; Blaze had to inhale deeply to digest the pleasing vision. He looked up at her revealing his dimpled smile. They stood there in the doorway, both still with the phones to their ears smiling at one another.

"May I come in?" Jack asked.

"Oh yes! Of course, come in!" Blaze said.

Jack walked towards Blaze who was backing up into the living room. When they finally stopped midway into the room, Jack pulled Blaze close to him and looked into her eyes. He kissed her nearly picking her up off the floor. When they finally came up for air, Jack released Blaze and stood back to look at her.

"Each time I see you—you're even sexier than before," he said.

Blaze smiled as she took his hand and led him over to the sofa. They both sat down finally turning off their phones.

"I can't believe you're here. I was just thinking about calling you," Blaze blurted.

"Well, I'm glad to hear that because I was hesitant about just stopping by without calling you."

"Can I get you something?" Blaze asked not knowing what else to say.

"No, thank you. I just want to look at you," Jack replied.

"I like your place. It's very cozy," Jack stated.

"Thanks!" Blaze felt awkward. She had never been alone in her apartment with any man aside from Clay. She somehow felt uncomfortable as if she was betraying him.

"What's wrong?" Jack asked. "Is it something I said?"

"It's nothing—really. I've had a long day is all and I just can't seem to wind down from it."

"Well, we can't have that," Jack replied. "Let's see what we can do about that."

"What do you mean?" Blaze asked.

Jack held out his hand to her.

"Come here and lay down on the floor."

"Lay down on the floor?" Blaze asked.

"Yes, here lay on this." Jack removed a throw from the sofa.

Blaze was puzzled as to what Jack had in mind. She did as she was told and laid down on her back.

"I think it would be better if you turn over," Jack said smiling.

Blaze immediately assumed that Jack wanted to have sex. She reluctantly turned over on her stomach expecting Jack to take advantage of her position. Jack began to massage her shoulders. She was taken off guard. Jack rubbed her shoulders and neck finding pressure points where the tension was prominent in Blaze's back. She began to relax and let Jack continue.

"How's that feel?" he asked.

"Devine," Blaze answered in an inaudible voice.

Blaze relaxed as Jack worked his magic. He then proceeded to rub Blaze's feet eliciting moans of satisfaction and pleasure from her. Jack knew what he was doing and soon Blaze was completely relaxed feeling relief from her stress-filled day. When Jack stopped, he completely covered Blaze's body with the throw blanket and sat on the sofa watching her. She turned on her side to face him. He was smiling at her, and she sleepily returned the smile.

"Where in the world did you learn how to do that?" Blaze was impressed.

"Just a little something I learned while in the Philippines," he answered.

"Are you serious?"

"No, I just know how it would feel to me if someone massaged me in that way, so I took a chance and tried it on you. I have read some about reflexology and how each area of the foot is connected to a part of the body. I find it fascinating that some cures are administered in that fashion."

"Wow! You really are full of surprises Jack Newman."

"Well, thank you! I aim to please," Jack replied.

"So, what's got you so tense?" he asked. "Is it work or personal?"

Blaze looked at Jack not sure if she should be honest with him about why she was stressed.

"Jack, I always want to be honest with you. I never want what happened between us before to occur again. So, I'm gonna tell you the truth."

Jack sat on the edge of the sofa, now intrigued.

"I haven't been able to tell Clay the truth about us. I spoke to him earlier tonight, but I couldn't bring myself to tell him the truth. I just couldn't find the right words."

Jack's expression immediately changed.

"Go on," he said trying to control his disappointment.

"I was all ready to tell him when he told me he had been invited to the Newman event this weekend. He thanked me for getting him invited, but I had nothing to do with that happening."

"How'd he get invited?" Jack asked.

"I was about to ask you that same question?" Blaze asked.

"Well, you know I had nothing to do with it, but I can surely find out just as easily. I'll just ask my mother's assistant, Pierre. He usually tends to those kinds of things. He would know if anyone would." Jack stated.

"I hope you're not angry with me, but you can see how this affected me being able to talk to him about us. It just wasn't the most appropriate time to do that."

"Come here!" Jack was calm, his temperament perfectly in check.

Blaze got up from the floor and walked to where Jack was seated. He held out his hand for her to join him there. Blaze sat down still nervous as to how Jack would accept the news.

"We're in this together. I told you that from the start. If you need more time to talk to Clay, then time is what you have. I can wait a little longer before staking my claim," he joked.

Blaze released a sigh of relief.

"Thank you for understanding Jack. This isn't easy for me. I want this to be over in the worst way."

Jack enveloped Blaze in his arms and kissed her forehead. They sat there in their embrace neither of them speaking to the other.

"You know this wasn't what I expected the first time that I had you here," Blaze confessed.

"It doesn't matter what the circumstances are, I'm just glad to be here," Jack sighed. "Speaking of this weekend; I would like to escort you to the event."

Blaze was surprised by his invitation.

"Are you sure that's a good idea?" Blaze asked. I need to talk to Clay before Friday and I'm not so sure how he's gonna take this news. The timing really sucks."

"You have a point about his reaction, but I want you with me," Jack begged.

"Why don't we just go and meet each other there?" suggested Blaze.

"You mean you're turning down my invitation?" Jack placed his head on her shoulder.

"I think it's best that we don't show up together is all. This doesn't seem like the appropriate time for you to be introducing me to your family as your love interest."

"Baby, my family will welcome you with open arms. My dad already admires you and my mother—well just leave her to me...she'll come around too!"

"I'm not so convinced of that. From what I've heard, your mother is very particular when it comes to whom her children date. I'm not sure I'm what she has in mind for you."

"Well, it's a good thing my mom doesn't make decisions for me, isn't it?" Jack replied.

"I'm very nervous about this, Jack. I'm not good at meeting family."

"Don't you worry your pretty self about this? Let me take care of everything."

Blaze settled back into Jack's arms and held onto him. After a few minutes, she began to relax again.

"Can I get you anything, Jack? I was just making some tea."

"There is something that I want more than a cup of tea." He looked at Blaze as she walked to the kitchen.

"Oh yeah? What's that?" she asked already knowing the answer.

Jack walked up behind Blaze and wrapped his arms around her waist. He kissed her neck and back.

"Do you really need me to answer that question?" he asked.

Blaze turned to face him and looked into his eyes.

"Do you only want me for my body?"

"Yep, that's it. I want your body, and this is a confirmed booty call, so let's get to it."

"Your wish is my command!" Blaze pulled her tee shirt over her head as she walked into the bedroom with Jack following close behind.

| 32 |

The Cocktail Party

The evening of the cocktail reception and awards ceremony was rapidly approaching. This was Kate's most cherished event of the year. She expected a spectacular presentation and would allow nothing to interfere with her vision. No detail was too minor for attention right down. Kate even controlled what each of the Newman family members would wear to the event.

Kate chose to wear a black knit ruffled cocktail dress that flattered her 5-foot 9-inch figure. She decided on a three-inch high-heeled shoe that complimented her long lean tanned legs. Her accessories included a pair of dazzling emerald green drop earrings and a cocktail ring that played nicely against her coca-colored skin. Her stylist elegantly pinned short-cut cut hair away from her face to emphasize her almond-shaped brown eyes that were accented with a smoky liner for a dramatic look. Her makeup was flawless and just enough to signify the evening with style and grace. Kate would be the center of attention and she was prepared to have all eyes upon her.

Once she was finished dressing, she checked on Thaddeus and the children making sure that they were presentable for the numerous photographs that would be taken of them. Kate entered Thaddeus's dressing chamber to hurry him along.

"Thad, are you ready darling?" Kate asked as she approached his bathroom.

"I'm having a little trouble with this tie?" he groaned.

Thaddeus wore a black designer suit, white shirt, and green tie to compliment Kate's emerald jewelry. He was a handsome man, thin in stature, but still, physically fit. Specks of gray flickered through his hair and mustache giving him a distinguished look, which was most appealing to women of all ages. Kate walked towards him to help him with his tie.

"You look stunning!" Thaddeus remarked as Kate approached him.

"Why thank you, dear. And you look delicious." She kissed him on the cheek.

"Delicious you say! Well, why not skip this joint and take a ride to the shore house and make out all night?" Thaddeus tried to pull Kate close to him.

"Oh no you don't," Kate laughed and pulled away. "We have the rest of the summer to get away. Tonight, we are going to be the model host and hostess and raise lots of money for those children in the city." Kate finished tying Thaddeus's tie.

"Hold still!" She tried to get the bow straight.

Just then, Elizabeth called from the bedroom.

"Mom, dad, you in here?" she yelled.

"We're in here Lizzy and stop yelling we can hear you just fine." Kate scolded her daughter.

Liz blew out a whistle.

"You guys look wonderful together." She walked over to kiss her parents. "Oh, mother! That dress is fabulous!"

"Thank you, my dear." Kate began to focus on Liz's attire.

"Liz, you look stunning! I told you that dress would be perfect for you."

Liz was the image of her mother; tall, lean, and beautiful. Her dark hair cascaded down her back covering the backless, form-fitting, long-sleeved, white silk dress. The dress had a high neckline and low-cut back with the bottom tapered just below her knee. She wore silver shoes embellished with Swarovski Crystals and she carried a small glass clutch purse in her hand. Her diamond earrings dangled close to her shoulders, and she wore only her diamond wedding band on her left hand. After three children, she still possessed the body from her youth. She enjoyed a more athletic lifestyle than most of her friends. She enjoyed being privileged, but never flaunted her wealth or behaved in an unflattering spoiled manner. She loved her husband, adored her children, and worked hard as an advocate for the children that her mother's youth organization serviced. She was well-liked by most and adored by her family. Liz was the apple of her father's eye.

"Well princess where's that son-in-law of mine?" Thaddeus asked as he kissed Liz on the forehead.

"He's downstairs, daddy."

"Good, I have some things I'd like to go over with him before we leave."

Hearing this, Kate interrupted their conversation.

"You will do no such thing. There will be no business transactions going on tonight. This is a family affair and I want happy humans at this party."

"Alright dear, whatever you say," Thaddeus agreed. He stood over Kate's shoulder making funny faces at Liz.

Whenever there was a party or function that involved the Newman clan, everyone gathered in the sitting room of Kate's and Thaddeus' bedroom talking and laughing. It was the official gathering place for all things Newman. After a few moments, Michael,

James, and his wife Becca joined the trio as the brothers taunted Liz while Kate scolded them all.

"Has anyone heard from Jack? I thought he would be here by now," Kate yelled over the noise.

"You know how Jack is mother," James said. "He'll probably meet us there."

Kate didn't look happy about that, but she wasn't about to let anything spoil this evening. Once Thaddeus was finished getting ready, everyone went down to the family room for cocktails.

"Has the car picked up Reverend Patterson yet?" Kate asked Pierre.

"Yes Kate, he's on his way. They should be arriving just about now."

The Reverend Timothy Patterson had been the pastor of the United Presbyterian Church of Greater Northwest Philadelphia since Kate was a young girl. Kate's family were life-long members of the congregation. Kate was active in many of the women's groups at the church. Reverend Patterson officiated over all the Newman family events and activities including baptisms, weddings, and funerals, so it was fitting that he delivered the opening prayer at the awards ceremony and dinner.

Once Reverend Patterson arrived, the family prepared to leave for the theater. Kate, Thaddeus, and Reverend Patterson, all rode together in the limousine, while the siblings all decided to ride in the second car. They arrived at the African Museum a little after six o'clock, which gave Kate time for some last-minute instructions before receiving her guests. The program was scheduled to begin at eight o'clock with cocktails at six-thirty.

The cocktail reception was held in the foyer on the main floor of the museum. A jazz quartet played rhythmic music while guests mingled enjoying cocktails and hors d'oeuvres that were served by the hired staff. Kate was in her element as she greeted everyone personally to remind them how much a donation from their organization would benefit the students. Many of Thaddeus's business associates were in attendance, as were city officials and politicians hoping to gain support for their reelection.

The Newmans had been greeting guests for about thirty minutes when Jack arrived—alone. His entrance went without fanfare as he made his way to the receiving line that his parents attended.

"Mom, dad—hey what's up?" Jack asked kissing his mother on the cheek.

"Mother, you look beautiful as always," Jack complimented.

"Oh, thank you dear and so do you, my handsome son."

Kate immediately excused herself from her guests as she embraced her son and looped her arm into his leading him away from the crowd.

"I'm so glad you came early." Kate smiled. "Did you come alone?"

"Yes, mother. I came alone." Jack knew where the conversation was headed.

"But I thought that you were bringing a date?"

"Yes. Well it just didn't work out that way, so here I am," Jack replied.

"Well, no matter. There are plenty of young women here to entertain yourself with for the evening. Don't forget that the Mitchells are coming, and Denise is expected to attend as well."

"Of course, mother. How could I forget that?" Jack was annoyed.

"Listen, I see a few people I'd like to speak with. Can we continue this conversation later?" Jack asked.

"Why, sure dear, but don't go too far. The photo session will begin shortly, and I want you all in attendance," Kate reminded Jack.

Just then a couple approached Kate as they exchanged greetings and Kate resumed her charming demeanor eliciting donations for her charity.

Jack walked to the other side of the room looking around to see if Blaze had arrived. He was quite handsome in his elegant black-tie attire and the women were mesmerized by his good, clean looks. He flashed his alluring smile making small talk when necessary, but his mind was elsewhere. He wasn't interested in talking shop with anyone, and he surely didn't care about socializing with this elitist crowd. He walked to the bar and ordered a Perfect Ten. Michael and James joined him at the bar greeting one another and toasting to the night. It was getting close to eight o'clock when the awards ceremony and dedication were scheduled to begin. Pierre was busy giving last-minute instructions to the stage crew and carrying out Kate's orders. An announcement was made to the guests that the program would soon begin, and they should make their way toward the theater area to take their seats.

"Jack, you coming?" Michael asked.

"Yeah. You go ahead. I'll be there shortly, just have to make a quick call."

"Well, you better make it quick before mother sends the cavalry out here for ya," Michael added.

"Don't worry. I'm not going far," Jack responded.

Jack walked outside to a garden area to get some air. The museum was located on the edge of the city and from the garden steps Jack could see the waterfront. Stars sprinkled the sky as the moon cast a brilliant glow upon the river. The air was balmy as the warm breeze blew softly through the night reminiscent of another such night not long ago in Atlantic City. He could see her image in his mind very clearly. He remembered her smile and the way that she looked at him that evening. Jack didn't like that he was so smitten with her. He had never been in love, and he didn't know if he was now, but it sure felt as if he was.

"Damn!" he said out loud. "This is crazy. I'm acting like a schoolboy."

Jack turned to walk back into the museum. Most of the guests had already gone into the theater to take their seats and the foyer was nearly cleared out with the exception of the servers and other staff. Jack walked back to the bar to order another drink as he tried to put memories of Blaze out of his head.

| 33 |

The Surprise in Bella Jewels

Blaze had been on edge all day. She knew that she was expected to attend the Newman event tonight, but she didn't know how she was going to do that. All week long she had tried to come up with a solution for not attending the cocktail party, but nothing seemed legitimate enough. Whatever her decision would be she would have to answer to three men: Sam, Clay, and Jack. Not going was out of the question unless she was on her deathbed. Sam made it clear that all his executives were expected to be in attendance. He bought a block of tickets for the three-day event, and everyone on his team would be there or they would be unemployed. Clay saw his invitation as the opportunity of a lifetime. He would be in the company of some of the most influential business leaders in the country. Not attending would mean career suicide. And then there was Jack who expected her to be on his arm and wanted to introduce her to his family.

Blaze tried to subtly suggest that Clay not attend, but he ignored her and didn't give it a second thought. She just couldn't embarrass Jack in front of his family, business associates, and friends by arriving on Clay's arm. She didn't know what she was going to do. She had two extra tickets and so she invited her mother and Misha to go along with her. Clay was not happy about the arrangement, but Blaze told him that she had invited Misha long before he received his invite, so he really couldn't protest too much. With any luck, she would be able to get away from Clay long enough to explain things to Jack, but something inside of her knew that no amount of planning would deter the inevitable outcome of this evening.

Blaze made appointments at her mother's salon for both herself and Misha. It was Blaze's treat to have facials, manicures, pedicures, and their hair styled. Although Friday nights were usually busy at the salon, Jewels rescheduled her usual clients so she could spend time preparing her daughter for the evening. Since she was attending the event also, it gave the mother and daughter a chance to catch up and hang out. Before Clay received an invitation, it was planned to be a girl's night out. A few select clients still held their standing appointments, but the salon was closed to everyone else.

Blaze arrived a little before two o'clock with Misha arriving shortly thereafter. Jewels' salon was in Center City in the prominent yet exclusive Rittenhouse area. She called her chain of salons *Bella Jewels,* a combination of Blaze's middle name and her own name, which she always found quite beautiful. Jewels specialized in servicing the total woman and she believed in a complete regime of treatments for the mind, body, and spirit. Her clientele included socialites, celebrities, politicians, and of course, the career woman. Her bookings were made well in advance with some waiting three months for an appointment. Although she was quite successful, Jewels maintained a simplistic lifestyle and was very down to earth. When Blaze arrived, her mother was in her office finishing a call from her New York salon.

"Hey, mommy!" Blaze said reaching over to kiss her mother.

"Hi, baby! Have a seat I should be finished in a second." Jewels covered the mouthpiece of the phone.

Blaze flopped down on the cream leather sofa and kicked off her stilettos propping her feet up. She was deep in thought when her mother finished her call.

"You look amazing!" Jewels said.

"I do?" Blaze asked as if surprised.

"Of course, you do! You're my child." Jewels joked.

"I wish I felt amazing," Blaze replied.

"Why? What's wrong?"

"Just about everything," Blaze answered sprawling out on the sofa.

"What could be so terrible? You have a great job, a wonderful fiancé, and you're a beautiful girl with your life ahead of you."

"Mom? Can I tell you something?"

"Mmhmm," Jewels mumbled without looking up.

Blaze didn't know how to say it so she just blurted it out.

"I don't want to marry Clay. I'm not in love with him. I love someone else."

Jewels looked at her daughter as if she were an alien.

"What do you mean you don't want to marry Clay and you're not in love with him? And who is this someone else? You never mentioned seeing anyone else before." Jewels' concerns grew by the second.

"I know. It just happened so fast and well, I wasn't looking for anything like this, but mom, he is so fine and wonderful and ahhh." Blaze said all in one breath.

Jewels got up from her desk and walked over toward the sofa where Blaze lay hopelessly.

"Blaze Bella Beaumont have you lost your mind? Do you realize that Cynthia and I have already started making appointments to meet with wedding planners and we are looking at venues next week?"

"No, mother. I haven't lost my mind. I know that this is sudden —but..."

"Sudden! This couldn't come at a worse time Blaze." Jewels sat down. "I thought this was what you wanted, Blaze?"

"No mom. It's not what I want. It's what you and Clay want. I never wanted to marry Clay," Blaze confirmed. I'm not ready for that kind of commitment and I'm not sure if I ever will be with Clay. Anyway, Cynthia doesn't even like me."

"Oh, my goodness!" Jewels said holding her head.

"Mother, just wait until you meet Jack. He's wonderful and successful and he adores me." Blaze held her mother's hands.

"Does Clay know that you don't want to marry him?"

"Not yet, but I'm planning to tell him. I just haven't found the right time," Blaze admitted.

"Oh, my goodness! Girl, you need Jesus." Jewels did not know what else to say to her daughter. "You were always a precocious child, and this tells me you haven't changed a bit. I guess it's my fault. I spoiled you kids rotten."

"No mom! That's not true. You've always told us to follow our hearts. You used to tell us to not compromise our feelings and values. You taught us to love God, have high morals, and be honest. Well, mom, I'm being honest. I don't love Clay enough to marry him and it wouldn't be right to marry him knowing that. He deserves someone who loves him completely and wants to spend the rest of her life with him."

Jewels looked at Blaze and she knew she was being sincere.

"I've always supported you in the things that you wanted to do. That's not going to change, but you must tell Clay as soon as possible. It's just not right to lead him on this way."

"I know and I will tell him. But with this event all weekend long, and him wanting so much to be a part of it, I just couldn't do it."

"Okay, but as soon as this thing is over, you sit down with him and be honest. Promise me you'll do that," Jewels insisted.

"I promise, mom." Blaze embraced her mother with a big hug.

"Okay—we'd better get started or none of us will be going to the Newman event. Jewels and Blaze left the office area and went into the salon where Blaze, Misha, and Jewels were pampered for the evening ahead.

| 34 |

Stay with me

After the salon, Blaze went home and immediately ran herself a bath. She was careful not to dishevel her hair and so she only stayed in the tub for a short time. By six o'clock, she was ready to go. Blaze chose an off-shoulder black dress with a form-fitting bodice and ostrich feathers from the waist to the mini-length skirt. The black crystal chandelier earrings just graced her neckline and framed her delicate face. She added a pair of black four-inch stiletto sandals that finished her attire nicely. Her hair was pressed straight and hung down her back with the addition of a few extensions that Jewels insisted she styled in her hair. It was a nice complement to her already full mane and added sensual style to her already sexy look. She was so nervous about the evening that she thought she was going to vomit. She hated that she was going to be arriving with Clay because she knew that Jack would not take it well. But she was more anxious to see Jack because she missed him so much that she ached inside.

Blaze suggested to Clay that they meet at the museum, but Clay insisted on picking her up at the apartment. He wanted her on his arm when he walked into the room with all eyes on them as they entered. He knew that Blaze was familiar with most of the people that would be present, and he wanted a proper introduction to everyone important. He also felt that his fiancé was an incredibly beautiful woman and that he would be the envy of every man in the room. Little did he know how true that was, at least to one man in particular.

Clay was late arriving which made Blaze furious. This only served to add to her frustration and so she found it hard to be cordial with him. When he arrived a half hour late, she was angry, and she did not hesitate to let him know.

"Baby, I'm so sorry I'm late. My mother asked me to come by earlier today and the time just got away from me."

This further fueled Blaze's anger since Cynthia, Clay's mother, was not very fond of her, which she'd just spoken about hours earlier in the salon.

"Look Clay, I'm expected to be on time for this function. My boss made it clear that he wants his staff present. It's not good practice to be late for these things," Blaze yelled.

"Okay, baby. I understand. I get it. Wow! Would you cut me a break? How do I look? Do I look alright?"

Blaze tried to be as civil as possible with Clay, but she was so angry she just grabbed her purse and headed for the door.

"What? No kiss. No hello? What's the matter Blaze?" he asked.

"Can we just go, please?" Blaze asked.

"Sure, baby!" Clay said as he walked towards the door. "You look beautiful baby—really, really sexy," he added.

"Thank you," Blaze responded without enthusiasm.

Clay held out his arm for Blaze to take after she locked her apartment door, but she walked past Clay and got on the elevator with him following. The drive to the museum was uncomfortably quiet for Clay who tried to make small talk while Blaze stared out of the window. When they arrived at the museum it was seven-forty-five. They had missed the cocktail hour and were being directed to the theater by an attendant when Blaze saw Jack at the bar. Jack was looking right at her, and his stare pierced through her like daggers. Her heart skipped a beat when she saw him standing there. She had to think of something, and quick.

"Clay, I have to go to the lady's room. Why don't you see if you can find my table? I'll be right there when I'm finished."

"No baby. I can wait here for you. I'll get a drink from the bar," Clay said.

"No. We don't have time for a drink right now. We have to get in there. Please go and smooth things over with Sam for me please?"

"Okay! I'll go find the group, but you hurry up and get in there," Clay demanded before leaving.

When Clay was inside the theater, Blaze turned her direction towards the bar where Jack was standing. His back was now turned to her, and he was nursing a drink that was sitting on the bar.

He could feel her when she approached him as he said in a low voice, "Hello, beautiful. Glad you could make it!"

"Hi, Jack." She could feel the tension in the room. "Jack, please don't be angry with me." Blaze gently grabbed his arm. Jack didn't respond to her. He just ordered another drink.

"Give the lady what she wants," he ordered the bartender.

"I don't want anything," Blaze replied. "Look at me, please?"

Jack turned to face Blaze. He was visibly angry but trying hard to conceal it.

"It hurts too much to look at you. You're too damn beautiful and I don't like sharing my woman, so forgive me if I don't seem happy to see you."

Blaze felt weak. She wanted to fall into Jack's arms and put her arms around his neck and kiss him deeply. He was so handsome standing there. His jaw was tightly drawn, and his fist was clenched by his side. He looked as though he had just stepped out of a magazine so suave and debonair—tall and sexy as hell. Jack looked Blaze up and down from head to toe.

"What are you trying to do to me?" he asked. "You can't come in here looking like that and expect me to be a gentleman. I wanted to deck that dude with his arm around you as if he owns you."

"Jack, it doesn't mean anything. You know that. I promised you I'd tell him about us, and I will."

"Yeah, like you told him months ago, and when you told him last week? Blaze, I'm no fool. This is bullshit!"

"Jack, please don't be upset with me!" Blaze pleaded with him.

She placed her hand on his chest and moved close to him. Even with heels she still had to tip-toe to reach him. She kissed him on his lips as he stood there without any motion at all. He looked into her eyes when she finished as if searching for the truth. Her eyes were filled with tears as she fought hard to hold them back.

"Jack, I love you."

Jack put down his drink and walked past her and out of the building and into the night. Blaze wanted to run after him, but she knew she couldn't reason with him at this moment. She had to get herself together and put on a brave effort to continue with the evening's festivities. Her job depended on it and the Newman account was a priority right now. Blaze went into the restroom and composed herself. She dried her eyes and put on a fresh coat of lip gloss. She smoothed her dress and headed out the door into the theater. Sam and the team were seated at a table close to the stage and one table away from the Newman table. Clay was seated in her seat but had to relinquish it when Blaze arrived.

"I had no idea we wouldn't be sitting together," Clay whispered to her.

"I think there is someone who can help you find your table," she replied.

Blaze beckoned to an attendant who escorted Clay to a table on the other side of the room. Blaze was relieved that he wouldn't be sitting with her. She sat down at the table speaking to everyone who was seated there. Z and Parks were nearby, and Sam was in conversation with a business associate who stopped by the table. Each table sat ten people so quite a few conversations were going on at the same time. The program had not begun, so people were still mingling although some had been served and were beginning their meals. Blaze looked around the room for Jack, but he was nowhere to be found. She noticed that her mother was seated not far from her, so she went over to her table to speak with her and Misha who was also there.

"Girl, where you been? It's some fine ass men in here," she commented in a flagrant way that was exclusive to Misha. Jewels was stunning in a stylish off-white pantsuit that fit her slender figure perfectly. She complimented the suit with a cream silk tailored blouse and a few strands of pearls. She sat crossed-legged at the table showing off a stunning pair of cream shoes. She laughed at Misha's outlandish show of expression about the men in attendance, but her maternal instinct gave way to concerns about Blaze's mood.

"Honey, you alright?" Jewels asked Blaze.

"Yeah, mom—I'm fine."

"So, where's your young man?" Jewels asked.

"Oh, he's here somewhere, I suppose."

"When did you arrive? We were looking for you earlier," Jewels inquired.

"I just got here. Clay was late so we missed the networking session.

Jewels noticed that Blaze was not happy about something, but she didn't want to pry so she let it go.

"Listen, mother, I've gotta get back to my table, but I'll see you as soon as the program is over."

"Okay." Jewels' concerns about her daughter grew.

Blaze went back to her table and sat down trying to look like she was enjoying herself. She couldn't help but glance at the entrance to the theater numerous times to see if Jack was coming back. Z swapped seats with one of the team to sit next to Blaze.

"Hey there. You look good tonight," Z complimented.

"So, does that mean that you don't think I look good any other night?" Blaze asked sarcastically.

"My! We're in a mood!"

"I'm sorry. This evening hasn't started the way I would have liked it to start. Clay was late and Jack...well Jack is missing."

"No, he's here. We spoke to him earlier."

"Yeah, but he left since then," Blaze added.

"What do you mean he left? He's a part of the program. The whole Newman clan will be on stage. Kate Newman likes to put on a display and have the entire family aboard."

"Well, unless Jack returns in the next few minutes, he won't be a part of the festivities."

"Don't look now, but the queen herself is headed this way."

"Queen? What queen?" Blaze asked looking around.

"Kate Newman. She's headed for our table."

Just then, Blaze saw the elegant and beautiful Kate Newman headed toward them. She was stunning. Tall, lean, and elegantly dressed, she looked like a vision as she approached the table. Blaze had seen pictures of the socialite on the society pages, but this would be her first face-to-face with the icon and mother of the man she had been sleeping with these last months. To say that she was a bit overwhelmed would be an understatement.

"Good evening, everyone. I hope that you are all enjoying yourselves!" Kate said smiling.

"Well, hello again, Kate," Sam said standing up to embrace her.

"Sam, please introduce me to your team. I've heard wonderful things about you all," Kate addressed the group.

"Well, you've met Xavier and Parks from our quality department, and most everyone else except for our lead executive on the Newman account, Blaze Beaumont."

Blaze stood up and extended her hand to Kate. Kate turned and looked Blaze directly in the eyes with a half-smile.

"Well, Ms. Beaumont! We finally meet," she said coyly.

"Please...call me Blaze," she said as she met Kate's stare with equal deliberateness.

"It seems as though both my husband and son have been keeping you quite busy," Kate said with sarcasm. "They are so much alike when it comes to the company business. Now, when it comes to lifestyle, I like to think that I play a major part in those decisions with them both relying on me heavily for direction...even if they think that they're the ones in control." Kate chuckled ever so gaily as she made a point to be direct. "Oh dear, I think that it's time to get the program started. Sam, I'll see you at the house tomorrow?" she stated more than asked.

"Yes, of course, Kate," Sam replied quickly.

"Good! Well then, it was a pleasure meeting you all," Kate said as she walked away.

Z whispered to Blaze as Kate began to walk away from the table.

"Wow! Did the temperature drop below zero just now? I felt a cold wind blow over this table for sure."

"Keep it down, Z. We don't want to get thrown out on our butts before we get started," Parks stated.

"You're right," Blaze added. "Is it my imagination or did she deliberately diss me just now?"

"Naw. You right! She definitely dissed your butt and good. She's smooth though," Z chuckled.

"Well, I don't think I'll be attending the barbecue tomorrow. She might have security throw me out. I've heard stories about how much of a diva she is, and now I've gotten to see it firsthand," Blaze scoffed.

Sam also noticed the apparent slight that Kate delivered to Blaze. "You are all committed to all three days of the festivities. Don't forget the Newmans are our client so whatever we must endure to keep this account, within reason, we will do," Sam stated firmly.

The conversations at the table ceased as the house lights were dimmed for the opening of the program. There was no doubt that Kate had it in for Blaze. She made it known that she didn't like her, which meant that she didn't think Blaze was good enough for her son. Blaze was disheartened. First came the blow-up with Jack and now this. What a horrible way to start the weekend off. As the program got underway, Blaze found an opportunity to sneak away from the table. She walked over to sit with her mother and Misha. They chatted for a while in between segments, and then Blaze excused herself to go to the lady's room. As she was walking towards the exit, she saw Jack standing in the back of the theater talking to a woman. As she got closer, she realized that it was Denise, the woman who came to Manny's birthday party. She was standing awfully close to Jack whispering something in his ear. He laughed at whatever she was saying as he bent down to whisper something back. They didn't notice Blaze as she walked past them since they were a few feet away from her and the theater was dark.

Blaze didn't want Jack to see her, so she quickly exited the room. Blaze wanted to run away and hide. She was devastated by the turn of events that occurred tonight. She went into the restroom and sat in the lounge. Instinctively at that moment, Jewels entered the lounge looking for her daughter.

"Blaze, Clay wanted you to meet some of his colleagues," Jewels said.

"Well, I'm not ready to meet anyone. I just had the worse experience with Kate Newman. She hates me," Blaze said.

"What do you mean she hates you? She doesn't know you, so how can she hate you?"

"I don't know, but she pretty much has it down to a science. She made it a point to let me know in so many words that she was a big influence in Jack's life and that he needed her to help him make important lifestyle decisions."

"Well, that doesn't mean she hates you, Blaze."

"Oh mom, you should have been there. Everyone that was sitting at that table caught on."

"Okay listen to me. It isn't the end of the world. You've worked too hard to let something like this ruin your evening. No Kate—or anyone is going to put my girl down. You go back out there and show them what you're made of. If you need me, I'll be right there. You understand?" Jewels asked.

"Yes!" Blaze exclaimed hugging her mother.

"Okay! Now you freshen up your face and go out there and wow them all."

Jewels left Blaze to get herself together. She knew her mother was right, and she didn't like the way she was behaving. Blaze never let anyone take her down, and she wasn't about to let it happen now. She gathered herself and went back into the theater. The program portion of the evening had concluded, and the guests were directed to the ballroom for dinner and dancing. Clay found Blaze talking with some of the guests and introduced her to some of his colleagues. He introduced her as his fiancé seeming quite pleased with himself. Blaze remained gracious although she tried to remove herself from the scene. Just as she was about to go back to her table, Thaddeus Newman approached the couple.

"Well hello, Blaze. Are you enjoying yourself thus far?" he asked in his usually stern voice.

"Yes, Thaddeus. It's a wonderful party," Blaze replied.

"You think this is a party, just wait until the barbecue tomorrow. That's more my kind of style and not so much this stiff shirt kind of affair. You'll see how much fun it will be. You are attending tomorrow, I assume?" Thaddeus asked with eyebrows raised.

"Why, yes! Yes, the team will all be there. Wouldn't miss it for the world," she said apprehensively.

Clay cleared his throat to gain Blaze's attention.

"Oh, I'm so sorry, where are my manners? Thaddeus Newman, this is Clayton Williams Randolph. He's with the Marshall Group."

Blaze was careful to say as little as possible.

"Well now, Clayton your firm has a good reputation with some of my associates. Glad you could make it tonight," Thaddeus stated.

"Oh, sir it is my pleasure, I assure you. I've followed your career and admired you as a businessman." Clay poured on the sugar.

Just then a voice interrupted the gathering.

"Thad dear there you are. I've been looking everywhere for you," Kate said as she joined the group.

"Well, hello again Ms. Beaumont. Are you enjoying the evening?"

"Yes, I was just telling Thaddeus what a lovely evening it has been," Blaze lied.

While speaking to Blaze, Kate held her hand out to Clay and asked, "And you are?"

Clay took Kate's hand into his carefully so he could give her a proper handshake as he said, "Clayton Randolph Williams III, Mrs. Newman. It's a pleasure to meet you!"

"And so nice to meet you as well, Mr. Williams." Kate smiled, then continued. "Are you with one of our affiliates?" Kate asked feigning ignorance.

"I'm with the Marshall Group," Clay replied.

"I don't believe I'm familiar with your company, but no matter all are welcome to our little gathering. Has your company made a donation to our organization?" Kate asked boldly.

"Absolutely!" Clay replied.

"Well, that's wonderful," Kate added holding her head high and completely ignoring Blaze. "We can never get too many donations and we will always welcome a new sponsor. Well, Thaddeus, we should be circulating a little, don't you think?" Kate asked in classic Kate style. "Let's go in and mingle a bit. Very nice meeting you, Mr. Williams," Kate said a bit flirtatiously. "We'll see you in there," she added. Kate held onto Thaddeus's arm.

"By all means," Clay replied happy to be considered at all.

"Lovely seeing you both," Kate said as an afterthought as she and Thaddeus walked into the ballroom.

Kate and Thaddeus disappeared into the crowd of guests and Blaze and Clay walked to her table.

"Are you feeling alright tonight?" Clay asked Blaze.

"Yes, of course, I'm fine," Blaze awkwardly replied.

"You sure? You sure don't seem to be yourself."

"I just have a slight headache is all." Blaze lied yet again. "Why don't you go and mingle and meet some of the guests? I'll be okay. Just give me a few minutes."

"Can I get you anything? I don't like leaving you like this," Clay was genuinely concerned.

"I'm fine, Clay! Just go," Blaze insisted. "I see Misha and mom, so I'm gonna go over and talk with them a bit."

Clay finally walked away as Blaze headed towards Mish and Jewels.

"Hey, girl! This is some party!" Misha shouted.

"Yeah, it sure is," Blaze responded.

"I saw you talkin' to Clay. Where'd he go?"

"I convinced him to go mingle a bit. There are a lot of people here that could help him in business."

"You alright honey?" Jewels asked concernedly.

"Yeah, mom. I'm fine. Come on. I'll introduce you to some of my colleagues."

Blaze took her mother and Misha around the ballroom and introduced them to her colleagues as well as some of her clients who were in attendance. The women were having a good time and for a moment Blaze forgot her circumstances. Z and Parks helped to lighten the mood with their antics making everyone laugh. It was Parks's goal to keep them laughing. Both men took turns dancing with the ladies making it a fun evening for all. After a while, Clay joined in as the group sat at the table talking and drinking their cocktails. Blaze never realized that she was being watched from afar by not one but two interested parties.

Jack had been summoned by his mother to join her at the table where she was talking with the Mitchells as Denise looked on. The two families had been friends since their children were born and they continued to spend time together vacationing and attending various functions. When Jack joined them, Kate immediately went into her meddling mother mode.

"So, Jack, why don't you ask Denise to dance? The two of you should catch up since you haven't seen one another in ages."

Daphne Mitchell agreed, "The two of you make a fantastic couple. Their husbands were conversing about their golf handicaps and did not catch on to what their wives were up to.

"How do you know that Denise wants to dance?" Jack asked annoyed.

"Well, you'll never know until you ask." Kate smiled.

Denise feigned ignorance although she was delighted that Kate wanted her and Jack to be together as much as she did.

She began to tug on Jack's arm, "Come on Jack! Dance with me. I'll show you a few dance moves," she teased.

Jack gave in as she took his hand and proceeded to the dance floor. It seemed that all eyes were on the couple as they danced to a very sexy Latin song. Denise was not shy as she conveyed her sexuality to Jack dancing provocatively for him. He was uncomfortable with her display but played it cool. She was a good dancer considering her parents doled out thousands to finance lessons for years. Jack couldn't help but laugh as she taunted and teased him on the floor. She was relentless in her pursuit of him, and she was not shy to let everyone know it.

"Oh, Jack! Come on. Loosen up," she commanded as she swayed this way and that.

Jack smiled and grabbed her around the waist commencing to a two-step. She enjoyed being close to him and pressed her thin body tightly against his. Her little black dress clung to her thin frame and her long legs were accentuated by the black stiletto heels she was wearing. Across the room, Blaze still sat with the group laughing and talking when someone mentioned the couple getting down on the dance floor. Misha, Jewels, and Blaze walked out to the dance floor to see what all the commotion was about. Misha was the first to comment on the handsome pair.

"Now that's what I'm talking bout. Damn, he's fine! She is one lucky girl to be with him tonight," Misha stated.

Blaze almost dropped her wine glass on the floor when she saw Jack and Denise on the dance floor. As she stood there watching them, she could feel the anger well up in her chest, but she decided to play it cool. Denise could see Blaze standing on the sidelines and overplayed her performance for the growing crowd. Jack not being one to back down from a challenge, and having had more than a few drinks, allowed her to continue her display while he maintained his decorum. The crowd began to clap when the music stopped as

Denise flung her arms around Jack's neck in laughter pleased with her performance. She kissed Jack on the lips for all to see knowing Blaze was watching. Jack noticed that Denise was eyeing the crowd on the sidelines looking in the same direction when he saw Blaze standing there. By the time he realized the game Denise was playing, it was too late—Blaze was gone.

Jack pulled away from the clinging vixen to search the crowd for Blaze. He left Denise alone on the dance floor as he realized how careless he had been in allowing her to taunt him into the dance in the first place. He walked into the lobby in search of Blaze to explain but she was not there. He retreated to the restrooms, but she wasn't there either. He continued onto the terrace and finally out onto the street, but Blaze was nowhere in sight. Jack stood on the sidewalk, hands in his pockets. The combination of night air and the numerous top shelf martini's caused Jack's head to spin, but he managed to regain his composure.

Somewhere across the ballroom, Clay was also looking for Blaze. He had gone over to converse with a colleague during the dance between Jack and Denise and wasn't aware of what was taking place. The only thing that he knew was that once again he had lost track of his fiancé. This was becoming a most annoying habit and Clay began to become suspicious of Blaze's disappearances.

The night air was warm as Blaze began walking without a destination. Tears blurred her vision as she made her way through Olde City passing outdoor restaurants and cafés full of carefree revelers out for a festive Friday night. A few catcalls and several propositions later she found herself on the steps of Jack's apartment.

"What am I doing?" she asked herself.

Blaze didn't know how she got there, but she felt as if destiny was pulling her there. She looked up at the building to Jack's floor and remembered the two nights that they spent together at his apartment. She went into the building and made her way up to the tenth floor. She didn't know what she was doing only that she wanted to be near Jack in the worse way. Although she knew Jack wouldn't be there, she somehow felt close to him being where he recently had been. She opened her small purse and took out her cell phone and dialed a number. After a few minutes, her call was answered.

"Hello.

"It's me."

"Where are you?"

"I'm at your apartment. I'm not sure why I'm here."

"Stay there. I'm on my way!"

Jack tore out of the museum and headed for his apartment. Although he was close enough to walk home, he hailed a cab for fear that Blaze might get anxious and leave. The traffic was heavy, and the streets were filled with people. There was a jazz show on the waterfront, so crowds of people filled the streets.

"There's an extra twenty for you if you can get me there quickly," Jack propositioned the driver.

The driver put his foot to the petal and within minutes he was pulling up in front of Jack's door. Jack handed the driver two twenty-dollar bills and jumped out of the cab not waiting for change. He looked around for Blaze but didn't see her anywhere.

"Damn!" he said. "Where is she?"

He pulled out his cell phone and rang her number. Blaze answered right away.

"Where are you?" Jack asked.

"I'm standing in front of your apartment door."

The elevator was waiting on the main floor, but it still wasn't fast enough for Jack. When he finally reached his floor and the doors opened, he saw Blaze making him stop in his tracks. She was standing in the hallway by a huge window that looked out over the city. Jack occupied the entire floor, so there was no one else but the two of them there. Jack walked towards Blaze and stood behind her.

When Blaze heard him approach her, she became nervous and her heart began to race. Jack stopped when he reached her and stood behind her not saying a word. He slowly placed his arms around her waist and bent down to smell her hair. Blaze closed her eyes and leaned back against Jack's chest. Tears ran down her cheeks as they stood there in silence. After a few moments, Jack turned Blaze around to face him.

"What were you thinking running off that way?" he asked her.

"I don't know why I did that. I just couldn't stand to watch you dancing with her," Blaze answered. "She was all over you like she was performing some sort of mating call, and everyone was being entertained at my expense."

"You know Denise doesn't mean anything to me."

"Do I? It seems that you were pretty ticked off at me tonight. I looked everywhere for you, but you disappeared and I felt bad about that."

"How was I supposed to act? There you are with what's-his-name all chummy, chummy like you and I don't matter or something."

"Jack, you know that's not true. We talked about this and decided that things could wait until after the weekend was over."

"Yeah, well I changed my mind. I don't appreciate that boy with his hands on you. I don't want to share you with anyone." Jack pulled Blaze close to him. He kissed her and she eagerly returned his kiss. Jack picked Blaze up into his arms as they embraced in a long and sensuous kiss.

"Take me inside," she whispered.

Jack made no haste in opening the door to his apartment and entering with Blaze in his arms. The enormously bright July moon was shining directly into Jack's living room. It cast a glow upon the two lovers as they quickly removed each other's clothing and lay on the rug on the floor. Jack kissed Blaze from head to toe paying special attention to his favorite parts of her body. She was overwhelmed by him as tears escaped from the corners of her eyes. They lay together making love for what seemed like hours, oblivious to the ringing of Blaze's cell phone. She didn't care if Clay or her mother was looking for her. She was where she longed to be, and with the man whom she longed to be with.

"You're staying with me tonight!" Jack boldly commanded.

"I know you don't want to hear this, but how will I explain where I've been all night to Clay or my mother? He's probably furious with me."

"I don't know, and I don't give a damn what he thinks! One thing I do know is that he'd better not even think about causing you any grief over this. I'm not gonna stand by and let him hurt you," Jack added.

"See! This is exactly what I've been afraid of Jack. I don't want there to be a confrontation between you and Clay."

"Baby, there won't be a confrontation. That, I promise you." Jack sounded confident.

"And what about tomorrow?"

"What about it?" Jack asked.

"Well, I'm expected to attend the barbecue with my company, and Clay is determined to be there."

"I'd still like to know who sent him that invitation?" Jack asked puzzled.

"It doesn't matter who sent it. What matters is that he'll be there, and I won't have time to spend with you," Blaze added.

"Look...I say you tell the man tomorrow morning. Maybe he won't want to come after you talk to him."

"I'm not so sure. What if he decides to come anyway and make our lives miserable in the process?"

"Then, he will get thrown out on his butt," Jack stated matter of factly.

"I'd better go," Blaze said.

"No. You're not going anywhere tonight or should I say this morning. If you do, I'm taking you home." Jack didn't want Blaze out alone at that time of night and in that state of mind.

"Why don't I just take a cab?" Blaze suggested.

"Because I'm not gonna have you traveling the streets this late at night alone. I wouldn't feel comfortable doing that. I mean it, Blaze. You're staying with me." Jack said firmly.

Blaze didn't want to argue, and she was actually glad that Jack insisted she stay. She didn't care what tomorrow would bring. She only wanted to think about that moment. She was exhausted from the events of the evening and so the couple retired to Jack's bed where she cuddled up to him and drifted off to sleep. Jack lay awake for some time holding Blaze in his arms. He knew that there were a few things that he was going to have to get straight with his mother, Denise, and Clay. He thought to himself.

I've never backed down from a fight...especially when it was over something that I wanted...and I don't intend to start now.'

Jack kissed Blaze as she lay in his arms sleeping. She was more beautiful than anything he had ever seen. He knew at that moment that he wanted her more than he could have imagined. She was his prize and he wanted to protect her and give her everything that she ever wanted. This was a new feeling for him...one that he was not accustomed to, but he welcomed it. He knew that this would compromise his relationship with his mother, but he was prepared to deal with that. He wasn't so sure how he was going to handle Clay. He had a hunch that it would be a challenge. Clay believed he had a claim to Blaze considering their history, but Jack wasn't about to let that get in his way. In the few short months that he and Blaze had come to know one another, they had an intimacy that was beyond compare. He knew the challenges that lay ahead, and he was ready to face the consequences.

| 35 |

Where's Blaze?

Clay, Jewels, and Misha were on the hunt for Blaze. They had exhausted the possibilities at the museum and so concluded that she had left and gone home. The evening was coming to a close and the guests were beginning to leave. On the other side of the room, Kate and Thaddeus were saying their goodbyes to the guests who were still there. They all promised to be in attendance the next day for the barbecue. Many of the guests were staying at nearby hotels, so they lingered a bit longer as Kate invited some back to their apartment for a nightcap. Since the Newmans lived in the suburbs of Philadelphia, they kept an apartment in the heart of the city for those times when they were having a late night out on the town. Although Kate was in a festive mood, she was still concerned about the whereabouts of her youngest son. She noticed that immediately after his dance with Denise that he disappeared and so had that Blaze woman. By all speculation, the two were together and that didn't sit well with Kate, or Denise, who managed to glue herself to the Newmans most of the night. Kate excused herself from a few of her guests to find Michael and James.

"Have either of you seen your brother?" Kate inquired.

"Not since that hot number he and Denise performed," Michael interjected.

Kate gave him a knowing look as James tried to ally her fears.

"Mother, you know Jack. He probably felt a little too much on display and decided to call it a night. Maybe he got lucky and didn't go home alone," James added laughing.

"Seriously!" Kate replied as she turned and walked away.

"Boy, mother is really ticked at Jack," Michael said. "I wouldn't want to be him when she catches up to him."

"Don't you worry about Jack. He's a big boy and can take care of himself," James added.

Just as Jewels, Misha, and Clay were leaving, Kate and Thaddeus were also heading for the door. Clay saw them and immediately turned to thank the couple for a lovely evening.

Extending his hand to shake hers, Clay proceeded to render his appreciation to Kate.

"Thank you for a lovely evening," he said.

"Why, thank you for attending, Mr. uhh?"

"Clayton Randolph Williams ma'am," Clay reminded her quite proudly.

"Oh yes! Of course. And where is your lovely date, Mr. Williams?" Kate asked coyly.

"Ah she ah had to leave a bit early tonight," Clay lied.

"Really? Well, that's too bad. I was hoping to get a chance to speak with her again before the evening was over. We didn't really have an opportunity to chat." Kate was fishing for more information.

Jewels watched Kate's mannerisms when talking about Blaze and remembered how distraught her daughter was earlier that evening.

"My daughter wasn't feeling her best this evening Mrs. Newman." Jewels said jumping in.

Kate then turned her attention to Jewels as if seeing her for the first time. Jewels continued her introduction to the Newmans.

"I'm sorry we didn't get a chance to meet. I'm Jewels Beaumont, Blaze's mother." Jewels extended her hand to Kate. Jewels knew how to be coy too and played Kate's little game. Jewels could very well compete with Kate on style, looks, and intelligence, so she had no qualms about dealing with the woman.

"Well Ms. Beaumont, your daughter is a lovely young woman as well you are...lovely that is," Kate said sarcastically extending her hand to Jewels.

Jewels looked at Kate smiling but burning within.

"It's Mrs. Beaumont," she said extending her hand too. Kate returned the gaze as if she could tell what Jewels was thinking. Thaddeus was aware of his wife's sharp wit and so jumped in to deter any further insult.

"It's a pleasure to meet you, Mrs. Beaumont. I'm Thaddeus Newman. Blaze is doing a wonderful job on our account. She's a fine asset to her firm."

In a warmer and more relaxed tone, Jewels replied, "Why thank you, Mr. Newman. I appreciate your confidence in my daughter and it's truly a pleasure to make your acquaintance," Jewels added.

For a brief moment, the group stood in the foyer of the museum in an awkward stance not knowing what to say next. Misha broke the silence with an off-handed comment.

"This was one hell of a party you guys put on here. The food was good and the cocktails the bomb," she complimented in typical Misha fashion.

"Aha," Kate said sizing up Misha. "We're thrilled that you enjoyed yourself."

"Well, we'd better be off dear," Thaddeus said to Kate. "We have a big day ahead of us tomorrow. You all will be coming to the barbecue I assume?" Thaddeus asked.

"Oh, most certainly we'll be there," Clay stated.

"Well, goodnight then," Kate said as she held onto Thaddeus's arm, and they exited the room.

"What a bitch!" Jewels said.

"Yeah, she was kinda uppity," Misha added.

"I'm gonna try Blaze's cell one more time before we leave," Clay stated.

"Nope...no answer," he said putting his phone away.

"Okay ladies...let me get your car for you."

Clay took Jewels' ticket giving both to the valet for their cars to be brought around.

"I guess Blaze took a cab home," Clay commented.

"Well, let's just leave her alone. We can talk with her tomorrow. I'm sure she's alright." Jewels assured Clay.

"Yeah...I'm beat, so I'll wait and call her in the morning," Clay added.

The trio said their goodnights with Jewels and Misha leaving together first. Clay took off behind them going in the opposite direction. Jewels was very uneasy about not hearing from Blaze, but she didn't want to exasperate the issue any further in front of Clay. She dropped Misha off at her apartment and drove home. Once she was home, she tried calling Blaze again leaving her an urgent message.

"Blaze, call me as soon as you get this message. I want to hear from you right away. We have a few things to discuss."

Jewels hung up the phone and readied herself for bed.

'No matter how old they are, you always worry about your kids,' Jewels thought to herself before turning out the lamp on her bed stand.

A few miles away, Kate and Thaddeus were headed for their apartment which was downtown from the museum.

"Did you enjoy the evening?" Thaddeus asked Kate as he held her hand.

"I did. I think everything went well. Don't you?" she asked.

"Very well," Thaddeus replied.

"If only our children behaved themselves accordingly," Kate added.

"Now Kate, I don't want you to worry about Jack. He's a grown man and can take care of himself."

"I'm not worried. I'd just like to know what happened to him is all?"

"Well, how about giving your husband some of that attention?" Thaddeus said kissing her hand.

Kate smiled at Thaddeus, snuggling closer to him as he placed his arm around her.

"Now isn't that better?" he asked her. "We have the whole night ahead of us. Remember the last time we stayed in town?" Thaddeus asked smiling.

"Oh, Thad...of course, I remember."

"Good...but I'd like to refresh your memory anyway." He rubbed her knee.

Kate smiled a familiar smile as the driver turned down the parkway and headed for their apartment building.

| 36 |

Blaze, it's time!

Blaze was awakened at 5:00 am startled by a weird squeaking noise coming from the living area. She reached her hand over to the other side of the bed, but it was empty. She then called out to Jack, but he didn't answer her. She sat there for a moment trying to compose herself. She threw the covers back on the huge bed, climbed down to the floor, and tip-toed into the outer rooms. There was Jack on his rowing machine, earplugs in his ears, dripping in sweat, wearing only a pair of shorts. His body was magnificent as the sweat glistened upon his smooth, brown, skin. Every muscle flexed with each movement, as he effortlessly rowed back and forth on the machine. Blaze stood in the doorway naked, observing the majestic view. Her body tingled with excitement at the raw magnetism that exuded from Jack's body. She was so aroused that she could barely control her emotions. She quietly walked towards him as he sat facing the window performing his workout. He made a sudden movement and leaped around tackling Blaze to the floor eliciting a squeal of surprise from her since she thought he didn't know that she was in the room. He straddled her snatching the earplugs from his ears as he bent down to kiss her passionately. Sweat was dripping from his body onto Blaze, but she didn't care. Jack buried his face between her breasts as his rapid breathing escaped from his mouth. He kissed Blaze as if she had just returned from a long absence, his strong arms balancing him so as not to crush her against the floor. Blaze threw her arms around Jack's neck and wrapped her legs around his waist. She matched his kiss with equal ardor as Jack lifted her body to meet his own. He made love to her right there in the first morning light.

Two hours later after Blaze arrived home, she listened to several messages from Clay, Jewels, and Misha all frantic as to her whereabouts. The calls all came in the night before so Blaze felt confident that she could feign being home with a headache and no one would know she'd been out all night with Jack. Jack dropped her off at her apartment promising her that they would meet at his parent's home later that day. Blaze immediately called her mother to get an idea of how Clay took her disappearance. The phone in Jewels office rang several times before she answered the call recognizing Blaze's number.

"Blaze Beaumont, where have you been?" she asked.

"Hi, mom."

"Blaze, where in the world are you?"

"I'm home."

"Do you know how worried I've been? Why'd you leave the party without telling me?"

"I'm sorry mom. I wasn't feeling very well, so I grabbed a cab and came home. I took a sleeping pill and turned off my phone so I could get some sleep." She lied.

"Clay was upset that you left him. You know you're gonna have to talk to him sooner or later. It's just not right to lead him along this way," Jewels scolded.

"Mother, I know. I intend on talking to him today. This week has been the week from hell and there was never a good time to bring the subject up."

"You mean you don't know how to tell him that you want to call off the engagement."

"Yeah, I guess you're right," Blaze admitted.

"Well, you have to face up to your decision and tell him as soon as possible."

"I plan on telling him today," Blaze repeated.

"Good. Then you both can get on with your lives!" Jewels exclaimed.

"So, mom what time will you be ready to leave for the barbecue?"

"I'm not sure, dear.

"I'll ride with you and Misha today," Blaze said.

"After Clay and I talk, I'll definitely need a ride."

"Okay. It's all set. I'll pick Misha up first and then we'll be by to get you around one."

"Okay. See ya then." Blaze hung up the phone.

Blaze showered and prepared to get dressed. She called Clay, but he didn't answer his phone. He normally played basketball with his friends every Saturday morning when he could so Blaze assumed that's where he was. She left him a message to call her immediately and then she went about getting ready for the barbecue. She decided to wear a turquoise dress, and matching sandals. She pulled her hair into a ponytail since the afternoon promised to be a scorcher. She carried a small handbag with her lip gloss, her phone, and keys inside. She tried calling Clay again, and this time he answered.

"Hey there!" she said trying to sound normal.

"Hey yourself," he replied. "Thought you'd left town," he said casually.

"No. I'm still here! What time do you plan to leave for the Newman's?" Blaze asked.

"Well, I just got home from the court. Man, Daryl and Booker tried to take me down today."

Blaze tried to sound interested but had more important matters on her mind.

"Clay, I need to know what time you plan on leaving?" Blaze asked again.

"I don't know! What time should we leave?" he asked still nonchalantly.

"Well, I was hoping that you and I would have a chance to talk before we left for the party." Blaze stated.

"Baby, it's getting late, and I haven't even showered yet. Can we talk when we get there?"

"This isn't a conversation we want to have at a social gathering."

"Then, can it wait until after?" Clay asked.

"I guess it will have to," Blaze reluctantly replied. "I'm going to ride with mom and Misha, so we'll see you there!"

"That's no problem since I'm bringing Daryl with me."

"Well then, it's settled. I'll see you there." Blaze ended the call.

Although she wasn't anxious to do so, Blaze didn't want to prolong breaking off her engagement to Clay any longer. She knew that her mother was right and that it wasn't fair to lead Clay on like this. Besides, the sooner she settled this, the sooner she could begin a relationship with Jack. That was indeed something to look forward to.

| 37 |

The Lady's Spoken For

The Newman home sat on 400 acres of reconstructed farmland in the exclusive suburbs of Blue Bell Pennsylvania. The stone home, built in the early 1930s, was home to Jack and his family for nearly 20 years. Jack and his siblings grew up wanting nothing. They were perfectly content to just be the children of Kate and Thaddeus not knowing the expanse of wealth from which they came. Kate liked that her children had a wholesome upbringing since her own was so sterile and precision-like.

When Jack arrived at his parent's home for the barbecue, he made his way to the back of the house and quietly walked toward the kitchen. This wasn't unusual for him since he never entered the house from any other entrance. He felt at home in the kitchen and had fond memories of coming home to a big bowl of stew or soup that Bertha made just for the children. They would all gather in the kitchen during the cold winter months and sit by the fire doing their homework, playing board games, or simply talking around the table. Since the formal dining room was too massive for these small family gatherings it became a tradition among the Newman clan to hang out with Bertha in the kitchen—after all, she was like family.

Jack entered the kitchen to a bustle of activity and tiptoed up to a woman who was directing the staff in an ever so familiar way. Jack planted a huge kiss upon the woman's cheek which elicited squeals of delight from her. Although she stood only 5-foot 2-inches in height, her massive frame more than equaled Jack's weight. Still, he hugged her nearly lifting her from the floor.

"Jack…you should be shame of yo self nearly scarin' an ole woman like me to death," she chuckled in a slightly southern drawl.

"Bert, I've missed you! When you gonna retire from this old place and come in town and cook just for me?" Jack teased.

"I'm retiring tomorrow 'cause your mother got all these folks in my kitchen wit they fancy dishes and such. How she expect me to supervise everything in here with folks all over my kitchen making a mess? What I know bout some supervisin' in my own kitchen? I'm ready to put them all out is what." she blabbered on and on as she turned to yell at one of the servers. "Don't put that there on my counter boy. Take it outside on the patio," she commanded rolling her eyes.

Jack laughed as the server scurried away with fear in his eyes.

"My parents around?" Jack asked.

"Yeah, they here—outside with the guests. Your mother running 'round here as usual making everyone in the house crazy. Now, where ya goin' wit that?" Bert asked all in one breath to a man in a chef's hat.

"Lawd, I reckon." She added shaking her head.

Jack smiled as he made his way to the patio, "Give 'em hell Bert," he teased before exiting to the pool area.

The blue and white table linen along with the matching-colored balloons made for a festive site as guests were lined up at each station waiting their turn to be served. Kate opted for a buffet-style meal as opposed to a sit-down fare. She wanted to stay within the cookout and picnic-style theme. Carving stations with blue canopies were manned by chefs in checkered pants and large white hats. There were ribs, chicken, and pork stations. Servers maintained the dozen or so tables that were filled with seven different salads, numerous types of grilled vegetables, corn on the cob, assorted cakes and pies, fresh fruits, and an old-fashioned ice cream stand complete with frozen yogurt, sorbet, and water ice. A floating bar anchored in the pool was a popular attraction for some guests, while others preferred to be grounded at a stool enjoying a libation of drinks with brightly colored umbrellas.

Activities for the children were relegated to the east lawn. Various arcade games: bouncy houses, pony rides, clowns, and puppet performances were all carefully monitored by attendants in white shirts, bow ties, and straw hats. On the opposite side of the property, decorated tents were assembled to shade the guest as they sat down to enjoy their meals. A large stage and dance floor were constructed for the entertainment which included a renowned jazz band intermingled with the sounds of a DJ. Everything was in its place and the afternoon was going very well, according to Pierre. Kate, on the other hand, being the perfectionist that she was, found something wrong here and there just to keep the staff on their toes.

Making his rounds through the crowd Jack spoke to colleagues, business associates, and guests as he perused the area to see who was there. He was fooling himself into believing that he wasn't looking for any way in particular, but in his heart of hearts, he knew better. He mingled and chatted and even made a few unofficial appointments to meet with potential business associates, but his mind was somewhere else. In a place where there were loads of people, Jack felt alone and melancholy, a feeling quite new to him. One of Jack's college buddies, Joseph Evans, arrived and the two began to catch up after not seeing one another for nearly a year. Joe was an athletic type who played football in college and was an All-American in high school. He was a lady's man and had a list of current and former conquests that he bragged upon. Joe was always on the prowl for something new.

"Hey man, what's goin' on?" Jack asked shaking hands with Joe.

"Boy, you know how we do!" Joe said.

They talked about old times and got caught up when Jack noticed that he no longer had Joe's attention. Joe's attention was diverted elsewhere and as Jack followed Joe's gaze, he realized why he was so preoccupied.

"Wow! Who's that?" Joe was nearly drooling.

Jack could see what elicited such a response from a guy who usually kept it so well together. He understood Joe's sudden interest immediately. There she was more beautiful than any woman should be on such a hot and muggy day. She was like a breath of fresh air, and it seemed that there were many who wanted to suck her right in. She was in the center of a group of men who were talking with her. The conversation seemed to be lighthearted as Blaze laughed at some comment made by one of the guys throwing her head back slightly. She stood with one hand on her hip. She was wearing a beautiful turquoise dress that complimented her auburn hair which was pulled back in a ponytail. The dress fitted her body ever so slightly giving a glimpse of her well-shaped figure. The turquoise chandelier earrings framed her face as strands of hair cascaded about. She looked cool and confident as she stood there in her sandals tapping her pedicured toes to the beat of the music that was coming from the stage. She was beautiful. Jack stood smiling at the way she worked the group. He thought to himself about the night they spent together and the way she felt in his arms. He smiled as he remembered the way she cooed when aroused and how much he wanted to hear her make that sound again. He was startled out of his self-imposed daydream as Joe smacked him on his back.

"Man, I've got to go over and make my introductions!" Joe's enthusiasm and confidence soared.

"Slow down, cowboy," Jack said. "The lady's been spoken for."

"Man, are you serious? That's you?" Joe gulped in surprise. "How come you always manage to get the most beautiful women, Jack?"

Without a word, Jack just smiled not taking his eyes off Blaze. When he finally caught her attention, she smiled at him and waved. He nodded to her and looked in the direction of the house leading her to meet him there with his eyes. She understood and watched him as he continued to talk to Joe and then excused himself while walking towards his destination.

| 38 |

Shade, Drama & a Flagged Denise

As the afternoon progressed, more and more guests arrived at the Newman home. Kate was in her element greeting everyone and being the ultimate hostess. Ed and his family arrived, and Kate greeted them with enthusiasm.

"Ed! Abby! Welcome, I'm so glad you could be here!" Kate smiled.

"This is quite a festive event." Ed looked around while holding onto Abby's hand.

"Yes, Kate! You seem to have outdone yourself this year," Abby agreed.

"Well, I couldn't have done it without the help of my staff, and of course Pierre, who is priceless."

Ed maintained a sense of decorum although he was reeling inside from the mere sight of Kate.

"Please make yourself at home and enjoy the afternoon." Kate walked away to greet more arriving guests.

Abby looked at her husband with a knowing glance as they walked in the direction of the tents. Kate continued her duties as hostess and mingled with as many of her guests as possible before retreating to the patio. She knew that Pierre had everything under control, so she was able to sit by the pool with her feet up if only for a moment. Ed watched her as she made her way to the patio and excused himself from Abby who was talking with a few women whom she knew through her own charity work. He picked up to beverages from the bar and sat down beside Kate.

"You look stunning!" he said.

"Why, thank you, Ed! You are very dashing this afternoon," Kate returned the compliment.

"Where's Thaddeus?" Ed inquired.

"Oh, he's mingling with our guests."

"I've missed you!" Ed did not hold back.

"Ed! Please! This is not the time or place for that." Kate felt uncomfortable.

"So, I suppose I should just ignore how beautiful you are and fight the feelings I have to take you into my arms and make love to you?"

"I really don't think we should continue this conversation, Ed." Kate stood up.

"Thaddeus will be here any minute and anyone can hear you and what will that serve...hmm?"

Kate walked back onto the grounds disappearing into the crowd. Ed felt rejected as he sat down his drink to go and find Abby. He didn't have to go far since she was standing nearby and witnessed the exchange between Kate and Ed knowing it was more than a friendly chat.

Blaze managed to finally get away from the group, amid protest from the men and made her way in the direction where Jack was headed. She followed the path that Jack took, which led her around to the front of the house. There was little if any activity there since the entrance to the event was relegated to the rear entrance. Blaze walked along the patio up to the front door. The huge iron door was reminiscent of the entrance to a castle. She turned the large brass knob and entered the foyer of the house. The marble floors were spotless as she stood beneath the 12-foot ceiling looking into a domed skylight. The massive hall led to a large living room to the right and on the left was another room with double doors that were closed. A huge marble staircase leading to a mezzanine provided an entrance to both the east and west wings of the upstairs rooms.

"Jack?" she called out as her voice echoed through the halls. There was no answer.

She tried calling out to him again. "Jack? Are you here?" she asked again. Suddenly his voice echoed a return.

"I'm here."

Jack emerged from behind the closed doors on the main floor.

"I'm here," he repeated walking towards her.

Jack took Blaze's hand and led her into the large room with the double doors and closed them behind her. He took her into his arms and kissed her, and she kissed him back matching his passion. They stood there in each other's arms for what seemed an eternity before either of them let go.

"You smell so good." He nuzzled against her ear.

"I've missed you," Blaze whispered.

"We've only been apart for a few hours," he said smiling.

"I know. I must sound foolish, but I've missed you." She looked into his eyes.

"Well, you could've fooled me from the looks of the entourage that was surrounding you."

"I couldn't tell you who half those guys were," she said nonchalantly.

"Come here!" Jack said pulling Blaze around the huge ornate desk in the room. He sat down in the oversized leather chair and pulled Blaze to his lap.

"This is where I use to hide when my parents were entertaining. This was my adventure room. You can go anywhere in the world that you want to from here. It's all right here in those books."

Jack pointed to the shelves of books that covered two of the four walls in the massive library. Blaze could see that there was a vast collection including various types of literature, beautifully bound classics, reference books, and trade manuals. The walls were papered with a light damask fabric that gave contrast to the dark brown and burgundy leather furniture. A world map was lightly etched on one of the walls adding a scholarly essence to the room, which smelled of leather and fine tobacco.

"Jack, this room is magnificent!" Blaze said.

"I know. It's my favorite room in the whole house. When I was young, my dad would sit in here on the weekends working on some business deal, and I would wander in watching his every move and gesture. After a while, he would end his calls and put aside his work and we'd talk for hours about everything."

"You love your dad a lot!" Blaze smiled realizing Jack's appreciation for Thaddeus.

"Yeah, he taught me everything I know about life, business, and love."

"Really?" Blaze turned to face Jack. "Love? Really?"

"Yes, love," Jack returned. "He taught all of us by his example. His affection and love for my mother was, and is, very evident which taught us how to be good husbands, fathers, and life partners."

Blaze smiled at Jack kissing him softly upon his lips. He held her tightly and kissed her face while his hands explored her body.

"Did you come to the party alone?" he asked.

"No, actually my mother, Jewels, and my best friend, Misha, are here. We came together."

"So I get to meet your mother?" Jack asked.

"Of course, you do. She's heard a lot about you, so I'm sure she is anxious to meet you."

"And what about Clay? Is he also here?"

"He said he was coming with one of his friends, but I don't think he's here yet."

"You know I don't like this," Jack huffed.

"Jack please…let's not talk about that now," she implored him.

Jack quickly dropped the subject and sat with his arms planted firmly around Blaze's waist.

"You know you're the first woman that I've ever brought in here."

Blaze was stunned and didn't know what to say to him. She wasn't prepared for his honesty and the level of intimacy that they were sharing.

"Well, I'm happy that you decided to share this with me," she said.

"Me too…but I must confess that I wanted to pull you away from those guys."

"Oh really? I'm flattered."

"I want you to enjoy yourself but remember who you're leaving here with!" Jack teased.

"Oh yeah. I'll be sure to remember that," Blaze said before kissing him again.

This time Jack didn't stop at kissing her. His hand was firmly planted upon her breast, and he held her buttock in his other. He was aroused which was evident to Blaze. He caressed her body as she responded to his touch.

"Jack, we shouldn't," Blaze objected.

"I know. I can't help myself," he said pulling her dress up and kissing her body. He untied her halter top revealing her taut breasts as she tried to control the feelings that now overwhelmed her body.

"Jack?" she whispered as he relentlessly explored every inch of her. His hands traveled up her thighs and into her panties as his fingers explored the channels of her wetness. Blaze moaned as his fingers entered her, his eyes fixed upon her face watching her expressions of ecstasy. Her skin was warm and smooth like silk as he touched her exploring every area of her body with patience and skill. He turned her body so that her back was against him, and he bit at her cheeks while continuing to caress her inside. Blaze held onto the desk afraid to let go for fear that she might tumble and fall from the sheer delight of his touch. No longer able to contain it she moved his hand and turned to straddle his lap. She wanted him inside of her—all of him. She felt him next to her ready to erupt from her touch as she placed her hands around him and stroked him with purpose. She took him inside of her as she moved with an intense rhythm to meet his own. They were oblivious to their surroundings and together they came in unison peaking heights of pleasure only known to lovers who were deeply impassioned by their lust.

After their encounter, they sat in the oversized chair panting and wet from their sweat and dew. Jack's face was buried in Blaze's chest as he savored her aroma. Her arms were around his neck, and her legs were straddled on each side of him. Jack's pants were now around his ankles, as he sat there bare-assed with his shirt open.

"You are truly my little minx," Jack said while kissing her.

Blaze smiled looking into his eyes and studying his face.

"I can never resist you, Jack. It's as if you know my body so well."

They sat there for a long time before they began to breathe normally again.

"Is there someplace that I can freshen up?" she asked.

"Sure...there's a shower right in there," Jack said pointing to the other side of the room.

"Wow, I didn't realize there was another room in here."

She walked into the bathroom complete with shower, fresh linen, and organic soap.

The bathroom was nicely appointed and smelled of fresh lavender. Blaze took a shower wanting to be completely fresh when she rejoined the party. Jack made sure he locked the door before joining her. They quickly showered and dried off.

"My dress is so wrinkled. It looks terrible," Blaze complained. "I can't wear this out there."

"Give it to me. I'll have Bert throw it in the steam dryer."

Blaze reluctantly gave Jack the dress as he made a call to the kitchen to have Bert pick it up.

"Don't worry. Bert's cool. She'll take care of everything."

Within minutes Bert was there to pick up the dress and handed Jack a bundle with a new shirt and pants and underwear for him.

Jack came back into the bathroom and told Blaze to help herself to whatever toiletries were in the cabinet. When Blaze opened the cabinet, to her delight were all kinds of deodorants, powder, perfume, and lotions in several fragrances. She chose a light floral scent that captured the mood of the afternoon. Jack opened a bottle of white wine that had been chilling since Blaze arrived and he poured them both a glass. Blaze wrapped a bath sheet around her while she combed her hair. She then relaxed on the chaise lounge sipping on her wine.

"I'm surprised that your father keeps so many toiletries in here."

"You can thank my mother for that. She's a stickler for that kind of detail."

"Jack, you're so good to me," she said. "I can't remember when I have had a lovelier afternoon."

"Oh, I can think of one or two that could equal or surpass it," he added with a devilish smile.

Jack turned on the stereo as they languished together sipping wine and talking intimately to one another. After about twenty minutes or so there was a knock at the door, so Jack went to answer it. It was Bert with Blaze's dress and a heads-up for Jack.

"Your mother's been looking for ya. You'd better get a move on," she said peering over her glasses before closing the door behind her.

Jack took the dress and gave it to Blaze.

"Here you'd better get dressed and we'd better get back to the party. It seems I'm being sought after by Kate."

"Okay, I should only be a minute."

Jack continued to dress, and they were finally ready to face the world…but not together.

"We'd better make separate entrances," Jack told her.

"Okay, but you must know how I hate this," Blaze frowned.

"Me too, baby. Me too." Jack replied. "You go on ahead. I'll be out in a few minutes."

Blaze kissed Jack and made her way out of the library and through the front door. Jack decided to make his exit through the house to the kitchen and out the back door. He thanked Bert again for her help as he headed out to the patio.

The party was in full swing as the sun was beginning to set. Colored lights decorated the patio, tents, and stage areas illuminating the jovial scene as the partygoers were in a very festive mood. Kate and Thaddeus were the perfect host and hostess as they made their rounds through the crowds of guests making each one feel at home. Kate was spectacular in her white slacks and a beige tunic top, making sure she elicited donations from everyone there. The tunic-style top with three-quarter-inch sleeves was stylish but casual. She wore a large three-strand coral necklace with matching earrings that complimented her tanned complexion. Her hair was brushed away from her face, which was bare except for a little mascara and tinted lip gloss. She was stunning and admired by many in attendance as she commanded the party with her natural elegance. She noticed Jack from a distance and gradually made her way in his direction. When she reached him, she grabbed his hand as he kissed her cheek.

"Hello darling!" she said in her throaty voice. "I haven't seen you all day."

"Well, I've been here just waiting to get you on the dance floor," Jack teased.

"You know I'm up for the challenge," she said with a smile.

"Then let's do it." Jack danced while leading Kate to the dance floor.

The music was Olde School R&B and Jack twirled his mother around the floor as they bopped to the beat. They were a striking mother-and-son pair. A few other couples joined them on the floor. A crowd of on-lookers gathered to clap to the beat while Kate showed her skill showing she still had it. When they were finished a loud applause ensued as Kate hugged her handsome son while laughing and thanking the cheering crowd. Blaze watched from a distance admiring the relationship that the two seemed to have with one another. From their interaction, it was obvious Kate adored Jack as much as he did her. Jewels stood next to Blaze as they watched together.

"He's definitely a handsome man. I'll give you that," Jewels said to her daughter.
"I can see why you'd be so attracted to him."

"He's more than good looks mother. He's simply wonderful." Blaze smiled.

"Uh oh!" Jewels exclaimed.

"What?"

"Don't look now, but Clay is trying to get your attention."

Blaze looked across the crowd of people to see Clay smiling and waving at her. She waved back and managed to put on a smile though she didn't feel happy to see him. He came over and kissed her and then kissed Jewels on the cheek.

"How are the two most beautiful women at the party?" he asked gleefully.

"Well, we're doing just fine!" Jewels replied.

"Hi, Clay," was Blaze's response.

"You look beautiful, baby," Clay said.

"Come on! I want to show you off."

Clay took her hand and tried to get Blaze onto the dance floor, but she protested.

"Clay stop, I'm not in the mood for dancing right now."

"Well, isn't this a party? I mean, let's have a little fun."

"Maybe later." Blaze let go of his hand and headed back to her table.

"What'd I do?" he asked Jewels.

"She's fine, just a little tired is all." Jewels tried to smooth things over.

Once back at the table, Blaze sat down and joined the group which included Misha and a few people from the office. Z and Parks were there as well as Sam and his family.

"So, I see your financé has arrived." Z looked at Blaze.

"Yes, Z, I know that!"

"Hey, don't bite my head off, okay?"

"I'm sorry, Z. I don't know what's gotten into me lately."

"I know what it is," Z chuckled. "It's all over your face. Better try and act like you're having a good time with Clay, or he'll surely know something is going on between you and Jack." Z placed an arm around Blaze's shoulder in a friendly and comforting way. Little did they know that someone was listening to their every word as Parks was standing close to the table and out of sight.

"Hmm," he said to himself. "So, Blaze and Jack are an item—huh? This should prove to be interesting." He scurried away before he was seen.

After a few moments, Jack walked over to the table where Blaze and her group were seated. He extended his hand to Sam and Z and spoke to the others who he knew from the company. Blaze became quite nervous as he went around the table speaking to each person. When he got to Blaze, he extended his hand to her.

"Ms. Beaumont, glad you could make it to our little cookout," Jack said smiling.

Blaze extended her hand to him, "Thank you, Jack. This is a great party!"

"Jack, I'd like you to meet my mother, Jewels Beaumont."

Jewels smiled as Jack shook her hand.

"I would have thought you were going to say this was your sister. I see the resemblance but had no idea this was your mother. I'm pleased to meet you, Mrs. Beaumont." Jack said in his most charming manner.

"Please, call me Jewels. Everyone does," Jewels insisted.

"Then Jewels it is," Jack agreed.

"Excuse me! Did you forget something, Blaze? Hi, I'm Misha Blaze's friend."

Misha stood up eager to shake Jack's hand. Jack took both of Misha's hands into his and greeted her warmly.

"Well, Misha, it's very nice to meet you," he smiled and nodded.

"The pleasure is all mine," Misha said grinning.

Clay walked over to the table just as Jack was greeting everyone and introduced himself to Jack extending his hand with a smile. Blaze was relieved that she didn't have to make the introductions herself.

"Clayton Randolph Williams—with the Marshall Group," Clay announced with pride.

Jack gripped Clay's hand with a rigorous shake and looked him directly in the eyes.

"Jack Newman," he said with authority.

Blaze sat motionless as the two men shook hands, with Jack more sternly focused than Clay. Jack was sizing him up for certain. He wanted to know about this guy who laid claim to his lover. Blaze tried to think of something to divert the conversation in another direction, but she was at a loss and could not think of anything. Just as she thought things couldn't get any worse, who should grace the group with their presence, but Kate.

"Well, hello everyone," she performed in her most noble voice. "I trust that you all are having a great time at our little soiree?"

Many affirmative acknowledgments were bestowed upon her as she quickly pursued the group.

"Sam, I wanted to thank you personally for your generous donation to our cause. It's sponsors like Brickhouse, Becker, and Shuman who keep our youth and scholarship programs afloat."

"It is my pleasure and the pleasure of each of us here to offer such a small token to such a worthy cause," Sam added.

"Well, hello, Ms. Beaumont! And Mr. Williams, it's a pleasure to see you here," Kate chided.

Kate nodded at Jewels who returned the disingenuous greeting. Then, she walked over to Jack placing her arm into his.

"The two of you make quite a handsome couple. Don't you think so Jack?" Kate chided holding onto Jack's arm.

Jack made no comment and did not respond to his mother's question.

"You must be excited? Have you set a date, Ms. Beaumont?" Kate asked Blaze.

Blaze's throat was dry, and she could hardly muster an intelligent response. Jewels, Blaze, and Misha were all looking as if they had seen a ghost. Clay, not being aware of anything unusual, jumped in to answer Kate. Planting his arms firmly around Blaze's waist, he eagerly offered a reply, "I would marry her tomorrow, but she has her sights set on a big, fabulous wedding."

Jack shifted his weight and tightened his jaw as Clay displayed a possessive stance with Blaze. Blaze was uncomfortable with the gesture, and she could see that Jack wasn't pleased. On the other hand, Kate was enjoying the power that she had making Blaze feel uneasy knowing that this was an uncomfortable moment for her. Jewels could see through the game that Kate played and came to her daughter's defense.

"I'm sure you understand the protocol and timetable for weddings Kate, and therefore, since they have just recently announced their engagement, they have a bit of time before committing to a date."

Kate and Jewels exchanged glances at which time Jack decided to pull his mother away from the group.

"Mother, I believe some of your guests are leaving. We'd better get you over there before they go," Jack said in his most compromising tone.

"Ah yes! Will you excuse me?" Kate asked. "It's been wonderful chatting with you. Please enjoy the rest of the evening," she said as she walked away head held high arm-in-arm with Jack.

"What a bitch!" Misha blurted watching Kate walk away.

"Misha, that wasn't very nice to say about your hostess," Jewels sarcastically replied. "Although you're right, she is a bitch!"

"She really is something else," Blaze added.

"I think she's a very elegant lady," Clay responded.

"She seems like she's got it in for ya or something," observed Misha.

Blaze and Jewels looked at one another and said nothing further.

"Well, I for one am ready to get outta here," Blaze stated.

"It's still early babe. Why you want to leave so soon?" Clay asked.

As if on cue, the fireworks display began illuminating the night sky with a myriad of colored lights marking the past moment with impeccable timing.

"I'm with you," Misha added. "Let's go."

"Yeah, I've had just about as much fun as I can stand tonight," Jewels replied.

"Well, I guess I'm outvoted. Since you girls drove in together, you go ahead. I'll be right behind you." Clay kissed Blaze. "I'm just gonna go and talk with some people and then I'll be on my way."

"No need to hurry, Clay. Enjoy the evening. I don't want to ruin it for you." Blaze said.

"Okay, I'll see you later."

Clay kissed Blaze and walked away never the wiser about what had just happened.

"She knows!" Blaze said.

"Knows what?" Jewels asked.

"Knows about me and Jack! It's obvious that she doesn't care for me at all," Blaze replied.

"Who cares what she likes? She probably doesn't even like herself," Jewels said as they walked towards the gate leading to where the cars were parked. As they walked out, both Kate and Jack watched but from different locations. Jack wanted to walk out to Blaze and ask her not to leave, but he knew that she was taken aback by his mother's incessant inquiries into her marriage to Clay. He knew that Kate made Blaze feel uncomfortable, and he also knew that it was deliberate on his mother's behalf. On the other hand, Kate felt a sense of accomplishment as she watched Blaze and her entourage leave the party. Kate felt relief and went back to her conversation with her guests.

Kate thought to herself, *'Another little gold digger bites the dust.'*

Jack no longer felt festive and decided that he too would leave the party before Kate could object. He didn't want to be there knowing that Denise was just waiting for an opportunity to pounce upon him. He didn't want to go home to an empty apartment either. He thought about catching up with some of his boys, but that wasn't appealing to him. Joe had already left and most of his boys were headed down the shore. There was only one thing he wanted to do. The only thing that would satisfy him was being with Blaze. He knew that she would be with Clay and that didn't sit well with Jack at all. He kept imagining her in Clay's arms and this gave Jack much to be angry about.

Jack entered the house from the back through the patio area. He'd left his keys in his bedroom and went up to get them. He walked into the room and entered his closet turning on the lights. Deciding to change, he took off the shirt he was wearing and went to his armoire to retrieve another one. Before he could find another shirt, he suddenly heard a giggle from across the room where his bed was located. When he took a closer look, there was Denise sprawled across his bed with just her bra and panties on. She was clearly intoxicated, and she smiled and beckoned for Jack to come over to the bed.

"Jacky baby…why you make me wait so long for you to get here?" she asked with slurred speech.

"Denise! What the hell?"

"I'm waiting for you,' she said as she laid back upon the bolster pillow her feet still in her stiletto heels.

"Put some clothes on girl," Jack said as he picked up her dress from the floor and tossed it to her.

Denise giggled and kicked the dress onto the floor spreading her legs in the most unflattering fashion.

"Okay, I'm gonna get you some coffee. Clearly, you're flagged," Jack said heading for the door.

Denise jumped up from the bed and ran in front of Jack placing her body across the door like a shield.

"No, no, no! You've gotta stay here with me. I've got something for you."

"Denise, stop playing, now. You're drunk!"

"I'm not drunk. I'm just a little tipsy is all." she hiccupped and swayed from side to side.

"Your parents are downstairs and so are mine, You want them to see you like this?" Jack asked trying to reason with her.

"You never said that before when you use to let me sneak in here and take it." Denise hiccupped again.

"That was a long time ago. We were just kids then. Things have changed since then Denise."

"What kinda things? I'm still the same nasty girl you liked. Want me to show you?" she asked.

"Okay, I'm gonna get you some coffee."

As Jack reached to open the door, Denise fell into his arms and began to kiss him. Jack tried to gently resist her, but she was all over him. Her arms were about his neck, and she tried to wrap her leg around him while attempting to stick her tongue down his throat. Jack quickly picked her up and threw her upon the bed but when he did, she held on tight pulling him down upon her.

"Now that's better," she said looking into his eyes.

"Come on, Denise. You don't want to do this." Jack said pleadingly.

"Sure, I do. I've never wanted anyone more than I want you, Jacky," she said before planting a kiss on his mouth.

Jack didn't resist and let her kiss him.

"Denise, you know that it has been over between us for a long time. Why the sudden interest now?"

"I've always wanted you, Jack. I never stopped."

"Okay. Then listen to me for a minute. You're a beautiful, intelligent woman. Any man would be lucky to have you."

"I don't want any man, Jacky. I want you!"

"But I'm not available, Denise."

"Why because of that bitch I saw you with at the party in A.C.?"

"She's not a bitch. Her name is Blaze, and yes, she is the woman in my life right now."

"Then why is she engaged to Clay what's his name?"

"Not for long! Anyway, I care about you, Denise, and I don't want to see you hurt. So as your friend I'm gonna say this; clean yourself up and act like a lady for once."

Denise looked at Jack and smiled, "Oh Jacky, are you really my friend?"

"That's right...and now your friend is going to get you some coffee so get dressed.

Jack was lying next to Denise shirtless as she tried to open his pants.

"Come on, Jack. Niecy wanna see big Jack," she said nearly falling from the bed.

Just then, the door of his bedroom opened, and in walked Blaze.

She stopped dead in her tracks as she witnessed the display on Jack's bed.

Blaze gasped at the sight.

"Excuse me...I thought you were alone," Blaze said. "Clearly, I was mistaken." She then turned and walked out of the room. Denise was still holding onto Jack who was now calling Blaze and trying to get up to follow her.

"Ooops," Denise said as she giggled and wrapped her arms around his neck again, but he forcefully extricated himself from her grasp eliciting a startle from her and then another giggle. By the time he got to the door and into the hall, Blaze was gone.

Jack went back into his room to grab his shirt. He had to find Blaze and explain, so he ran down the stairs and out to the back of the house where the cars were parked. He got there just in time to see Jewels pulling off with Blaze in tow. He yelled after them, but they were too far ahead to hear, so Jack walked back into the house and headed for the kitchen.

It was nearly 10:00 pm and the kitchen was empty except for two men from the catering company who were cleaning and wrapping up leftover food. Many of the guests had left the party, except for a few people on the patio who were talking and enjoying the music. Jack poured a cup of black coffee that appeared to be quite strong. He took the cup back up to his room, but when he arrived Denise was sound asleep and snoring. Jack sat the cup down and covered her with a comforter. He grabbed his keys, turned out the light, and went back downstairs. He informed Bert that Denise was in his room and asked her to look in on her from time to time. He then slipped out the back to the garage, got in his car, and drove into the city. He thought of going straight to Blaze's apartment, but he knew Clay would be there. He had to get to her to make her understand. He tried calling her cell but got her voicemail. By the time he got home, it was nearly eleven and he wasn't in the mood to be around anyone...that is anyone except Blaze who was having her own trials uptown.

| 39 |

Plotting Parks

Once Blaze left, Parks went into overdrive trying to get information from Z.

"Hey man...nice party, huh?" Parks said to Z.

"Yeah, sure is," Z replied.

"Looks like it's only a few of us left from the office," Parks added.

"Yep...just about everyone has gone," Z stated.

"Did Blaze leave?" Parks asked.

"Yeah, she left a few minutes ago."

"So...I guess she left with Clay?"

Z gave Parks a quizzical glance.

"You seem to be full of questions tonight. What gives?"

"I was just wondering where everyone is...that's all," Parks stated guardedly.

"Parks! Man, you never just ask something for the sake of asking."

Parks knew that he wasn't going to get much from Z especially since he protected Blaze like she was his own woman. He decided to give up and leave.

"Well, I'm taking off too." Parks stood up from the table.

"Alright man...take it light," Z said shaking his hand.

As Parks walked away, Z shook his head as if he knew that Parks was fishing for dirt and he too picked up his keys and headed out. Parks wasn't finished yet as he decided to make one last attempt at sabotaging Blaze and her reign at the firm. He spotted Kate who was conversing with a group of people on the patio. He decided to get a drink and then saunter over towards the group waiting for an opportunity to get a word in with Kate. After a few minutes, he saw his chance and took the opportunity. Extending his hand to Kate Parks smiled before he spoke.

"Mrs. Newman—I just wanted to extend my appreciation for your hospitality this evening.

"Why thank you, Mister..."

"Parker Johnson of Brickhouse, Becker, and Shuman Inc.," he stated in a weasel-like way.

"Mr. Johnson," Kate smiled.

"Please call me Parks."

Kate smiled and answered him.

"Mr. Johnson you're quite welcome."

Kate turned to walk away when Parks spoke again.

"Ah, Mrs. Newman...a word please?"

Kate turned and looked at Parks a bit annoyed, but she obliged his request.

"I think that we may be able to assist one another with a small intrusion."

"Really?" Kate asked.

She looked at him with superior regard.

"May I?" Parks asked gesturing to two chairs on the patio inviting Kate to join him.

Most of the guests had drifted on to other areas of the party or were leaving, and Thaddeus was off entertaining clients in his game room, so the two were left alone to talk.

"So, Mr. Johnson, what is it that you think we have in common?" Kate asked crossing her legs and looking directly at Parks.

"Well from your conversation earlier, I get the distinct impression that you're not very fond of Ms. Beaumont."

"I hardly know the girl. She's of no interest to me."

"Really? I got a different impression," Parks stated boldly.

"And why would you think that Mr. Johnson?"

"Because she has caught the eye of your youngest son, and you don't approve of her."

"I'm sure I don't know what you mean," Kate continued to look directly at Parks.

Parks leaned forward speaking to Kate in a low whisper.

"I can help you get her out of your son's life."

Kate stared at Parks with a mixture of distrust and intrigue.

"Assuming that your theory is correct, how will this benefit you?" Kate asked.

"For one, she would be removed from the Newman account, and I would take over as the lead. Two, this will help me towards a partnership at my firm, and three, I would be forever grateful to you."

Kate studied Parks intently for a moment.

"Mr. Johnson, I think that you have underestimated my intentions. I'm not in the least bit interested in supporting your scheme to elevate your status at your firm."

"But you would like to see Jack with someone other than Blaze...right?" Parks continued pressing the issue with Kate.

"What do you want, Mr. Johnson?" Kate asked, clearly bored with his game.

"I believe, Mrs. Newman, if we work together, we can both achieve our goals. I'm on the inside and can feed you information that may be useful to you," Parks insisted.

Kate got up and Parks stood up to face her.

"As I said before Mr. Johnson—your assumptions are miss guided. Now if you will excuse me, I have guests to attend to," Kate walked away leaving Parks to stand there with a look of disbelief. He watched her as she walked toward a group of guests who were preparing to leave. Parks headed to the valet to retrieve his car.

| 40 |

It's Over

Jewels dropped Blaze off at her apartment and took Misha home. Blaze was angry at what she witnessed between Denise and Jack. She couldn't believe that he was half naked with Denise—her arms and legs all around him. Her head was reeling, and she couldn't make sense of any of it. Just hours before she was with Jack in his father's study making love.

"How could he be with Denise after that?" she asked herself.

On top of everything else she wasn't feeling up to dealing with Clay, but she knew it was inevitable. There was no right time in her mind to tell him about Jack, but she knew that it had to be done. She entered her apartment, showered, and put on a pair of sweats and a tee shirt. She was exhausted from everything that had transpired earlier. All she wanted was to curl up on the sofa and unwind before bed. Before long, Clay arrived. He let himself in with his key and began to make himself at home.

"Wow! What a day?" he said removing his shoes. "Nice party, huh?"

Blaze sat quietly on the sofa anticipating his every move. He reached over to kiss her, and she kissed him lightly upon his lips.

"What? You mad at me or something?" he asked.

"Clay, sit down please." Blaze's tone was serious.

"This sounds serious," he said sitting next to her.

"There's something that I have to tell you. I've been putting this off for too long, and after today I know that I have to be honest with you."

"Okay. Now I'm concerned." He frowned.

"You've been special to me. We have been through a lot since school, and I know that you love me so what I'm about to say has nothing to do with you or anything that you might have done. The thing is...I don't think we should get married."

Clay just looked at her as if she were speaking in another language.

"What...why... I thought this is what you wanted...what we both wanted?"

"No, Clay. Actually, it's what you wanted. I could have gone on and lived with you forever without ever needing to marry you, but you insisted that was what we should do. The truth is that I'm not ready to be married. There's so much that I want to accomplish."

"What? And you don't think that you can do those things with me?"

"It's not like that, Clay."

"Oh no? Then you tell me how it is Blaze...cause I'm not sure I know anymore."

"Clay, it wouldn't be fair to you. I love what I do, and it takes up a lot of my time. I wouldn't be able to give you the attention you deserve and be the kind of wife that you need."

"Bullshit! I don't believe that's why you don't want to get married. It doesn't make any sense. We're good together and we could be a power couple you and me. Where the hell is this coming from?"

"I just don't think a good marriage can be based on that kind of relationship, Clay. I wouldn't be fulfilling your needs."

Clay got up and walked into the kitchen and took a beer from the refrigerator. He turned the bottle up to his mouth and drank until it was nearly empty. When he walked back into the living room, he stood in front of Blaze and stared at her. She looked up at him and could see that he was hurt and furious. For the first time in their relationship, Blaze was afraid of what he might do. He sat down beside her and took her hands into his.

"Baby, I know that you're scared. I'm scared too, but we can make this thing work."

Blaze jumped up from the sofa wringing her hands. She turned and faced Clay.

"I'm not scared, Clay. I just don't want to marry you!" she nearly screamed.

Clay looked at Blaze and sat back on the sofa. He was startled by her boldness. There was silence between them for a few minutes until Clay spoke.

"You know, I knew that there was something different about you these last few months, but I couldn't put my finger on it. You've been distant and unavailable. I overlooked it thinking that after this account with Newman was stabilized that you would get back to the business of you and me. I guess I was wrong, huh?"

"Clay, I—"

"Don't say another word, Blaze. It'll only make things worse. I thought that we were happy. I thought you loved me and wanted to be my wife. How could I have been so blind?"

"Clay...please listen to me."

"Naw, I've heard enough! You don't want to get married. Hell, I'm not gonna twist your arm. We just won't get married. Will that make you happy?"

"Yes...I mean no...Oh, Clay! This isn't how I wanted things to go."

"I'll bet! Tell me this Blaze...is there someone else?"

Blaze stood silently not looking at Clay. She lowered her gaze unable to look him directly in the eyes. An expression of awareness and realization spread across Clay's face drawing anger to his words.

"Well...I guess I got my answer."

Clay slipped into his shoes and grabbed his keys and went out the door. Blaze stood in the middle of the floor tears welling up in her eyes. She felt awful as if a piece of her was torn away. She wasn't prepared for feeling this way. She fell to her knees and sobbed uncontrollably. Clay was standing on the other side of the door and heard her from the hallway. He wanted to return and comfort her. He wanted to take her in his arms and console her. He wanted all this to be some bad joke, but it wasn't. He was losing his best friend and soul mate, not to mention the woman he chose as his future wife. Clay walked towards the elevator and pressed the button. He wasn't even aware of what he was doing; his movements were mechanical at best. He got on the elevator and as the doors closed; his gut told him it was over.

Blaze spent the night crying herself to sleep. She was extremely distraught over her encounter with Clay. She was not so sure she had done the right thing by telling him she didn't want to marry him. She felt an emptiness inside that she wasn't prepared for, and her heart ached like someone had died. After a fretful night's sleep, Blaze lay in bed trying to bring herself to face the day. She reminisced on how she and Clay would spend Sunday mornings by going out to get coffee and muffins for breakfast, and then lying in bed talking, reading, or making love. She usually slept in on Sundays with Clay by her side, but this Sunday was different from the last four years that she had with him.

'How am I supposed to do this without him? What is it going to be like not seeing him or talking with him every day?'

She wept on her pillow until her eyes burned and her tears dried up.

| 41 |

Nightcap

Overall, the Newman barbecue was a raging success, and Kate couldn't have been happier. As Kate and Thaddeus said goodbye to their last guest, the Newman children gathered in the family room. It was well past midnight. Michael and James were playing a game of cards while Becca napped on one of the three Italian leather sofas that complimented the well-lived-in room. Kate gave her staff some last-minute instructions before retiring for the night. She closed the door to the east wing of the home and headed for the family quarters. The roaring sound from the theater system nearly gave her a fright.

"Please turn that down!" Kate shouted as she entered the room.

"Anyone want a nightcap?" Thaddeus asked.

"No thanks, dad. I'm fine," Elizabeth replied.

"None for me," Michael said as he entered the room.

"Well, I'll have a sherry," Kate answered.

Thaddeus made Kate's drink and joined her on the leather chaise.

They all began to trade stories of the night's event, who was there, and how much of a success the event turned out to be.

Kate felt a sense of accomplishment knowing that everyone had a great time and that her family was all together.

"Hey, where's Jack?" Liz asked.

"I think he may have gone to bed," Michael replied knowing full well that Jack had left.

"Okay, Michael. I'm sure you know as we all do that Jack left hours ago," Kate added.

"Okay. Sorry! Did he go home?"

"Who knows! You know how Jack is," Liz stated.

"Well, he's a grown man so I'm sure he can take care of himself," Thaddeus said.

Kate gave him a raised eyebrow and got up from the chair.

"Well, I'm going to bed. I've had a full day and tomorrow we still have the prayer service and brunch, so everyone should be heading up as well," she commanded.

"Goodnight mother," Liz said.

Everyone else chimed in saying their goodnights as Kate and Thaddeus retired for the evening. Holding onto her husband's arm, Kate voiced her opinion regarding Jack as they approached the stairs.

"What's gotten into Jack these days?" Kate asked.

"Don't you worry about Jack. He'll be just fine! Now, maybe you can display some affection for me." Thaddeus tapped Kate on her behind.

"Thaddeus!"

| 42 |

Solitude

Day three of the festivities on Sunday morning began with a prayer service on the Newman estate grounds followed by a brunch immediately after the benediction. The blue and white tents shaded the guests as the wait staff prepared their meals. A traditional brunch was served to more than 200 guests through the early afternoon. Kate was once again stunning in her wide-brim hat and pastel silk taffeta dress and pale blue sandals. She donned a pair of large black sunglasses to block out the sun's glare as she went around to each guest to thank them for their patronage of her event. A tiny gold chain adorned her neck, and her signature gold bangles graced her arm. She extended a warm and gracious welcome to her guests as she extolled her appreciation to everyone for attending. While the guests were being entertained on the South lawn, the children of the guests and the Newman children were busy enjoying an afternoon at the family pool. They were tended to by two nannies Maria and Eileen as their parents enjoyed the festivities. The entire Newman family was present and accounted for—that is everyone except for Jack.

Jack didn't feel like being around anyone, so he decided to sleep in and get some much-needed rest. When he woke up, he read a bit and watched some television before showering and getting dressed. He decided to take a walk through the city and maybe get a bite to eat at one of the pubs on the way. He thought of calling Blaze but couldn't bring himself to do so. He knew that the incident with Denise was hard to explain and looked as if they were having an intimate moment. Nothing could have been further from the truth. Jack wasn't going to address this problem right now and so he decided he would spend the afternoon alone. It was past noon when he left his apartment and made his way through the city. Although it was a very warm July afternoon, the streets were full of people. The outside cafés were busy and the lines of people at the shops along the way seemed to overflow out into the streets. The only time that Jack wore shorts was when he was playing basketball, or some other sport, so he wore a pair of khakis and a white cotton shirt that hang outside of his pants. He was very casual with his cap covering his eyes and dark sunglasses. He could have been mistaken for a tourist himself. He grabbed a cup of coffee at a local café and read the paper for over an hour. Nothing seemed to keep his interest, so he headed back home to catch up on some work. When he got back to his apartment, there were two messages on his phone—one from Kate and the other from Manny. He decided not to call Kate but made a return call to Manny who was inviting him to hang out. He decided to do just that.

Meanwhile, Blaze was still in bed and having a slow start to her day. By eleven o'clock, she decided to pull herself out of bed. It was such a beautiful day and she needed to get out of the apartment. She checked her phone to see if she somehow missed a call, but there were no messages. She thought about Jack and when she last saw him. She cringed at the sight of him lying on the bed with Denise wrapped around him like some octopus—all legs and arms.

"I can't stand this," she blurted out. "I've got to get outta here."

Blaze took her shower and put on a pair of jeans, a white tee shirt, and her tennis shoes. She pulled her hair up covering it with a hat, and then she put on a pair of dark sunglasses. She grabbed her keys and left her apartment. She drove the ten blocks to the center of the city and parked her car in a lot. She decided that she needed some retail therapy and went shopping along the Square where several boutiques carried one-of-a-kind items. She went in and out of the shops hoping to find something that would strike her interest, but nothing seemed to suit her. She was so emotionally distracted that not even a new dress could ease her mind. She thought of calling Jack, but she immediately decided against it. Since shopping wasn't having the desired effect that she had hoped for, she headed home picking up something for dinner on the way. She made it an early night to get a head start on the next day which she anticipated would be busy.

The next few days Blaze submerged herself into her work with full force. After work every day, she went straight to the gym where she worked out for an hour. She made an appointment with her trainer for two days each week. She wanted her mind, body, and spirit to be in good form. She then went to a small café near the gym and had a light supper. She took homework with her to occupy her mind. There was no time for idleness, and she wouldn't be victim to some memory of Clay, or Jack for that matter.

In her solitude, Blaze did some soul-searching, and she decided that for a time she wanted to be alone. This came as a surprise to even her, but she was determined to take a new lease on her life. She called Jewels up to discuss her new-found project entitled, Simply Blaze. Jewels laughed when she heard that her daughter called her life a project and even named it, but deep down she was relieved and proud of her decision. They talked for an hour before hanging up promising to meet for dinner sometime within the next week.

Blaze went home and prepared to retire for the evening. She took a shower and turned on the television to watch one of the late-night talk shows. She checked her messages and had four calls to return. One of the calls was from Jack asking her to call him when she came in. The other three were from Clay asking her when he could get the rest of his things. She didn't return the calls to either of them opting for once to concentrate on her own needs and desires. After her shower, Blaze sat on the sofa and flipped through the channels. Before she retired to bed, she prayed to God for guidance that she'd make sound, sensible choices and that she could find peace in her life. She dozed off into a peaceful and restful sleep with her dreams full of promise and renewed purpose for a future she had faith in.

| 43 |

An Impromptu Meeting

At work, Parks was careful before making any kind of move against Blaze. He wanted her position and to become a partner in the firm. There really wasn't any ammunition against her that he could use to pull her down from her high horse. She was well-liked by everyone at the firm, she had a solid reputation in the business, and she did her job exceptionally well. She brought new clients earning the firm millions of dollars and recognition in the industry. There just wasn't an opportunity to cause her a problem—that is until Jack Newman came on the scene. Parks had an idea that they were involved, and he also knew that Kate Newman didn't approve. Parks thought that he might capitalize on this bit of information and so he went about devising a plan to bring Blaze to her knees...a place that he thought she deserved to be in more ways than one.

On this particular day, Parks had been in the office most of the morning and was now sitting at his desk in deep thought. He picked up the phone and dialed out waiting to speak with the person he called.

"Good morning, Newman residence!"

"Good morning! Mrs. Newman, please?"

"May I tell her who is calling?"

"Yes, this is Parker Johnson."

"One moment, please. I'll see if she's available."

After a few moments the woman who answered the phone returned.

"I'm sorry, Mr. Johnson. Mrs. Newman's not available at this time. May I give her a message?"

"No, thank you." Parks hung up the phone and sat at his desk with his hand on his chin. He smiled at the thought that Kate was avoiding him. It didn't make a difference to him because he knew in time, she would take his call. Parks sat in his chair for a moment pondering his next move. He enjoyed a good challenge, and he was especially up for this one. A thought suddenly occurred to him that caused a stir in his devious little mind. He turned in his chair and proceeded to make another call. The phone rang a few times before a woman answered.

"Hello, who dis?"

"Hey, girl! How you doin'?" Parks asked in a sly voice.

"I'm fine. And you?" the woman asked.

"Good. Really good." Parks answered. "Listen I was wondering if you could do me a favor?"

"I don't know. Depends on what it is," she said.

"Remember the guy that you were talking with at the club a few weeks ago who said he was a stylist?"

"Oh, you mean Pierre!"

"Pierre! Yeah, that's right darling. Didn't you tell me he worked for Kate Newman?"

"Uh-huh. He's exclusive to her though. He don't work with any clients but her."

"That's fine! Do you know how I can reach him?"

"Well, I know he be in the club sometimes. I usually see him on Wednesday nights."

"Great! Are you working tonight?" Parks asked.

"Yeah. You comin' to see me dance?"

"You bet your sweet ass I'll be there tonight," Parks smiled an evil smile.

"Okay. I'll do something special just for you."

"See ya then," he replied.

"Yeah, honey. You certainly will," Parks said before hanging up.

With his hands crossed behind his head, Parks smiled a sly and devious smile of achievement.

That evening, Parks entered the Tail Winds Club at half past ten. There were approximately twenty people all of whom were enjoying the floor show. There was a stage in the middle of the floor with a bar that wrapped completely around it. A woman with a tiny waist and huge breasts was swinging around a poll with nothing but a g-string and platform shoes. Parks sat at the bar when instantly a buxom red-headed woman asked him, "What's your pleasure?"

Parks ordered beer and watched the show. Minutes later a young woman wearing a black bralette and red mini skirt with clear platform shoes approached him with a hug.

"Hey suga!" she greeted him with a smile.

"Hey there," Parks returned. "What ya drinking babe?" he asked.

"I'll have a champagne cocktail," she told the bartender.

"So, where ya been? I ain't seen ya in a while." The girl slithered up to Parks.

"I been busy working."

"Well, if ya want, we can go in the back and get more comfortable," she offered.

Parks looked around. "Maybe later."

"Okay." The girl sipped her drink.

The two of them sat and talked for a while until it was time for her to dance. She got on stage and performed her routine mostly strutting and grinding for Parks. He put some money in her G-string, and she continued to dance for him until another man on the other side of the bar beckoned for her to come and retrieve the money he had for her. Just then, the person that Parks was really there to see appeared. Pierre entered the club dressed in a flashy red suit and a wide-brim hat. His pants were tight, and his purple shirt was open at the chest. He looked like a chicken without the feathers, as he sat down at the bar eyeing some of the male patrons. When Parks noticed him, he sent Pierre a drink who quickly accepted it thinking it was an invitation for something more. He moved his seat down closer to Parks and struck up a conversation. Parks was cordial to him and ordered Pierre another drink. After a few minutes of small talk, Parks changed the subject.

"So, Pierre where do you work?" Parks asked already knowing the answer.

Trying to look important, Pierre answered Parks.

"Well, if you must know, I work for a very wealthy family."

"Oh really! And just what is it that you do for this family?" Parks asked attempting to sound intrigued.

Pierre was naturally suspicious, "Why, sir, are you so interested in my work?"

"Well because a person of such style as you obviously must be a designer or stylist." Parks quickly replied. Taking the bait with all the gullibility he could muster, Pierre smiled and responded.

"My how perceptive you are! I am a designer. Well, more of a stylist at the moment," he said cheerily.

"Really? I'm impressed!" Parks exaggerated.

Pierre was eager to relay his achievements and went on about who he worked with throwing around important designer names. Parks had a feeling that although some of what he said may have been true, Pierre was nowhere near the sought-after talent that he envisioned himself to be, but Parks played along.

"Well, I am impressed with you Pierre. Not only do you have style, but you also have your pulse on what is important in fashion."

Pierre was thrilled at Parks's acknowledgment of him. He ordered another drink for himself and one for Parks as well. After three rounds, Pierre's tongue began to loosen; he did like to hear himself talk. He boasted about the Newman family, their wealth, and how he was privy to all kinds of information about their private lives.

"If you only knew the half of it."

Pierre laughed as he waved his manicured hands in the air. Parks became more intrigued with Pierre's stories but played it cool trying not to tip his hand about why he was there.

"You know I work directly with Mrs. Kate Newman. I'm her stylist! When you see her in magazines and newspapers looking fabulous you can bet, I'm the one who dressed her. Yeah, she's quite the lady, so everyone thinks...but I know a few things about her that would make your hair stand on end."

"Really? What kind of things?" Parks asked cautiously.

"Well, she dyes her hair for one. That's not her natural color. And she's had some work done, but she'll never admit to it." Pierre went on and on about Kate's clothes and shoe collection.

Parks was beginning to regret that he initiated this whole thing. He was just about ready to call it a night and leave this harpy to spew his venom at someone else. Parks began to get up from his stool when Pierre said something that finally caught his attention.

"Yeah, and she thinks no one knows that her old friend Mr. Thompson is more than an old friend. She been sneaking around with him for years behind Mr. Newman's back."

Parks's ears stood straight up like a German Shepard as he quickly sat back down on his stool. Parks was once again interested as he goaded Pierre to go on, but an alarm went off in Pierre's head as he noticed that Parks was a little too interested in what he had to say.

"Maybe I'm talking too much," Pierre said. Parks tried to salvage the moment by pretending to be interested in Pierre.

"Nonsense. You tell a great story."

"Well, why don't we take this little party somewhere more private?" Pierre suggested leaning on Parks's arm.

Parks immediately became uncomfortable and feigned an excuse for why he had to leave.

"Boy—ahh, I wish I could, but I have an early call in the morning. Maybe we can continue this another time," Parks said getting up from his stool.

"Well, if you have to go—"

"Yes, I'm afraid I do, but I'll see you again." Parks nearly ran out of the club. Pierre sat on the stool dumbfounded at Parks's exit.

"Well, I never! Some people have no manners," Pierre scoffed before drinking all that was in his glass.

More than wasted he said in a commanding voice, "Bartender! Another round please!"

| 44 |

Summer Vacations

It was a busy morning as the Newmans were preparing to leave for a month-long vacation at their summer home on Stone Harbor, an exclusive stretch of beach with a million-dollar mansion that lined the Jersey Shore. The house, which sat on a few acres overlooking the Atlantic Ocean, was left to Kate by her grandparents. Being an only child, she inherited quite a bit of property from her parents as well.

Kate gave the staff instructions before closing the main house and driving to the shore. Except for Bert, Kate gave each of her staff three weeks of vacation with pay and informed them of when they were expected to return. She wanted them to reopen the house before she arrived at the end of August giving them a week to get things ready for her return. Bert traveled everywhere the family went since both Kate and Thaddeus felt as though she was family. They also preferred Bert's cooking to anyone else. She was paid handsomely for her services and Thaddeus also set up a very generous trust for her retirement which they all hoped would never come.

Most summers, the family usually spent a few weeks in Barbados as well, but Thaddeus was unable to get away this year, and Kate didn't want to be away that long without him. She opted to have him with her a few days out of the week when she stayed at the summer house. Liz and Bradley would be joining the family bringing their children, of course, and James and his wife Rebecca who would also be there. Michael planned to spend some time with the family as well, but Jack had yet to commit to a specific time feigning business as the reason for not being able to commit.

Kate decided to drive herself with Liz, the children, and Bert joining her for the car ride down. Kate loved the family outings, which gave them all a chance to catch up and spend time together. Once everyone was settled, Thaddeus said goodbye to his family promising to drive down by the weekend. He preferred staying at the apartment in the city instead of rattling around alone in the big house when Kate was away. He definitely had his reasons, but ones he dared not share with the family. Kate promised to call when they arrived and made him promise to look in on Jack while he was staying in the city.

Ever since the Newman's event-filled weekend and his fall out with Blaze, Jack had been arriving in the office early and staying quite late. His mood had been somber though he managed to remain his usual congenial self with staff and colleagues. His father noticed that he had been driving himself pretty hard, but he never mentioned any of it to Kate or Jack for that matter. Jack was finalizing a deal that would give Newman ownership of three prime pieces of real estate and several vacant lots that had been on the market since the beginning of the year. Cementing this deal would be a major acquisition for Newman. Ordinarily, this would be cause for celebration, but Jack wasn't feeling very festive. He was planning a trip to the West Coast on business and thought how good it would be to have Blaze join him, but since the night of the barbecue, she had become distant and unavailable. Blaze assured him that she believed when he said that nothing happened between him and Denise, but he wasn't convinced she was telling him the truth. Jack engrossed himself in his work and was determined to stay focused. He had several messages from Kate requesting that he make an appearance at the shore house with the rest of the family, but Jack was still furious with his mother after her behavior at the barbecue. He made his required appearance at brunch at the house, but he hadn't stayed at home since the party. He worked all day and then retired to his apartment in the city at night. It had been this way since he last saw Blaze over a week ago.

It was a habit for Thaddeus to arrive early as well, but on this day, it was well past mid-day when he arrived in the office. He made some calls and attended a brief meeting before heading to his son's office to catch up on things. When he arrived, Jack was just finishing up a telephone call with the finance division of Newman. Thaddeus walked in motioning for Tommy to not get up as he went directly into Jack's office and closed the door.

"Hey, Pop! When'd you get in?" Jack asked.

"Hey, son! Just been here a few hours. Sounds like things are going smoothly with the acquisition!"

"Yeah, in fact, we signed the papers yesterday, and finance just received copies of everything. I was just talking with Marcus when you came in."

"Good, good! That's what I like to hear. So how is everything else with you?" Thaddeus asked before taking a seat.

"Things are good, Pop." Jack's tone was dismissive.

"Your mother is worried about you son."

"Pop it's not up for discussion, so let's just skip it!"

"Okay, but you should make a point of getting down to the house this week or next. The girls left this morning. Kate called me about a half hour ago to say they made it down safely."

"That's good," Jack replied while studying some papers on his desk.

"Well, I'm staying in the city until they return if you want to stop by."

"That sounds good, Pop, but aren't you going down to the house too?"

"Yeah, I'll make it down by the weekend. I need to be here for some meetings and other business," Thaddeus said almost apologetically.

"Well, I thought I might hang out on the deck tonight and throw some steaks on the grill if you want to join me," Jack stated.

"Okay, you're on!" Thaddeus smiled.

"I can DJ while you cook," he offered.

"Okay, see ya round seven."

"Seven sounds good," Thaddeus said before leaving.

As Thaddeus walked through the double glass doors of Jack's office, he took out his cell phone to make a call. The phone rang several times before someone answered.

"Hello!"

"Hey, gonna be late tonight. Gotta go to Jack's. I should be there by ten. Wear something nice for me," Thaddeus requested.

"Can't wait to see you," a woman replied.

"Sure thing," Thaddeus said before hanging up as he walked into his office.

After a few hours, Jack left the office and headed home. He showered and changed into a pair of sweats and a tee shirt before preparing the steaks for the grill. He had corn on the cob, salad, and plenty of beer on hand for both him and his dad. Once he was finished prepping the meal, he sat on the deck beer in hand enjoying the Philadelphia skyline. Thaddeus arrived a little later and began to sort through the albums playing classics and funky jazz rhythms while the two talked about everything from sports to stock options.

They had dinner on the deck laughing, talking, and reminiscing. Jack and Thaddeus always enjoyed each other's company.

When the subject changed to the campaign that Brickhouse, Becker, and Shuman Inc. were handling, Blaze's name came up in the conversation.

"So how do you think Ms. Beaumont and her team are managing the account?" Thaddeus asked.

"I'm very satisfied," Jack replied.

"That Ms. Beaumont is very sharp. I'd love to steal her away from Sam and bring her into Newman."

Jack didn't like the sound of that, and he made it apparent from his answer.

"Pop, that's a bad idea."

"Why?" Thaddeus asked.

"Because it just is!" Jack said reaching for another beer.

"Jack is something going on between you and Blaze Beaumont?"

"Look, Pop—we went out a few times, and well, yeah. Something is going on, but for the life of me I don't know what."

"So that's why you've been so grumpy."

"Grumpy? Pop I ain't never been grumpy in my life," Jack laughed.

"I thought that she was engaged to what's his name. You know, we met at the barbecue—Clay something?"

"She broke it off!"

"Just like that? She broke it off?"

"Come on, Pop. What is this? The Inquisition?"

"Jack, this is cause for concern. Blaze Beaumont is your employee. You can't mix business with pleasure. Trust me it never works."

"Oh yeah?" Jack asked smiling. "How do you know?"

They both burst into laughter.

"Just you never mind how I know. All you need to know is that I know."

"I suggest that you get whatever it is out of your system. Go down to the shore and stay at the house for a few days. Take a trip to AC and do some gambling. Do something but don't let this thing get to you. Understand?"

"Pop, I'm fine! I'll be alright and I'll think about going down to the house. Okay?" Jack answered with a smile.

"Okay, son! I'm gonna get outta here, but you get some rest and think about what I said."

Thaddeus stood up, hugged his son, and shook his hand. He left a little after nine, so it was still early in the evening. After Jack cleaned up, he sat on the deck listening to music in deep thought. He was just about to head in when his phone rang. Recognizing the number, he decided not to answer. He wasn't interested in talking with any of the women that he knew. Jack was an eligible bachelor, and there was no shortage of women who would jump at the chance of spending time with him. But he was determined to give up women altogether, at least for a while. He concluded that he would visit his parents at the summer house and spend time with his family on the weekend.

It'll be good to sit on the beach and relax for a few days,' he thought. Jack closed the doors to the deck and turned in for the night.

Every summer, Jewels and her children retreated to the beach house for a few weeks. It was an annual event that they all looked forward to. Since Jewels enjoyed entertaining, she didn't mind that her children would be inviting their friends to join them. They all had a good time when they were together. Kush was single and loving it. He always had some new girl to introduce to the family. This month it was a model who did catalog and television work. Although Jewels hoped that he would one day settle down, Kush had no intentions of doing so anytime soon. He was having way too much fun.

Peyton and Sydney both had boyfriends who would be visiting them at the beach and Blaze was newly single—a concept that she was not familiar with. She had been dating and living with Clay since college, so it took some getting used to not having him in her life. She told everyone she was fine and that being single meant that she had more time to devote to her career. In some ways, she was enjoying her newfound freedom, but she was conflicted when it came to Jack Newman. She felt as though she fell too hard for Jack too fast. Jewels agreed with her and encouraged her to take her time and enjoy her life before making any permanent decisions. Getting away for a while was just what she needed, so Blaze packed her things and headed to the shore. She loved being there with her family and she felt so much at home at the beach. Z, from work, had a standing invitation to join them for a few days. The two of them would go to the casinos and hang out at the clubs. She knew if Z came, it would be like old times and Blaze couldn't wait to hang out with her good friend.

When Blaze arrived, Jewels had a buffet of food waiting. Jewels always placed an order in advance and had the food delivered upon the family's arrival. The summer house wasn't huge, but it was comfortably adequate. Jewels bought the property after her salon in Baltimore began to turn a profit. She also owned a home in Ocean City, Maryland. She was quite frugal with her money and spent every penny wisely. Jewels kept up with the trends and read all she could about finances and the economy. She made sure that she had enough money put away to send her children to college and provide herself with a handsome retirement. She knew very well what it was like to be penniless with four small children to care for. When Malcolm died, it was nearly two years before she was awarded any money from the company he worked for. They tried to hold the money up in court proceedings and didn't want to pay out the full amount offering her a small settlement instead. Jewels obtained legal aid to help her fight for the entire amount since the company was negligent. She sued the company and won. She was so happy that she would be able to take care of her children and that they wouldn't have to be without. So, she held onto her funds, invested some, and spent the rest on continuing her education. She bought her first salon when Blaze was three years old, and she soon became one of the most sought-after stylists within the next few years. Jewels' priority was her children and for that reason, she had not been in a serious relationship for a long time. There were occasional dates, with one man in particular, but because she wouldn't allow herself to get too serious, so he decided to move on. Jewels had a full life with a successful business and four wonderful children. She had everything that she needed except for a love life.

Over at the Newman's summer house, Kate, Liz, and Becca were getting settled while Bert took inventory of the kitchen pantry. The children immediately found their way to the beach accompanied by their nanny. The house had been opened a week before their visit so all the rooms were ready to be occupied. The house featured a huge airy living room and dining area with a view of the patio through two sets of large French doors. Natural light covered the main floor through several large windows. Stained hardwood floors were immaculately polished and adorned with oriental rugs in hues of plum, coral, and cream throughout the entire house. The furniture was simplistic and covered in cream canvas fabric featuring overstuffed sofas and chairs. Depictions of brightly colored bohemian artwork lined the walls of every room in wooden frames of varying designs. The six bedrooms were decorated with mahogany tables, dressers, and four-poster beds that sat upon plush rugs. All the bedding was white even the towels except for the ones in the beach house which were blue and white striped. The bathrooms were completely white with porcelain sinks and tubs, porcelain and chrome fixtures, and mahogany shelves and cabinets. Kate chose simplistic lines for the house mimicking the richness of Thaddeus's Barbados culture making it comfortable and homey. She only entertained family and close friends when she was there, making it completely off-limits for anything related to business.

The property offered a view of the ocean and an expanse of beach that could be seen for miles from the large wrap-around deck. Huge blue and white awnings shaded the back of the house as the family relaxed on the lounge chairs while the children played along the beach. A large fenced-in pool featured a waterfall and alcove that presented a cool atmosphere and a pleasant sound as the water trickled down into the Olympic-sized pool. Huge flowering tropical plants surrounded the stone-paved patio and outdoor fireplace as azaleas, petunias, and daylilies lined a path that traveled out past the garage and onto the private beach. Soft jazz music played throughout the house from hidden speakers offering a soothing sound that complimented the relaxed environment. Kate decorated the house herself maintaining much of the old charm and adding new pieces here and there for ambiance. This was her sanctuary and she loved being there even during the winter months. She and Thaddeus often got away together and would spend hours at the beach house languishing in bed and enjoying each other's company. Many fond memories were made here for the Newman family where Kate was her happiest.

Kate went into the kitchen and uncovered a plate that Bert had previously prepared for her before she left for her bingo game in town. She sat down at the table and began to nibble from her plate sipping on her favorite wine. She was lonely for Thaddeus's company. She tried him on his cell phone and at the apartment, but there was no answer on either one. She retired to the family room turning on the television for a mere diversion from her thoughts. After flipping through the channels and not finding anything worth watching she decided to take a hot bath and retire. Just as she was getting ready for bed, the phone rang. It was Thaddeus. Although she pretended to be cross with her husband, she was happy to hear from him.

"Thad, I tried calling you hours ago."

"I know dear I was over to see Jack and we had dinner together. Time just got away from us somehow."

"Well, I guess I forgive you since you were spending time with our son. How is he by the way?"

"He's good! He's busy, but doing well I would say," Thaddeus lied.

"Is he taking care of himself, Thad?"

"It appears that he is. He grilled steaks for us and made a salad. We had a good evening listening to music and talking. He seemed in good spirits."

"Will he be making the trip down, do you think?"

"Now, that I can't say," Thaddeus replied.

"Maybe I should give him a call."

"Listen. Why don't you leave it to me? I'll talk with him again tomorrow and get him to drive down with me in a few days."

"That would be wonderful. I'll have Bert plan some of your favorites and we'll have a cookout just for the family. Michael and James will be here as well," Kate added.

"Okay then!" Thaddeus answered. "I'm gonna call it a night, but I'll call you tomorrow sweetness."

"I love you, Thad. Hurry down and spend some time with me. I miss you terribly," Kate replied.

"Goodnight, sweetness."

"Goodnight, my love," Kate replied.

Kate felt better after her conversation with Thaddeus. She threw a summer comforter over her bed snuggling in for the night and within minutes she was sound asleep.

Thaddeus hung up and walked back into the bedroom.

"Come back to bed," requested the woman who was in bed waiting in bed for Thaddeus to return. Removing his robe, he walked over and climbed into bed with her. She eagerly turned to him wrapping her arms around his neck and kissing him aggressively. The covers fell away from her naked body as she continued her quest to arouse Thaddeus into another session of sex. He grabbed her around the waist pulling her on top of him as he smacked her behind.

"Ooh that hurt," she giggled.

"Aw, baby, that was just a love tap," he said rubbing her behind as he eagerly returned her kisses.

| 45 |

Pierre

When Pierre woke up, he was not alone. His head throbbed as he tried lifting it from the pillow. He tried opening his eyes, but the light in the room was blinding and he retreated under the covers. It was then that he noticed that he was not alone. A young man not more than twenty years old was lying next to him completely naked. Pierre tried to focus, but all he felt was the pain. He tried remembering the events of the last night, but he could not. He dragged himself up from the bed and went into the bathroom to look for aspirin. He managed to find some and filled a glass with water quickly throwing back the pill. He returned to his bedroom and stared at the young man sleeping.

"Well now...who the hell are you?" he whispered. "I must have really tied one on last night since I don't remember bringing this one back here."

He began to shake the bed waking the young man from his sleep.

"What?" he asked annoyedly. "Why you gotta be shakin' the bed that way?"

"It's time for you to go," Pierre replied.

"Go? Go where?" The young man rubbed his eyes.

"You gotta get up," Pierre commanded.

"Wow, you sure are mean in the morning."

"I'm not a morning person and you are invading my space."

"Well honey, you weren't so particular about me invading yo space last night."

Pierre stood his ground, "Get up! Get your things and leave my apartment now before I have someone remove you from here." Pierre yelled.

"Well, can I at least use the bathroom?"

"Yeah, but make it quick," Pierre said. "I have to get ready to meet someone."

The young man dragged himself out of the bed, picked up his clothes, and took them into the bathroom with him. Before too long, he reappeared fresh-faced and angry.

He picked up his cell phone from the coffee table and turned to look at Pierre.

"Pops, you got issues honey and next time you lookin' for some fun...try the circus." He said as he exited the apartment slamming the door.

Pierre didn't care what the man thought he just wanted him out of his apartment. He sat down and tried to close his eyes to relieve the throbbing in his head. He had no recollection of how he came to be with this person in his apartment and he wasn't up for entertaining. Pierre was infamous for getting intoxicated and waking up the next day with no memory of the night before. This time he had outdone himself.

Later that evening, Pierre arrived at the Trade Winds decked out in a fuchsia-colored silk shirt and tan pants. It was a hot night and he wanted to be as cool as he looked. A gold medallion hung around his neck shimmering on his chest as he entered the club. He carried a small clutch under his arm as he traipsed past the entrance smoking a cigarette and greeting everyone along the way. He was eager to get his night started ordering a cocktail and asking the barmaid to run a tab for him. The Trade Winds Club was uptown away from the ambiance of downtown Philadelphia. It was located on a busy avenue that had rows of shops, and businesses, many still open. The hustlers on the corner were shooting craps as the old heads hung out in front of the local barber shop that was still open with clients waiting their turn to be groomed. This was Pierre's roots where he felt very much at home. Sure, he had been to France and Rome and had met many well-known artists and designers, but he was most comfortable right here.

It had been nearly an hour since Pierre arrived and he was no longer feeling any pain. Just as Pierre had hoped Parks walked into the club. He was standing at the entrance talking with a few of the patrons. Pierre straightened up and glanced at himself in the huge mirror that was over the bar. He wanted to look his best since he hoped Parks would hook up with him. Parks noticed Pierre at the bar and made his way over.

"Hey, Pierre. Good to see ya, man," Parks shouted over the music.

"Well, Mr. Parks! Nice to see you again," Pierre said coyly trying to remain uninterested.

"What you drinkin'?" Parks asked.

"Grand Marnier," he replied.

Parks ordered another drink for Pierre and a beer for himself. He sat down beside Pierre who was ecstatic that he remembered him. They sat at the bar for a while making pleasantries and watching the show. When the first set was over, the DJ took a break as the noise in the room came to a more tolerable level.

"Wow, now we can actually hear one another," Pierre laughed and threw his head back.

"Yeah, this is much better," Parks added feigning a smile.

Parks bought another round as the two chatted about little or nothing. Parks asked Pierre about his work and pretended to find it interesting. Pierre liked the way Parks looked and made no attempts to hide it. Although this made Parks feel uneasy, it was worth it to get information that he could use against Kate. Pierre was on his fourth cocktail as he loosened up a bit. He was quite boisterous and made gestures to Parks that indicated he wanted to take their conversation in another direction.

"Whew, I'm toasted," Pierre said.

Parks was getting impatient with Pierre. He wanted to get more information about Kate and Ed Thompson but didn't want to set off any alarms so that Pierre would get suspicious. He knew that Pierre was no fool. He had to outsmart him. Parks decided to use the direct approach and ask Pierre out right about Mrs. Thaddeus Newman.

Parks ordered another round of drinks.

"Oh, that's very decent of you Parks to order me another drink. You are quite the gentleman." Pierre sat down.

"So, Pierre what do you like to do for recreation? Do you play tennis? Like to swim? What do you enjoy doing?"

"Well, I do play tennis and I haven't been swimming at all this year. I have access to the Newman courts, but I'm usually so busy that I don't get much time to play."

"Wow, that must be nice!" Parks took that opportunity to dig in deeper. "Do the Newmans play a lot of tennis?"

"Why, yes! Especially Mrs. Newman. She's an avid tennis player. That's how she and Mr. Newman met."

"Really?" Parks asked.

"Who's the better player you or Mrs. Newman?"

"Why, me of course!" Pierre exclaimed.

"So does Mrs. Newman have a tennis pro to keep up her game?"

"No, she's very good—though she does often play with Mr. Newman."

"That's Nice! So, does she ever play with Ed Thompson?" Parks asked setting Pierre up.

"Why, yes, how'd you know about Mr. Thompson?" Pierre asked curiously.

"I just remembered that you told me they were friends."

"Chile…they are more than friends. They were an item in college. He wanted to marry Kate, but when Thaddeus came on the scene girlfriend fell head over heels. The rest is history," Pierre blurted all in one breath.

The wheels were turning so fast in Parks's head you could nearly see the smoke.

"So how is it you have the night off?" Parks asked.

"Baby, I'm on vacation for three whole weeks."

"Really? That's a long time to be away from Mrs. Newman."

"Oh, she's at her summer home in Stone Harbor for the month. She'll be back after Labor Day."

"Wow! That must be nice! Did she go with her family?"

"You sho do ask a lot—a lot of questions bout the Newman's. You a reporter or something?" Pierre asked stumbling on his words.

"Who me?" Parks chuckled. "No, I'm just a lowly clerk just interested in how the other half lives is all," he smirked.

Parks drained his glass and got up from his stool.

"Well, that's it for me. I gotta be getting home. Don't want to oversleep for my big day tomorrow."

"Hey, don't leave so soon. Have another drink with me," Pierre begged. "What's so special bout tomorrow anyway?"

Parks leaned in and whispered into Pierre's ear, "It's the day I become a rich man."

Pierre gave Parks a blank stare as he stumbled almost falling off his stool.

Parks paid his tab and walked out of Trade Winds confident that he had Kate Newman in the palm of his hand.

| 46 |

Surprise, Surprise

Jack and Thaddeus arrived at the shore house around midday just in time to have lunch with the family. Bert prepared a spread of seafood favorites. They had clams, oysters, crabs, and lobster salad. The beer was cold, and the wine chilled as the family retreated to the patio. Michael and James made the trip down as well, so everyone was there as Kate requested. The patio was cool and serene as the family relaxed and caught up with one another.

"Jack, let's hit the casinos tonight!" Michael suggested.

"You're on, man. I haven't gambled since..."

"Since when?" Michael asked.

Jack stopped in his tracks when he realized the last time that he played was when he and Blaze were in Atlantic City together. His expression changed quickly as he excused himself from the group.

"I'm gonna take a walk. See you guys later." Jack walked out of the gate and onto the beach.

"What'd I say?" Michael was confused.

"Nothing, Mike." Thaddeus chimed in to answer. "It didn't have anything to do with you or what you said."

Kate gave Thaddeus a knowing glance as she attempted to finish her meal.

"Leave your brother alone. He's had a hard week. Let him unwind in own his way. He'll come around," Thaddeus insisted. Everyone agreed to give Jack his space—everyone except Kate who would have her say one way or the other.

Over at Jewels' beach house, Blaze decided to take a nap before she and Z went to Atlantic City for the evening. Her bedroom was in the back of the house, so she received an ample breeze from the ocean. She loved how peaceful it was at the beach. She often sat in her window daydreaming for hours on end. Z had the spare bedroom and was glad that Blaze would be hanging out with him. They decided to leave at eight to drive into Atlantic City to do some gambling and hit a club or two. It was Friday night and most of Z's friends were down for the weekend. They planned to meet up with them once they arrived at the casino. Blaze wore a blue form-fitting dress that hugged her curves and didn't apologize for how much it revealed. She complimented the dress with a pair of four-inch nude-colored sandals. She pinned her hair up leaving a little bang that brushed her eyelids. She used a little mascara and lip gloss just enough to complete her very sensuous and smoldering look. When she emerged from her room, Z whistled while her siblings and mother applauded her as if she were some celebrated actress on stage. Blaze blushed at their antics all the while confident that she deserved their accolades.

"Whoa! Don't hurt nothing!" Kush yelled. "My baby sista is fine yall," he added getting reassuring confirmation from the group.

"Okay, who's the designated driver tonight?" Jewels asked.

"That would be me," Blaze said. "And if by some chance I do have a few drinks I promise to just stay in Atlantic City or call for a car."

Blaze hugged her mother and told her not to worry and then she and Z took off for Atlantic City ready to do some serious partying with the music blasting all the way.

Meanwhile, Jack was also meeting friends at the Ocean Club a favorite hangout in Atlantic City. These were the guys from Jack's fraternity that had become lifelong friends since college. They met several times a year to do a weekend either in Las Vegas or Atlantic City where they gambled, picked up women, and got wasted. They claimed that whatever happened on those weekends would remain exactly where it happened. There were to be no discussions of the events once the trip was over. Jack usually ended up being the one who took care of everyone else. He rarely left with anyone but preferred to be sociable with caution. It wasn't that he didn't like women; on the contrary, he liked them very much. He just wasn't willing to deal with the possible consequences of a one-night stand. He was looking forward to unwinding and enjoying himself. As per his usual, he decided to call the hotel and have them reserve a room for him in case he couldn't make it back to the summer house. He arrived in Atlantic City at eight-thirty. He was meeting Manny to gamble before they went to the club. The rest of the crew would join them there. They decided to go to the casino to shoot some craps and play Roulette. Manny was shooting craps while Jack observed his friend's winning streak. After they played Roulette, a couple of girls came over and introduced themselves. Jack brought them a drink and invited them to join them at the club later. The girls told them they were staying at the casino hotel, and that maybe they could come up to see them later. Manny liked the idea, but Jack decided to play it cool not offering any promises.

"Man, what's wrong with you? Those honeys ain't fine enough for ya?" Manny asked jokingly.

"They're alright," Jack smirked. "You know me, Manny. I like to be selective."

Manny patted his friend on the back and smiled, "Come on boy let's go have some fun."

They arrived at the club around ten-thirty with most of the crew already there. They had their usual spot in VIP, and the champagne and women were flowing, in that order. Jack knew the DJ, so he went up into the booth to say hello. From the booth, it was easy to get a view of the whole club since it was packed. It was the height of the summer season and everyone who was anyone was there. Jack was talking and having a blast when he noticed the group of people who occupied the other VIP section. It didn't take him long to recognize the body of the woman in the blue dress. Jack couldn't believe his eyes when he saw her standing there. He stood there motionless just watching her. He studied the way that she moved or threw her head back when something was funny. He took advantage of his position as if he was observing some beautiful wild creature in her natural habitat. He smiled as she shook her head to the music closing her eyes and singing along. He decided to take his time and continue to observe her to see if she was on a date. She danced with her friends and seemed to be having a really good time. It didn't appear that she was with anyone. Jack grew tired of his voyeurism and wanted a spot front and center, so he finally descended the steps of the DJ booth and went back to where his friends were.

"Manny, you got a pen?" Jack asked.

"Yeah, I got one. You finally gonna give some honey your number?" Manny asked playfully.

"Something like that," Jack replied.

Jack wrote something down on a napkin, folded it up, and beckoned to one of the waitresses. He told her to give the note to the woman in the blue dress in VIP. He then stood back and watched as Blaze accepted the note. She took the napkin from the waitress and unfolded it to read what it said. She instantly started to smile and then continued to read the note. She looked around the club and then towards VIP where she saw Jack standing. Just then the waitress brought over a very expensive bottle of champagne and showed it to Blaze. She looked over and Jack raised his glass to her smiling. She leaned over to whisper in Z's ear and then proceeded to exit the VIP section. She walked directly over to where Jack and his friends were seated. Jack walked down to meet her, and they stood in front of VIP looking at one another. Jack took her hands into his and leaned down to kiss her. Blaze smiled and kissed him back.

"What are you doing here?" she asked with a wide smile.

"I guess the same as you, hanging out with my boys."

Manny interrupted and came over to kiss Blaze and welcome her.

"You look amazing!" Manny held her hand and twirled her around.

"Alright man, that's enough," Jack laughed.

"It's good to see you too, Manny!"

"You staying down here this weekend?" Manny asked.

"Yeah, I'm vacationing with my family. We have a house in Cape May.",

"Must be nice," Manny replied giving Jack the eye.

"I guess our moms have something in common., Jack said. "My family is down here for the rest of the month as well," Jack added.

"Wow, this is deep." Blaze smiled.

"Come on. Have a seat," Jack said while leading Blaze into VIP. Jack was smiling and leaned in to whisper in Blaze's ear.

"You look amazingly sexy," he said slightly buzzed from his drink. Blaze blushed at his remark.

"How long are you gonna be down here?" Jack asked.

"Probably for a few weeks at least. You should come by the house tomorrow. Jewels is throwing a summer bash at the house. Bring Manny and your friends it should be really fun," Blaze added.

"Definitely!" Jack was still smiling. "I can't believe you're here."

"Me either...I mean, that you're here too."

"What you drinkin', Blaze?" Manny asked.

"Oh, I'm not drinking I'm the designated driver for the night."

"Don't worry about it. You can stay with one of us if you can't make it back, right Jack?"

Jack looked at Manny and replied, "If she stays with anyone, it's gonna be me."

Manny and the guys laughed as Blaze blushed yet again.

"You know I'll drive you back if you can't drive yourself," Jack said in a serious tone.

"I don't think you're in any condition to drive anywhere. I think I'll just chill for right now."

"So, when'd you get in town?" Jack wanted to know every detail and Blaze didn't mind sharing.

"We got here about eight-thirty, went to the casino, and then came here."

"Did you gamble?" Jack asked.

"Of course!" Blaze smiled.

Manny grabbed Blaze's arm, "Come on darling. Let's dance!"

Manny took Blaze onto the dance floor, and they danced for at least three songs. When they got back Blaze excused herself and went to the lady's room.

"Man, she is one beautiful girl," Manny said to Jack.

"Yes, she is," Jack said watching her as she disappeared into the crowd.

"You better claim that or somebody else damn sure will be trying to hit on that."

"You don't claim a woman like Blaze," Jack stated matter-of-factly. "She deserves to be wined, dined, and treated like royalty."

"Well then, I suggest you get to it 'cause here comes that beautiful creature now. Damn!"

Jack intercepted Blaze and took her hand to dance with her to a slow song. She placed her hand on his chest as he wrapped her in his arms.

"So, how have you been?" he asked.

"Fine!" she said before she realized.

"I know that you're fine, I want to know how you've been?" Jack teased.

"I've been good."

"Now that's what I wanted to hear. You've been busy!" Jack stated.

"Of course, gotta make sure my clients are happy," Blaze responded slyly.

"You've done an awesome job on the account. We're all quite pleased with the final product."

Jack was trying to make small talk. Blaze was smiling looking at Jack while he tried desperately not to seem overzealous. He could hardly keep his composure with her so near to him. Her body was warm and inviting and she smelled so tantalizing to him. Blaze knew the effect that she had on him, and she enjoyed tormenting him. She moved her body as close to him as possible lightly brushing against his strong lean frame. She awoke his passion and he wanted to kiss her as they danced but he kept his cool.

"So, Jack, how have you been?" Blaze asked seductively.

"I've been good. Trying to keep busy."

"Did you miss me?" she asked playfully.

"What kind of question is that?" he asked.

"It's a genuine one that requires an answer." She continued with her ploy.

"I don't know. It seems like a loaded question to me."

Blaze threw her head back letting out a little giggle.

"Why Jack, I'm being sincere here, just look at me," she pouted and gestured toward her face.

"Baby, you don't have to convince me to look at you. You're too hot for words. But that ain't all I want to do is look at you."

Jack held her at arm's length gazing at her from head to toe. Blaze smiled her most alluring smile.

"What do you say we get outta here for a bit?" Jack asked.

"Where do you want to go?" Blaze asked still teasing him.

"Baby, I'd go anywhere you want." Jack looked into her eyes.

Blaze was done. She couldn't play the game any longer, not with him looking at her in that way. She relinquished control and responded in kind.

"Okay, just let me tell Z since we came together."

Blaze walked to the VIP section where her friends were partying.

"Z, I'll be back in a few. I'm gonna take a ride with Jack," she said smiling.

"Aw, sooky sooky now," Z was excited for Blaze. "Don't worry bout ya boy. You know how we do. I'll stay with Isaac or Lisa, but you'd better call Jewels if you plan to stay in town." Z said.

"Yeah, your right! I don't want her to come looking for me," she laughed. You do the same if you do decide to stay," Blaze returned the command. "Keep your cell phone on so we can connect later," she added.

"Okay, babe...talk to ya later."

Blaze joined Jack who was telling Manny he was taking off.

"You ready?" she asked.

"Yep, let's go," he said.

Jack shook hands with the guys and then led Blaze out of the club. The club was open until 4:00 am so there were lines of people still waiting to get in when Jack and Blaze were leaving. Blaze was glad to get out of there and be with Jack. As she passed the women in line, she could see the envy on some of their faces as Jack held her hand and they made their way down the street together.

"Where would you like to go?" Jack asked.

"I don't know. What'd you have in mind?"

"Well, why don't we go over to the casino? They have a decent cocktail lounge where we can relax and talk."

"Sounds perfect."

Blaze could not stop smiling. When they arrived, Jack gave the waitress a tip and asked her to find them a cozy table. They were seated in a booth in the corner where they had a good view of the stage but far enough away to have their privacy. The casino lounge featured an R&B band with a female singer who was unquestionably talented. They sat on opposite sides of the booth facing one another not knowing what to say or how to break the ice. Jack was the first to speak.

"Pretty good band! They sound good."

Blaze nodded her head in agreement since she was nervous and excited at the same time. She didn't want to seem too eager, but she longed for Jack to kiss her.

"So, who's minding the shop if both you and Z are here on vacation?"

"Well, our team is very capable of handling the final phases of your account, and of course, Sam is there too leading the troops," Blaze confirmed. "What about you? Who's holding down Newman while you're partying with your boys?" she asked playfully.

"They can manage for a week without me. My family is at the summer house in Stone Harbor, so I came down for a few days to unwind, get some golf in and take the boat out."

"Sounds like you pretty much have an itinerary."

"Seems that way doesn't it, but something is missing from my plans."

"Really? And what's that?" Blaze asked relaxing back into the booth.

"I don't have anyone to share my time with while I'm here—no one to make plans with or play with." Jack pretended to be sad.

They looked at one another and both burst into laughter.

"You know you're full of it right?" Blaze asked.

Jack smiled that deep dimpled smile and shrugged his shoulders as if innocent.

"Did I tell you that you look beautiful tonight?" Jack asked.

"Yes, but I never get tired of hearing you say it."

The band delivered their rendition of a slow jam 'Let Me Make Love to You,' which inspired Jack to take Blaze's hand and lead her to the dance floor. Jack wrapped Blaze into his arms as he sang the words to the song. Blaze smiled as she closed her eyes being so near to him. They were both feeling the mood and the music added to their euphoria. Blaze loved the way Jack smelled and she felt so good being close to him. He caressed her back as his hand traveled to her butt. He rubbed his hands along her buttocks which sent shivers through her entire body. She tried to play it cool, but she was so aroused by him; she loved to be touched by him. Jack could sense the response to his touch as his voice resonated in her ear.

"Stay with me tonight!" Jack suggested.

Blaze closed her eyes as the warmth of his breath made her dizzy with delight. She hesitated for only a moment before she spoke.

"Why'd you wait so long to ask me? Of course, I will," she whispered. It didn't take Jack long before he led Blaze away from the dance floor. Jack took her hand before going into his pocket to leave three twenties on the table as they made their way out of the lounge. They didn't speak another word to one another as they walked through the casino reminiscent of their first night together. Blaze leaned upon Jack as they waited for the elevator never letting go of his hand. She closed her eyes burying her face in his shoulder. The ride to the suite felt endless, as the elevator stopped on almost every floor packed with guests. Blaze and Jack stood motionless in the back as they approached Jack's floor. When they got off the elevator this time, Blaze took the lead remembering where Jack's suite was located. Her heart was racing, and her breathing was rapid as she pulled him down the corridor. Jack fumbled through his jacket and retrieved the room key opening the door to his suite. Once inside he leaned upon the door as he closed it watching Blaze move across the floor. Blaze pulled her dress over her head as she boldly stood in front of him half naked in her stilettos and sheer black panties that barely covered her cheeks. Jack stood there as Blaze walked towards him and wrapped her arms around his neck kissing him with deep unadulterated passion. She was relentless as she pressed her body against his in a rhythmic motion as she craved his body like never before. She removed his jacket and opened his shirt revealing his smooth broad chest. She licked and kissed his nipples and ran her hands along his rippled stomach. She continued her exploration as her hands traveled to open his pants where she unbuckled his belt and loosened his pants. Her hands traveled into his pants where she freely fondled his erection with skill. She delighted in what was waiting inside for her.

"Oh, Jack! I've missed you so much!"

She let go of his pants gazing upon what he had to offer her. As he stood naked before her his pants around his ankles, she continued to relish in his masculinity.

"You are magnificent," she said kneeling before him.

She took him into her mouth giving him so much pleasure that he could not contain himself. He called out her name pulling her up from her knees and turning her around so that her back was against his groan. He pulled at her panties until they fell to her ankles, and she kicked them away. He lifted her body to gain position as he entered her from behind eliciting cries of pleasure from her. Jack held her waist as his stroke gained intensity and Blaze met his rhythm with equal ardor. Their primal lust engulfed them as they broke long enough to make their way to the chair. Blaze pushed Jack down into the chair straddling his lap. She mounted him taking his penis and guiding it to her place of pleasure. She grabbed the back of the chair to gain position as she took total control of her stroke. She rode him with precise movements as he allowed her to have her way. Blaze was relentless as her stroke became ever more demanding and he met her thrashing which drove her to complete rapture. She pressed her breast against his lips as he took them one then the other into his waiting and warm mouth, his lips, and tongue excited in their play.

"Oh Jack, Jack." She was not able to complete her thoughts. She gained momentum and drove harder. When she reached her climax for the third time Jack could no longer control his desire as he let go and enjoyed the raw ecstasy exploding deeply within her relinquishing his passion and his control.

Blaze was drenched with perspiration as her hair fell wildly about her shoulders and into her face. She lay upon Jack with her breast pressed against his face. He picked her up with her long legs wrapped around his waist and carried her into the bedroom placing her on the bed. Jack lay down beside her equally as spent and drenched with sweat.

"Wow!" Jack let out after some time.

"What is it?" Blaze asked turning to look at him.

"Who was that?" he asked half smiling catching his breath.

"Who was who?" Blaze asked.

"That woman that came in here with me," he replied.

"What are you talking about?" Blaze asked laughing.

"I feel like I was taken advantage of," Jack joked.

"I'm sure I don't know what you mean," Blaze replied indignantly.

"Oh really...you don't know what I mean?"

Jack turned to Blaze with a serious expression. "Blaze Beaumont, you a little whoa!"

"What did you say?" Blaze asked before jumping on Jack and tussling with him. Jack flipped her over to the other side of the bed as they engaged in an old-fashioned pillow fight throwing pillows and play fighting under the covers. Blaze tagged Jack and ran into the shower turning on the water.

"You stink, Jack Newman! Better get your butt in here and wash," she yelled from the shower. Jack soon joined her continuing their play as they washed each other's backs and lathered one another clean. Once they were finished, they returned to the bedroom remaking the bed before they collapsed back into it. Blaze sat up on the edge of the bed drying her hair with a towel as Jack watched her. His eyes were full of desire for her although he hesitated to admit that he was hooked.

"Come here!" he said to her.

"No way. I know your moves, Jack Newman."

"No, seriously. I'm not gonna do nothing," he said. "Come here!" he said again, this time sternly.

Blaze crawled over to Jack on all fours.

"Okay I'm here...now what do you want?" she asked playfully.

Jack took her face into his hands and kissed her sweetly. Blaze threw her arms around his neck, and they lay back on the bed in an embrace.

"Do you know how angry I've been with you?" Jack asked.

Blaze didn't answer but continued to lie in Jack's arms.

"You're something else, Blaze Beaumont! What do you think I should do with you?" he asked stroking her back."

"Love me," Blaze blurted out before she thought about it.

"Just like that huh? You want me to just love you after the stunt you pulled."

"Are you sorry that we're together now?" Blaze asked sincerely.

"Naw, I'm glad we ran into each other. This was the best surprise I've had in a long time." Jack embraced her.

"Then just for tonight can we pretend that we just met and there is no past or unhappiness, just two lovers enjoying their time together?" Blaze asked.

"Sure, why not. I think that would be a good thing," Jack replied in a low tone.

"Good, then it's settled!"

Blaze sat up and extended her hand to Jack, "Hi...I'm Blaze Beaumont."

Jack looked at her smiling before he extended his hand to her.

"Jack Newman."

"Pleased to meet you, Mr. Newman. Come here often?" she asked.

"As a matter of fact, I do. What about you, Ms. Beaumont? You come here often?"

"No this is only my second time being here. The last time I was with a very handsome and sexy stranger who kept me in bed for three days," she said smiling.

"Smart man. I envy him. Any chance you might want to stay with me for a few days?" he asked playfully.

"I don't know. He's a hard act to follow. Think you can keep up?" she asked.

"Only one way to find out," Jack said before pulling Blaze down upon him and kissing her neck and shoulders.

"Mmm...that's nice! I say you're off to a good start," she teased as she nuzzled up to him before they made love again.

| 47 |

Prepping for the party

Jewels' party was an annual event that she hosted for a small group of family and friends. Although a few of her friends did attend, most of the guests were friends of her children. She had the party catered by a local company. The theme was casually chic since she liked making everyone feel at home. Jewels was putting some last-minute touches on the decorations on the deck as Blaze arrived home. With hands on her hips and a knowing look in her eyes, Jewels began questioning her daughter.

"Well did you have a good time?"

"Yeah, I really did." Blaze had happiness written all over her face.

"I invited some friends to the party, mom. I hope you don't mind."

"Of course, not! The more, the merrier. Anyone I know?" she asked.

"A guy named Manny and a few of his friends, and Jack," she said quickly.

Jewels stopped what she was doing and looked up at Blaze for the first time.

"Jack Newman?" she asked.

"Yes...Jack Newman, mom."

Jewels put her hands up in the air.

"Okay... none of my business. As long as you're fine with it, then so am I."

"By the way, where did you stay last night?" Jewels asked.

"Mom, I'm a big girl now. Just know that I was with friends."

"That says it all." Jewels turned to go back into the kitchen from the deck.

Blaze knew that her mother had reservations about Jack, but she wasn't going to let anything spoil this evening.

"Mom, did Z get back yet?"

"No, but he called and said he's on the way."

"Okay. I'm gonna change so I can help you," Blaze added.

"No need honey," Jewels replied. "Everything's under control! You just go and relax, take a walk on the beach, or sit by the pool. You're on vacation, remember?"

Z walked in just as Blaze was on her way to her room.

"Hey girl! How was your night?"

"Good!" Blaze replied.

Z burst into laughter, "Girl, is that a hickey on your neck? What are we seventeen again?"

"Boy, you better shush. Is there really a hickey there?" Blaze asked rushing to the mirror.

"Naw just putting you on," Z laughed hysterically.

"How's Mr. Newman?"

"Mr. Newman is just fine! But you can see for yourself. He'll be here later."

"Aw shucks now. You must've laid something on the brotha," Z teased.

"I don't know about that, but he sure laid something on me," Blaze whispered.

"This should be really interesting. By the way, Parks called said he was in the area, and asked if he could come by," Z said.

"Really? I wasn't expecting him to show up."

"Yeah, I thought he was gonna stay in the city this weekend."

"He mentioned that he had plans. Guess his plans changed. Well, whatever. All I know is I'm planning to have a good time tonight. Look, we have a couple of hours before the guests start to arrive, so I'm going to shower and take a nap," Blaze added.

"Yeah, I guess you probably do need one by now," Z said as they both laughed at his insinuation.

"See ya in a bit." Blaze headed for her bedroom.

Jewels' party was an annual event that she hosted for a small group of family and friends. Although a few of her friends did attend, most of the guests were friends of her children. She had the party catered by a local company. The theme was casually chic since she liked making everyone feel at home. Jewels was putting some last-minute touches on the decorations on the deck as Blaze arrived home. With hands on her hips and a knowing look in her eyes, Jewels began questioning her daughter.

"Well did you have a good time?"

"Yeah, I really did." Blaze had happiness written all over her face. "I invited some friends to the party, mom. I hope you don't mind."

"Of course, not! The more, the merrier. Anyone I know?" she asked.

"A guy named Manny and a few of his friends, and Jack," she said quickly.

Jewels stopped what she was doing and looked up at Blaze for the first time.

"Jack Newman?" she asked.

"Yes...Jack Newman, mom."

Jewels put her hands up in the air.

"Okay… none of my business. As long as you're fine with it, then so am I."

"By the way, where did you stay last night?" Jewels asked.

"Mom, I'm a big girl now. Just know that I was with friends."

"That says it all." Jewels turned to go back into the kitchen from the deck.

Blaze knew that her mother had reservations about Jack, but she wasn't going to let anything spoil this evening.

"Mom, did Z get back yet?"

"No, but he called and said he's on the way."

"Okay. I'm gonna change so I can help you," Blaze added.

"No need honey," Jewels replied. "Everything's under control! You just go and relax, take a walk on the beach, or sit by the pool. You're on vacation, remember?"

Z walked in just as Blaze was on her way to her room.

"Hey, girl! How was your night?"

"Good!" Blaze replied.

Z burst into laughter, "Girl, is that a hickey on your neck? What are we seventeen again?"

"Boy, you better shush. Is there really a hickey there?" Blaze asked rushing to the mirror.

"Naw just putting you on," Z laughed hysterically.

"How's Mr. Newman?"

"Mr. Newman is just fine! But you can see for yourself. He'll be here later."

"Aw shucks now. You must've laid something on the brotha," Z teased.

"I don't know about that, but he sure laid something on me," Blaze whispered.

"This should be really interesting. By the way, Parks called said he was in the area, and asked if he could come by," Z said.

"Really? I wasn't expecting him to show up."

"Yeah, I thought he was gonna stay in the city this weekend."

"He mentioned that he had plans. Guess his plans changed. Well, whatever. All I know is I'm planning to have a good time tonight. Look, we have a couple of hours before the guests start to arrive, so I'm going to shower and take a nap," Blaze added.

"Yeah, I guess you probably do need one by now," Z said as they both laughed at his insinuation.

"See ya in a bit."

Blaze headed for her bedroom.

| 48 |

Uncle Jack

Kate spent the morning lounging in bed as she and Thaddeus decided that they would spend the afternoon playing golf at the nearby country club. Kate was happy that her husband and son could join the family for the weekend and so she planned a family cookout for the evening. She had Bert prepare all the family favorites with the help of a local caterer. Kate wasn't surprised that Jack didn't come back home since he always reserved a room at the casino when down the shore. As usual, the children were up and just about to head to the beach by the time she came down to brunch. She entered the kitchen all dressed for a round of golf with her husband. Thaddeus was in the shower, so she plated some fresh berries, yogurt, and a bran muffin for him. She knew he would complain that there were no eggs, bacon, or biscuits for him to eat. She read the paper as she sipped her black coffee while Bert worked around her complaining about the kitchen being a one-stop shop for everybody there.

"I swear y'all must think all I have to do is wait around for each one of ya to decide when ya want ta eat. Seems like no one gets up at the same time down here," Bert complained.

Seconds later, Jack arrived home to be greeted by excited squeals from his nephews and niece as they ran to him begging him to go hunting for treasure with them on the beach. Jack walked into the kitchen with both boys in his arms and Lacy hanging onto the back of his shirt. He tickled them as he entered the kitchen while they both begged him to stop with giggles and screams of laughter.

"Well, this is nice to see," Kate commented. "Uncle Jack, go treasure hunting with them." Kate mocked the children's request.

"Can't do it today guys, maybe tomorrow." He flipped them in the air.

"Oh, Jack stop it. You're gonna make them sick," Kate chided.

Jack let the boys down and they dashed out of the back door and out to the beach with Lacy following to join the rest of the family. Jack gave Bert a big kiss and a hug.

"How's my favorite girl?" he asked teasingly.

"I'm just fine if people would get outta my kitchen for a while," she answered annoyedly.

Jack shrugged his shoulders smiling at Kate who was also smiling.

"I didn't expect to see you today," Kate said as she accepted Jack's kiss on the cheek.

"I thought I'd hang out with the family for a while, maybe get a few laps in the pool."

"How was your evening?"

"It was good," Jack answered.

"So, what's on your agenda for this evening?" Kate asked.

"I have a cookout to attend!"

"Really? On the island?"

"No, it's in Cape May!"

"Cape May! Who do you know that lives over there?" Kate was surprised.

Jack hesitated before speaking, "Blaze's family owns property there and her mother is throwing a party."

Kate was silent for a moment thinking it was best not to speak too quickly on the subject.

So as not to arouse any unpleasantness between them, Kate took a positive approach to the news.

"Well, that sounds like fun! I didn't know Ms. Beaumont's family had a house in the area. I thought I knew everyone who had property on the islands."

"Well mother, just goes to show you that even you can be surprised every once in a while. I'm gonna hang out with the boys on the beach. Where's Pop?" Jack asked all in one breath.

"He's upstairs getting ready to play a round of golf with me."

"Okay, I'll go up and see him before you guys head out."

Jack ran up the steps two at a time just like he did when he was younger even though he knew it drove his mother crazy. He went into his parent's bedroom and greeted his father.

"Hey, Pop!"

"Jack! What you up to?"

"Just came home to hang out with the kids. They want to go treasure hunting on the beach."

Thaddeus laughed as he began to share a few stories about the boy's antics with Jack. Jack hung out with his dad while he continued to dress for the afternoon. They briefly discussed some business before going down to meet Kate in the kitchen. She was giving Bert some instructions about Sunday brunch and the family cookout she was planning for Sunday afternoon. They were finalizing the shopping list for the local grocer. Thaddeus finished his brunch before heading out with Kate to the club. As promised, Jack spent several hours with his niece and nephews until their nanny

Maria called them in for their bath. Jack retreated to his bedroom for a shower and to relax before he readied himself for the party at Jewels' house. He was looking forward to seeing Blaze again, more than he ever thought could be possible. He realized that it would take some doing to get his mother to agree, but he would get her to see it his way in time. For now, he was going to enjoy the evening and his woman.

| 49 |

Love on the Beach

Parks's decision to attend the Beaumont party was strictly for selfish reasons. He had no love for Blaze or her family but knew that if his plan was going to work, he would have to play nice. Showing up at the event was painless. Putting his plan into action would prove to be profitable. Sam and his family would be in attendance so the timing would be perfect to execute some mischief and mayhem. He wasn't worried about Z either, though he knew that Z was Blaze's greatest ally. He packed a leather satchel full of designer pants, shirts, and shoes. Then, he headed for the shore. He booked a room at the Park Place Casino Hotel and planned to drive to the party after he checked in. He made sure that the package containing some important documents was packed securely in his briefcase so that they would be handy once the timing was right. With any luck, he would be able to kill two birds with one stone. As he entered the Atlantic City Expressway a wicked smile like a Cheshire cat emanated across his narrow, chocolate face. He felt confident that everything was finally going to go his way.

It was seven o'clock and Jewels' party was well underway. The guests were beginning to arrive as the evening sun began to set in the southern New Jersey sky. It was a beautiful evening with just enough breezes from the ocean to cool off the hot weather of the day. A huge tent was set up which housed tables for the guest, a bar, a stage for the DJ, and a large dance floor so everyone could party. Music echoed through the house and out to the backyard where most of the guests were gathered under the tent as they nibbled on hors d'oeuvres. The bar was open, and the atmosphere was festive.

Jewels entered the party looking stunning in a long tan and black linen tunic and white linen pants that she accessorized with wooden beads around her long neck and bangles that cascaded up and down her lean arm. Tan leather sandals complimented her casual but elegant style and completed her attire as she greeted her guest with hugs and genuine words of welcome. Sydney donned a saffron maxi halter dress which accentuated her long sandy-brown locs casting a ray of sunshine upon everyone while Peyton decided on a turquoise mini that clung to every curve of her bronze naturally thin body. She wore her hair cut in a short pixie style that complimented her almond-shaped brown eyes and sultry full lips. Jewels' children were attractive, taking after her late husband who was said to be 'as fine as he could be.' But the most beautiful of them all and the one who looked most like her mother was Blaze. She had the same keen features as Jewels, but her complexion was a deeper hue than the caramel color of her mother's skin tone. She joined the party a little after eight wearing an aqua mini dress and high-heeled jeweled sandals, which were tied around her ankle accentuating her long lean legs. The sleeves of the dress were slightly flared giving it a 1960's appeal and the jeweled embellished neckline showed just enough of her cleavage to be sexy and alluring. She gained quite a bit of attention when she entered the party receiving looks of appreciation from many of the young men in attendance. She wore her hair piled high atop her head with whispers of curls that lay ominously along her neck and framed her face. She had that certain something that was breathtaking and inviting all at the same time. Within a matter of minutes, she was cruising the party welcoming guests and catching up with relatives and friends she hadn't seen in a while.

Blaze and Z caught up with Kush who was holding court amidst a group of his friends as he listened to one of his boys defend his recent one-night stand. Kush was handsome. There was no doubt about that. He was tall, naturally lean, and muscular. His skin was the color of warmed milk chocolate, and his hair was cut close trading his natural curls for waves. His brown eyes twinkled when he smiled which he did quite often and his broad nose much like Blaze's made him nonetheless attractive. Kush sported a pair of jeans, which was typical of his style that hung low on his waist, and a white shirt that was only buttoned once above his rippled stomach. His signature medallion, one he wore all the time, hung around his neck laying splendidly upon his chest. He stood tall with his hands in his pockets as he presented an opposing view, which kept the group debating the pros and cons of casual sex. A few of the young women admired his position as he espoused the benefits of a monogamous relationship knowing they were listening. He winked at one girl who had been invited by Kush after he met her in town while on an errand. He told her to come and bring a few of her girlfriends, which she so willingly obliged. Blaze joined her brother who was eager to get her to discuss the present topic of conversation.

"Okay, okay. Let's get another opinion here. Blaze what do you say about all of this?" he asked placing his arm around his sister's shoulder.

"Look at my sister, Kush said with admiration. She's beautiful, so what better opinion could we seek in such matters?" he teased.

Before Blaze could answer, Jewels with the microphone in hand, asked for everyone's attention as she announced that the dance floor was now open signaling the DJ to begin spinning the sounds getting everyone up and out of their seats. By eight-thirty the party was officially underway.

When Jack arrived, Blaze was engaged in a lively conversation with Z, her sisters, her brother, and his friends. With the exception of Z, they had all practically grown up together and so each was very familiar with one another. They were laughing and talking about old times and marveling at how much Blaze and her sisters had grown from the pesky little brats that they use to be, to the beautiful and vivacious women standing before them. Jack smiled to himself as he watched Blaze work the group. He leaned upon the door admiring the woman he had recently taken to his bed. He felt privileged at what he knew about her that others didn't, how she purred in bed when she was satisfied, and when she was aroused and took control of their lovemaking. It didn't bother him that she was a flirt. He sort of enjoyed the way she manipulated her way through a conversation. When Blaze finally noticed that Jack was there watching her, she excused herself amidst protest from the group but promised to return. She sauntered over to Jack and on tiptoe, she pressed her hand against his chest and kissed him upon his lips.

"How long have you been here?" she asked trying to talk above the music and smiling at him.

"A few minutes," he replied loudly.

"Why didn't you come over and let me introduce you to everyone?" Blaze asked.

"I much rather enjoy watching you work your magic," Jack answered.

"My magic?" she asked leaning into him and laughing.

"Yes, your magic," Jack said as he pulled her to him and kissed her again.

"Wow, you smell so good." Blaze nuzzled into his neck.

Jack caressed her lower back traveling down to her generous bottom.

"You look fantastic in that dress, or should I say shirt?" he whispered in her ear.

Blaze leaned away from him a scowl on her face.

"This is a dress and a very expensive one at that," Blaze replied.

"Oh no doubt—no doubt." Jack twirled her around noting his approval.

Jewels noticed the two lovers as they were engaged in conversation with one another. She watched Jack with Blaze to get a better idea of the man who had stolen her daughter's heart. She noticed his attentiveness to her and the way he looked into her eyes, the smile that made the corners of his eyes twinkle when he laughed at something she said, and the way he touched her as if she was some priceless artwork that need to be handled very carefully. After a few minutes of observation, she walked toward the two of them.

"Jack, welcome to our home," she said sincerely while extending her hand to him.

Jack reached over and gallantly placed a kiss on Jewels' hand.

"Thank you for having me." He smiled.

"There's plenty to eat and drink. I want you to enjoy yourself and meet the rest of the family too," Jewels added.

"You look stunning by the way," Jack added, complimenting Jewels. "I see where Blaze gets her good looks."

"People often say she looks like me but if you knew Malcolm you wouldn't say that. I think all of my children take after their father and Kush is the spitting image of him," Jewels replied proudly.

"I'm anxious to meet him," Jack said.

Jewels placed her arm into Jack's arm smiling. "Well, come with me. Let me introduce you to everyone."

Jewels turned to look at Blaze with a nod of approval as she walked ahead with Jack in tow to introduce him all around the party. Blaze followed closely behind but with enough space to give Jewels her props. She smiled and was thrilled that Jewels liked Jack. She wanted them to be fast friends and she felt very comfortable with him there as if he had been in their lives forever. Jewels introduced Jack to Kush who heartily shook his hand welcoming him to their home. Jack was so handsome with his All-American good looks and winning ways. He was charming, funny, and very personable. The contrast of his sun-warmed skin against his white shirt was extremely sexy. His sleeves were casually rolled up as his shirt hung loosely over the pants that fit his waist perfectly falling loosely through his toned butt and long legs. Jack was 6-foot 3-inches tall and had a rather large foot, so all his shoes were made by an Italian shoe manufacturer who kept him in the most stylish footwear.

"Man, the footwear is slammin'. You gotta hip me to the manufacturer so I can cop me some of them jawns," Kush stated.

Jack nodded in approval. He could easily model for any magazine with his dimpled smile and air of confidence. As Jewels showed him around the grounds, he endured her introductions and the alluring eyes of some of the female guests. Blaze could see he was growing weary of the attention, so she stepped in and rescued him.

"Okay mom," she said possessively, "Do you think I can have my guest back for a moment or two?" Blaze asked jovially.

"Oh, of course, but you two better not disappear on us. We have much to talk about," Jewels added before walking away.

"Come on. Want to escape for a few minutes?" she whispered in his ear.

"What took you so long?" he asked taking her hand as she led the way out to the beach.

Parks arrived at Jewels' party a little after nine o'clock. He brought Jewels an expensive bottle of wine to thank her for the invitation. He was a good-looking man who thought he could charm the panties off of just about any female. Jewels could see right through his slick demeanor but accepted his gift graciously. She remembered meeting Parks at the Newman barbecue and decided that there was indeed something about him that made her uneasy. Parks entered the party attracting the attention of several of Peyton and Sydney's female guests. He wore his beige Italian-made slacks and tan knit shirt with confidence and ease. He liked the way he looked and was told more times than not that he was good-looking. The contrast between his dark skin and the fine-gaged fabric made his appeal even more alluring, but only to some. There was no doubt that he was attractive and stylish in his own way and that he often used those attributes to his advantage.

"You have a lovely home, Mrs. Beaumont."

"Thank you, Parker, and please call me Jewels. Everyone does."

"Then Jewels it is," Parks said smiling as he took Jewels' arm.

"Where's Blaze?" he asked.

"She'll be back in a bit," Jewels replied.

Just then, Z approached Parks and Jewels as they were conversing.

"So, man I see you made it." Z gave Parks a handshake.

"Yeah! I just got into town a few hours ago. I'm staying in A.C. at Park Place."

"Cool! Want a drink?" Z asked.

"Yeah, man. That'd be great!" Parks replied.

"What about you, Mrs. B?" Z asked Jewels.

"No, thanks, Z. I'm fine for the moment," Jewels added.

"Well then, I'll show you where the bar is," Z said leading the way for Parks.

"Talk with you later," Parks said to Jewels as he followed Z to the bar.

After exchanging pleasantries, Parks gave Z an update on the office activities and news regarding the campaigns. He assured Z that everything was running according to plan and that all was under control. The two men joined the rest of the party enjoying the food and company of several young ladies.

Blaze and Jack walked down to the beach not far from the house to an area where she had a couple of chairs set up and a few bottles of beer on ice. She carried her shoes in her hand to walk barefoot in the sand. Two large lanterns illuminated the area as they sat down together. They were close enough to the house to see the lights that traveled along the deck and backyard which presented a festive backdrop to their intimate setting. Stars twinkled in the clear sky providing an even more romantic mood for the couple. The breeze from the ocean was pleasant and calm as the waves met the shore only to retreat again with a promise to return.

"This is really nice, Blaze." Jack took her hand into his own.

"Come here!" he said before he picked her up into his arms to kiss her.

"I thought you might like to get away for a moment or two. This is one of my favorite places to just sit and dream or sort out things when they become too complicated for me," she revealed.

"I like that you brought me to your private place. Reminds me of other private places that you let me into," he said.

Blaze sat on Jack's lap sipping her beer and looking out at the waves.

"How was your day?" she asked.

"Good! I spent the better part of it with my nephews who have so much energy. It's amazing.

"Sounds like fun, Uncle Jack," Blaze teased.

"Your mother is beautiful! I appreciated her receiving me with such kindness. I know it couldn't have been easy seeing me with you so soon after your breakup with Clay."

"She doesn't fault you for that. I explained to her that I didn't feel the same as Clay did. I wasn't ready for marriage, and he wanted that more than anything."

"Wow, and here I thought it was because you fell in love with me," Jack laughed.

"You're not the least bit conceited, are you?" Blaze asked sarcastically.

"No, not the least bit."

Blaze got up from Jack's lap and held her hand out to him, "come on we better get back before they send out the troops for us."

Jack pulled her back upon his lap, "not until you kiss me like you mean it."

Blaze kissed him deeply and passionately.

"How's that for a kiss?" she asked.

"Kiss me like that again and we'll never make it back to the party."

Jack ran his hands along Blaze's legs, leaned down, and kissed her thigh as she sat on his lap. Shrills of delight ran through her body from his touch. He ignited a flame within her like never before with any other man. She wanted him right there on the beach. If it hadn't been that they were so close to the house, she would've given in to her desire. She pulled her dress up around her waist as Jack nuzzled her thighs and then her belly, kissing and licking her body. He ran his hands inside the tender area of her thighs eliciting moans of enjoyment from her as she sat on his lap with her back pressed against him.

"I love the way you smell," he said his hand traveling the length of her neck pulling her face towards him kissing her deeply thrusting his tongue inside of her mouth. They were both aroused beyond measure as they kissed and played with one another as only lovers do. Finally, Blaze broke away from Jack and stood up to put some distance between them. Her breathing was rapid, and her dress still hiked up around her waist.

"Aw come on baby. Don't do that. You can't leave me like this." Jack pointed to his manhood to show her his erection. Blaze obliged him and kneeled before him in the sand servicing him right there on the beach. She was more skilled than she knew as he reached a climax of sheer proportions. After his release, Blaze laid her head upon his lap as he stroked her hair and caressed her back.

"That was totally unexpected," Jack whispered in a hoarse voice.

"I'm as surprised as you are," she replied.

Jack relaxed in his chair taking in the sky which was full of stars.

"This is one of those nights for the memory banks!" Jack stated. "What more could a man ask for? Soft music flowing in the background, my favorite beer, and most of all, my beautiful woman to share it all with."

"We better get back to the party!" Blaze stated.

"Yeah, I guess you're right."

Jack buttoned his shirt and pants as Blaze attempted to pull herself together as well. She turned the lanterns off as they began their walk back to the party.

"Do I look alright?" she asked Jack smoothing her dress.

"You look beautiful," he answered before kissing her again.

They walked up to the house hand in hand. As they approached the house, Parks was inconspicuously standing near the deck. He backed away from the light so as not to be seen. He watched the lovers intently as the wheels spun around in his mind.

'Well, well, well,' Parks thought to himself. 'This will definitely prove to be very useful.'

When they reached the back of the house, Blaze turned on the outside shower and rinsed the sand from her feet.

"Wow seems like we were missing quite a party," Jack said as he observed the revilers enjoying themselves. They entered the back-yard to see people eating, drinking, and dancing and just having a great time.

I'm gonna go freshen up." Blaze told Jack. "Will you be okay for a minute or two?"

"Sure, I'm fine," he said.

"I know you're fine, I was asking if you would be alright," Blaze smiled.

Jack smiled too.

"Go. I'll be okay!"

Blaze disappeared into the house as Jack walked into the party watching people on the dance floor. Jewels noticed so she walked over to greet him.

"Are you hungry yet?" she asked.

"Yes, I am," he rubbed his hands together with enthusiasm.

"Come on. We'll get you a plate."

Jewels took Jack's arm and led him to the buffet table. There was an array of dishes to choose from including grilled fish, chicken, steaks and burgers, seafood, salads, grilled vegetables, and an assort-ment of pies as well as a special punch made by Jewels. Jack eagerly sampled a little of everything before sitting down to eat. When Blaze returned, she looked refreshed and vibrant as if just beginning her day. As she approached the table, Jack stood up and pulled out her chair much to the affirmative nods of approval from Jewels and a few of her friends. They were soon joined by Kush, Z, and Parks who were definitely in party mode. Jack and Blaze looked longingly into each other's eyes sampling food from one another's plates and whispering things that only lovers shared. They danced to a slow song as if they were the only ones on the floor.

"This has been a very nice evening," Jack said to Blaze.

"I'm glad you're enjoying yourself," she replied.

"So, are you coming back to the hotel with me tonight?" Jack asked.

"I'm not so sure that I should," Blaze said in an unassuming tone.

"What do you mean you're not sure? What do I have to do to get you to trust me?" Jack asked with sincerity.

"You must give me your firstborn son and then I will never doubt you again." Blaze smiled and reached over to place her slender hand upon his.

"You are very wicked, Blaze Beaumont. You've bewitched me to fall for you and I am now bound by that elixir of love that I so readily drank. Just looking at you hurts baby. I want to touch you every second of every minute," Jack exaggerated.

"Just let me pack a bag and I'll be yours for the rest of the night." Blaze got up from the table and disappeared into the house. When she returned, she beckoned to Jack to come into the house. Once inside, Blaze gave him her bag and told him to put it in his car while she went to tell Jewels that she would be staying with Jack in AC for the night. After speaking to her mother, she met Jack who was waiting patiently by his car. When Blaze appeared, he smiled and held the car door open for her. She walked past him as he inhaled her sweet scent. He quickly closed the door and retreated to the driver's side nearly jumping into his seat. He reached over and kissed Blaze on her lips before disappearing into the night with excitement and anticipation.

| 50 |

Kate's Adventure

Kate was in her element. Her family was all together in the one place that she most loved to be. Everyone gathered on the patio after a light supper prepared by Bert. Thaddeus was out front having a cigar with James as other family members played cards or video games with the children. Liz and Becca were making plans to take the children to the amusement pier in Wildwood and conspired to drag their husbands along for the trip. Kate and Thaddeus were invited as well. Michael made plans of his own to meet friends in Atlantic City, so everyone was on their way to doing something for the evening. Kate went to her room to change for the outing as Thaddeus relaxed on the patio. She went into her bedroom and into the bath to take a shower. Suddenly, she realized that her cell phone was beeping because the battery was low.

'Now where is my charger? It's got to be in my bag. I know I packed it,' she thought.

After a few minutes of searching, Kate found her charger.

"Got it!"

Kate plugged the charger into the phone and when the phone powered on, three messages instantly appeared on the screen. She listened to the first message.

"Kate, it's Ed. I'm here in Atlantic City and wondered if you could meet me for a drink. I'm at the Flagship Hotel, room 830. You can call me back on my cell phone if you can make it. Call me even if you can't!"

Kate looked at the phone as if it were talking directly to her. She instantly deleted the message and went on to the next.

"Kate, it's me again. I thought that I'd hear from you by now! I guess you must be busy, or Thaddeus is around, and you can't talk? When you get this message call me." Kate deleted the second message.

"What in the world has gotten into Ed? He knows that I'm here with the family and couldn't possibly get away. What's he doing in Atlantic City anyway?"

Kate went on to listen to the third message.

"Kate...I must sound a little desperate by now. I really need to see you. Please call me back!" Kate unplugged her phone from the wall socket and went into the bathroom and locked the door behind her. She plugged her phone into the socket above the face bowl and dialed Ed's number. He answered on the second ring.

"Hello!"

"Ed, what has gotten into you calling me so many times?" Kate was clearly annoyed.

"No hello, Ed, or even a how are you doing?" he asked.

"Ed, I don't have time for this. You know that the entire family is here with me. How do you propose that I get away without suspicion?"

"Kate, you're a resourceful woman. I know that you'll think of something so that you can get away."

"But I don't want to get away Ed. What has gotten into you? You're acting like a schoolboy."

"I assure you, madam, there's nothing school-boyish about my request. Either you find a way to get here, or I'll come and get you and bring your ass here."

"Ed, have you been drinking?" Kate asked astonished by Ed's behavior.

"Well, yes, I have as a matter of fact. I've become acquainted with the bartender a rather nice fellow who wants to escort me to my hotel room."

"Well, I think that's a good idea. You should take him up on the offer. Where's Abby? Is she with you?"

"She is and she's in her suite at the Flagship. We have separate rooms, as usual, so you don't have to worry about her finding us together."

"Ed, you need to go back to your hotel room and get some sleep. We can talk about this in the morning."

"Kate, I'm not that drunk. I want to see you tonight!"

"I can't do that! Thaddeus and I have plans for the evening and I just can't get out of them."

"Oh, no? Well then you better make room for three 'cause if you don't get here, and I mean soon, I'm coming out to the house to get you."

Ed hung up the phone as Kate stood staring into the mirror in horror. The phone still lay on her ear. She couldn't believe what she just heard. Kate had rarely been so hard-pressed to know what to do in any situation, but she was not prepared for this. She hit redial and tried calling Ed back, but the calls went straight to voicemail.

"Shit!" Kate said, clearly agitated by this turn of events. She sat at her dressing table trying to come up with a plan to get into Atlantic City and deal with Ed. She knew him well enough to know that he meant what he said inebriated or not. She was still in her underwear when Thaddeus entered the bedroom.

"Kate, you in here?" he yelled.

"Yes, Thaddeus. I'm in the bathroom."

She tried to put on her best face so that he wouldn't detect there was something wrong.

"Are you almost ready to go?" he asked.

She hesitated before speaking.

"Oh Thad, I have such a headache," she said holding her hand to her head.

"When'd you get a headache? You were in good spirits not so long ago," he said as he stood in the doorway.

"I don't know. Maybe I got too much sun this afternoon. I think I'm going to lie down. Would you mind terribly if I didn't go with the family tonight?" she asked in her most sympathy-seeking voice.

"Well, if you're not feeling well of course we don't have to go. You just lay down and I'll get you a cool cloth for your forehead."

Thaddeus helped Kate to the bed and then returned from the bathroom with a cool cloth. He sat beside her on the bed as she lay there with her eyes closed. She couldn't face him directly knowing that she was lying to him. Her conscience was getting the best of her.

"Why don't you go with the children to Wildwood and have some fun? No sense in us both being here miserable."

"I have no intentions of leaving you here alone when you're not feeling well."

"I'm fine, Thaddeus. Really! Nothing a good night's sleep won't cure. Now you go with the children and have some fun for a change. They will love having their grandfather along for the evening."

"Maybe that's not such a bad idea. I haven't been to the pier in a long time. Maybe I'll win one of those huge bears and bring it home to my girl," he joked. He kissed Kate on the forehead.

"Don't worry about me, Thad. I'll be fine. Both Bert and Maria are here and if I need anything, I'll call on them." she added.

Thaddeus left the bedroom and headed out to the patio to tell the family he would be joining them. Liz was excited to have her dad along as it reminded her of the days when she was still his little girl, and they spent their summers at the beach. Thaddeus would place her upon his shoulders as they walked along the boardwalk. Before long, the group was on their way to the pier as they piled up in two of the five vehicles owned by the family. When Kate knew that they were well on their way, she got dressed and went down to Bert's room. Bert was watching one of her favorite reality shows when Kate knocked on her door.

"Bert, may I come in?" she asked.

"Sho Kate. Come on in. What you need?"

"Listen, I have to run into town on an errand."

Bert immediately looked at the clock, "At this hour? What you need at dis hour?" she asked.

"Well, I wanted to purchase something for Thad that I saw when I was at one of the boutiques yesterday. I know that they're open and it was the only one that they had. The family has gone to the pier for the evening, so you and Maria will be here by yourselves until someone gets back."

"Okay! You sho you don't want me to pick that up fo you?" Bert asked suspiciously.

"No. I'll do it! I need to get out for a while anyway. If Thaddeus comes back before I do, just tell him I went out to get some fresh air."

"Okay...I'll do that," Bert said.

Bert had a feeling that there was more to Kate's story than she was letting on. She watched her as she climbed into one of the family jeeps and took off down the road.

"All this comin' and goin'...might as well have stayed at home. Don't seem like no vacation to me." Bert shook her head as she walked back to her room.

When Kate arrived in Atlantic City, she drove directly to the Flagship Hotel, but she didn't park at the hotel. Instead, she found a parking lot a block away where she parked the car herself and walked the rest of the way. She needed to be as discreet as possible both for her sake as well as Ed's. She went into the hotel and dialed Ed's room from the house phone. The phone rang several times before he picked up.

"Who's this?" he asked in an abrasive tone.

"Ed, it's me. I'm in the lobby."

His words were slurred.

"Well, come on up then," he mumbled before hanging up. Kate knew from Ed's voice that he had been drinking and she was cautious as to what his mood would be. She took the elevator up to the eighth floor and walked to Ed's suite. Before she could knock on the door, she noticed that it was slightly ajar. She walked into the dimly lit room where Ed was sitting nursing a drink in hand. His crisp white shirt and black pants were unbuttoned as he sat there with an intense look on his face.

"Lock the door," he commanded.

Kate felt strange as she approached him. She could not quite make out his face, but she knew that something was wrong. When she got closer to him, he was staring directly at her. Ed got up and walked past her to the bar to make himself another drink.

"Are you gonna join me?" he asked his back to Kate holding up his glass.

"No, Ed. I'm driving tonight and maybe you should think about slowing down yourself."

"I will if you promise to stay with me."

"Ed, don't be foolish. You know I must get back. I barely made it here. I had to convince Thad that I was ill and then I had to convince him to spend the evening with the family on their outing. I must get back before they return!"

Ed put his glass down on the table and walked over to Kate. He took her in his arms and kissed her. He tried to push his tongue into her mouth, but she retreated. He pulled her to him again but this time she turned her head away to avoid his kiss.

"What? I suddenly repulse you, Kate?" Ed asked.

"No, but you reek of alcohol."

"Oh, so you've never had a drink before?"

"Okay, I'm leaving." Kate playfully pulled away from Ed pretending to leave.

"Where do you think you're going? Ed was enjoying her presence as his hand traveled the length of her body returning to her neck and then down into her cleavage. Kate no longer resisted but held her head back as Ed unbuttoned her blouse running his hands along the outline of her breast. She relinquished herself to him completely as he led her to the bedroom. She lay on the bed as Ed took off her skirt and blouse spreading her legs as he touched them inside and out. Kate tingled from his touch as all resistance fled from her. She waited for him to remove his clothing and lay beside her. She admired his large physique and relished in his strength and power. She wanted him to ravage her completely. Ed made love to her with aggression and passion, sucking her inner thighs and buttocks until she squealed from the pleasure he gave her. He was rough with her, but she enjoyed his manipulation of her body. He grabbed her by the hair and lifted her body with the other to meet him as he entered her. They engaged in raw passion until igniting in unison leaving them spent and exhausted as they succumbed to their exhaustion. The sweat between them matted Kate's hair to her head. She was soaked from head to toe as the sheets clung to her naked body. Ed lay beside her eyes closed as he was aware of her movements when she tried to leave the bed. He reached out for her, but she bolted into the bathroom. When she returned, she lay upon her belly beside him kissing him on the lips.

"So, did you like our game?" Ed asked.

"Yes, I rather enjoyed it very much," Kate said nuzzling her head into the crook of his arm. She lay on her stomach facing Ed as he rested his head upon his other arm.

"What took you so long to call?" she asked.

"I had a few things to do and you know I had to spend some time with Abby."

"I wish you didn't have to bring her," Kate pouted.

"Don't you think that's a bit selfish of you Kate?"

"No...I don't! I want you all to myself. She has you every night and I only get to be with you once a week."

"Well, didn't I come all this way to see my sweet Kate?" Ed kissed her. "It wasn't easy getting away from Abby."

"Really? And where is the pathetic little thing anyway?"

"Now, there's no reason to be unkind Kate. You're getting what you want...right?"

"Well, it wasn't easy to get away from Thad either, but I wasn't gonna let anything stop me from being with you tonight and after what I just had I'm certainly glad that I did," Kate said with no remorse. Ed smacked Kate's behind before getting up.

"Well, you've gotta be getting back soon. Thaddeus will be looking for you and Abby will be calling here any minute now." Kate sat up resting her head on one hand while placing the other on her hip.

"What? You ready to throw me out? You got what you wanted and now it's time for me to go?" Kate asked indignantly. Ed shook his head as he put on his clothing.

"Sweetheart, you knew that we couldn't be together long while down here with both our families here too. Why you trying to start trouble where there really is none? Ed walked over to Kate and picked her up into his arms. He kissed her reassuringly and looked into her eyes.

"You know you're it for me. There's nothing left in my marriage and there's no other woman for me besides you. You have my heart, Kate. God help me, but you do!" Kate threw her arms around Ed's neck and kissed him passionately. She lay on his shoulders as he let her down to stand on her own feet. Lifting her chin in his hands, he spoke to her softly.

"Now go get cleaned up so you can get back before Thaddeus does." Kate nodded to him being as cooperative as a child that had been scolded and then comforted by his or her parent. Ed smiled as he smacked Kate on her behind when she walked into the bathroom to freshen up. She rubbed her bare bottom as Ed laughed heartily at the grimaced face she made.

"I couldn't resist. You know I love your ass," he added.

When she finished dressing, they hugged and kissed one another as if they were parting for a very long time.

"Remember," Ed warned. "No stopping anywhere. Go straight home and call me when you can."

Kate agreed and kissed her lover one last time before she reluctantly left the hotel room without him. They had to be cautious that they were not seen together so she took the stairs down to the next floor and then the elevator to the lobby. The lobby was crowded with people coming and going with some checking in, so it was easy to go unnoticed. When she got off the elevator, she stopped to search her handbag for the parking ticket. When she retrieved it, she covered her hair with her silk scarf and left the hotel to walk the one block to where her car was parked. As she turned into the parking lot and made her way to her car, she was ambivalent that she was being watched. A man lurking in the shadows of the dark street had followed her from the lobby of the Flag Ship Hotel. He looked at his watch observing the hour as he made a mental note to himself.

It was well past ten and Kate had little time left to beat the family home from their outing, but she didn't care about that. The only thing on her mind was Ed and the way that he made her feel. She loved their trysts and looked forward to them each week. Ed helped her to unwind and escape the daily issues that life placed upon her. It was not easy being the wife of Thaddeus Newman. People expected a lot from her and for the most part, she obliged them. She was revered in her social circle and she wanted to maintain that status. With Ed, she could let the real Kate loose. With him, she could be the vixen or harlot and not be judged. Ed liked when she would play along with his games and she enjoyed being his toy. But if their affair were ever revealed, it would mean the end of her marriage and all the benefits that come with it. Kate was too proud and too vain to give all that up—but she had an insatiable sexual appetite and Ed kept it in check. When she arrived at the summer house, all was quiet. The family cars were not in the lot, so she was safe for now. She went into the house from the patio going right to her room. Everything was as she left it and so she removed her clothing, threw everything into her hamper for cleaning, and jumped into the shower. She washed her hair and scrubbed herself until she felt clean as if she could wash the smell of Ed from her. She applied an expensive cream to her body and donned a silk nightgown. It didn't take her long to dry her hair and finish grooming herself. She threw on a cashmere robe and went to the kitchen for a cup of tea after which she returned to her room and climbed into bed. She decided to read until Thaddeus and the children arrived home. It wasn't long before she could hear them drive up and unload the vehicles. She heard Thaddeus bid everyone goodnight, so she lit the two candles that were on the nightstand and turned out the lamp. She heard Thaddeus's footsteps as he came down the hallway towards their bedroom, so she prepared herself in bed. When he entered the room, she was lounging on the bed with her leg exposed up to the top of her thigh waiting for him. He smiled at her when he entered the room. He walked over to the bed and leaned down to kiss her. Kate reached up and placed her hands around his neck drawing him near to her. He knew that she wanted to make love, so he lay down beside her taking in her sweet scent. She let the strap from her gown fall off her shoulders revealing her breasts that were still quite perky for a woman of her age. Thaddeus kissed her as his hand fondled her breast.

"Hey! How you feelin'?" he asked clearly aroused by her.

"I'm good, really good," she said in a sultry tone.

"You smell delicious," Thaddeus said sniffing at her neck and cleavage. Kate took his hand and placed it between her legs.

"Make love to me, Thad," she sighed breathlessly. His hand caressed her gently as she opened her legs to better accommodate him. Thaddeus made love to his wife enjoying the pleasure that she gave him. He quickly fell asleep as she lay happily feeling victorious in her conquest.

| 51 |

Let's do brunch

The next few days were heaven for Jack and Blaze. They slept late, ate, shopped, gambled, languished in the cabana enjoying the ocean breeze, and made love every second in between. Blaze relished in the pleasure between her and Jack, and he was equally as pleased. This was indeed the first time that he had spent so many days in the company of any woman, and he liked the experience more than he could have imagined. A few times he went to the gym leaving Blaze to her own devices, only to return shortly after with an eagerness to be near her. Blaze ventured out to shop and spent time at the salon having herself beautified for her lover. She found it difficult to be away from Jack for too long and anticipated returning to him shedding her clothing immediately upon entering the suite anxious to partake of the splendor of lust that awaited her there.

Blaze didn't go back to the beach house the next day or even the next. She stayed with Jack for the entire week, and he was quite pleased with the arrangement. Jack checked in with Kate to ensure that she wouldn't spoil his time with Blaze by showing up unannounced at his hotel suite. Kate was fine on the condition that

Jack would make an appearance at Sunday brunch. Before he could protest, Kate hit him with an unexpected suggestion.

"Why don't you invite Blaze and her family to brunch?" she suggested. Jack was apprehensive about his mother's sudden invitation to Blaze for brunch at the house. He hesitated before answering her.

"Okay, I'll extend the invite, and let you know if she can attend." He thought it was best to play it safe and not engage his mother in conversation about the matter.

"Good! I'll see you on Sunday." Jack hung up the phone and did not immediately tell Blaze about his conversation with Kate or the invitation.

Kate planned an intimate, but lavish Sunday brunch for her family and a few of her closest friends. Her attention to detail was methodical at best as she planned the sumptuous feast as meticulously as she did any five-star event that she was known for organizing. Bert's services were enlisted to assist with the preparations as was Marcel Caterers who she often used when staying at the beach house. The patio was transformed into a tropical paradise right down to the minutest detail. Bert had been in the kitchen since early morning baking bread and her special cinnamon buns that the children loved. The caterers arrived early to set up along the patio arranging tables and setting up each station. A display of fresh fruits, exotic cheeses, crepes, bacon, sausages, lox bagels, cream cheese, and an omelet station was generously filled. A carving station with beef brisket and ham, jumbo shrimp and lobster tails, chilled asparagus with hollandaise sauce, several salads, chilled desserts, coffee, tea, and orange juice for the mimosas. Fresh pastries were delivered for the occasion with delectable choices to appease the most discriminating palate. Kate loved the idea of planning another social event, even if it was small. She also had both the men in her life nearby so that she could have her cake and eat it too. She never gave it a second thought that there just may be something wrong with that arrangement—she only thought to herself, 'It's good to be privileged.'

| 52 |

Vacation Interrupted

Pierre was enjoying himself with the endless parties, drinking, cruising and nameless faces he picked up during the night while he was out wandering. He had been to every club, in every corner of town, giving new meaning to the term party animal. He also had his fair share of casual sex with whoever was willing. He slept late, had coffee at the local café near his apartment around 2:00 pm where he entertained a few locals, and after a few hours made his way back to his apartment to get ready for his evening out. This was his routine, and he loved every minute of it.

On this particular morning, Pierre was sleeping in after having another night of partying, when the loud ring of the phone startled him awake. He tried to ignore the sound and let the call go to voice mail, which it did. He dozed back off to sleep only to be awakened a second time by the ringing of the phone. Now quite annoyed and wondering who on earth could be calling him at this hour, he pulled himself up and snatched the receiver into his hands.

"Who is this?" he asked with contempt in his voice.

"Pierre, is that you darling?" the voice said on the other end. There was no question of who the caller was. He should have known that Kate would be the only one with the gall to call him during the day. He squinted through tiny slits of his red, swollen eyes as he attempted to sound upbeat and awake.

"Kate, what a surprise! How are you?"

"I'm doing well, Pierre. How are you enjoying your time off?"

"Oh, just relaxing and taking in some sites. You know, museums, catching up with old friends," he lied.

"Well, that's wonderful! I'm so sorry to call you on a Sunday morning at the last minute but I'm just desperate for your help."

Pierre knew by the sound of her tone that he wasn't going to like what was coming.

"Well, of course, I'll help in any way I can. What's going on?" Pierre asked although annoyed.

"Well, I'm having a special brunch for family and friends, and well it's just so impossible for me to pull this all together without your expertise and assistance. You always manage to make any event a special and perfect affair. It seems that once again I've over-extended myself and will have more people than originally planned. I could certainly use your support."

"Well, if you really need me, I guess..."

"Oh, good Pierre—I was hoping you'd say that. I'll send a car for you right away and have Bert make up the spare bedroom for you as well. You're a lifesaver," Kate said all in one breath. "Well let me go so that I can have the car ready for you. Let's say about an hour?"

Pierre agreed half-heartedly and then hung up the phone. Forty-five minutes later a town car pulled up in front of Pierre's apartment building as the driver called up to him. Pierre had the driver come up for his bags. Donning his sunglasses, Pierre took a long last look around before locking his door and entering the elevator.

"If I'm going to end my vacation, then I'm gonna do it in style." He held his head high as the driver opened the door for him to get in the car. He took his scarf and threw it around his shoulder.

| 53 |

Unannounced and Uninvited

Jewels enjoyed having her children and their friends along for vacation which made for a festive time and kept her entertained. She enjoyed relaxing by the pool or the beach, playing cards with friends, or sometimes just being alone reading a novel. During the evening hours, either she and her friends would meet up in town or she would take a walk along the promenade at night. Other times, she traveled to Atlantic City for cocktails and dinner, shows, gambling, and shopping.

Jewels kept her body and mind in shape through a healthy regime of eating right, exercising, and a strong spiritual lifestyle. She had a glow about her that was warm and welcoming, but she was assertive and a force to be reckoned with when warranted. Not only was she smart, but she was also very fashion-conscious keeping up with the trends since makeup and hair went hand in hand with fashion. Although she attended hair shows and fashion shows on a regular basis, her real source of information was her three daughters who kept her aware of what the younger generation liked. Jewels emerged from her bedroom and went out onto the deck. Greetings from all were heard as she returned them one by one kissing her children good morning and brushing her hand along the shoulders of her guests. Everyone was on the deck having breakfast talking all at once about their plans for the day. Z had been a regular guest at the Beaumont summer house for the last two summers, so it wasn't unusual for him to stay with the family even when Blaze was away. Z had become one of the family and he and Kush had become fast friends from the start. The family was all set to go to church service when the phone rang with Jewels taking the call.

"Hello!" she said.

"Hey, mom!" Blaze said jubilantly.

"Well, who is this? Could it be my long-lost daughter?" Jewels teased.

"Very funny. Is all the family there with you?" she asked.

"Yes, we're all here heading out to church. Even Z is attending the service with us." "How'd you manage that one?" Blaze asked laughing.

"Wasn't hard. I just made a little wager with Mr. Z and I won is all."

Blaze laughed along with the rest of the family.

"Mom, I called to tell you not to make plans today; we've been invited to brunch this afternoon at the Newman's summer home."

Jewels hesitated before answering.

"Really? What brought that on?"

"I'm not sure, but Jack is here, and he says to say hello."

"Hello, Jack. What time is this brunch?" Jewels asked.

"Guests should be arriving around one," Jack yelled.

Jewels tried to hush the comments coming from the noisy group as she replied, "Does his mother know that we're all coming?"

"Yes, mom. It was her idea."

"Really?" Jewels sounded surprised. "Well okay then! Just text me the address and we'll be there."

"Okay, mom."

After they hung up, Jewels took a few moments to consider the invitation before she ushered everyone up from the table and grabbed her purse to head out the door for church.

It was nearly one o'clock and everything had been arranged to Kate's satisfaction. Pierre had arrived amid a flurry of caterers, wait staff, and of course, Bert ordering everyone from her kitchen. Kate was indeed happy to see him, as he knew exactly how she liked things to be. This gave her an opportunity to prepare herself for her guests. She decided to wear a white one-shoulder summer dress with a full princess-length skirt. Her white sandals were encrusted with a crystal jeweled heel and her accessories included a stunning pair of crystal drop earrings and a diamond tennis bracelet. Her freshly washed hair was left to dry naturally as ringlets formed a frame around her face emphasizing her newly tanned skin and revealing several freckles along her thin nose. She was stunning and Thaddeus was pleased as he walked over to her kissing her shoulder and complimenting her on her choice of fragrance. She was delighted that her husband still found her to be as attractive as the day they met. Everyone was gathered on the patio as guests began to arrive including the Steinbergs, Mitchells, Andersons, and the Coopers who were all incredibly good friends of the Newmans. Champagne was flowing and the music relaxing as the informal affair got underway. When Jack arrived with Blaze on his arm, Kate greeted them warmly. She was quite gracious as she made the usual fuss over Jack.

"Oh Jack, I'm so glad you decided to come," Kate said hugging her son. Jack kissed his mother's cheek never letting go of Blaze's hand. Kate turned to Blaze and offered her hand welcoming the young woman into her home.

"Ms. Beaumont, it's a pleasure to see you again," Kate smiled. "Please—call me Blaze, Mrs. Newman—and thank you for having me and my family in your home." Blaze's tone was sincere.

"Well, of course, dear," Kate said. Jack knew his mother well and could tell that she was putting on an act for appearance's sake. Blaze was so enthralled in being with Jack at his parent's home. The pretentious behavior went right over her head.

"Please make yourself comfortable and enjoy the afternoon." Kate left to greet more guests. Michael was the first of the family to come and introduce himself to Blaze.

"Hi! I'm Michael Newman, Jack's brother." He took Blaze's hand into his own. Michael was soft-spoken and the quietest of the Newman clan. He was handsome in a more refined way than Jack. He had his mother's features that appeared too delicate for a man to have. Not as tall as either of his brothers, Michael was smaller and thinner and was not as athletic as his other siblings. He enjoyed literature and the arts as much as his mother and studied abroad for some time taking an interest in art history. He was a gentle sort of man who took comfort in his books and the arts. He was on the board of Kate's foundation, *Les Petites,* which he was totally involved with and very hands-on when it came to the program at large. He was responsible for acquiring sponsorship and endowments from some rather influential benefactors and was well-known in the charitable community. Michael made Blaze feel welcomed and she immediately felt comfortable with him. They chatted briefly as the rest of the clan joined them. Soon, James and Rebecca, and Liz and Bradley were welcoming Blaze and taking total control of the conversation. Blaze soon discovered that the Newman offspring were extremely competitive and even Liz challenged her brothers to games of backgammon and chess. Sometime later, Jewels arrived with her children and Z as they were warmly greeted by Thaddeus and Kate. Kate escorted the Beaumonts to the patio where Blaze and Jack were hanging out. Blaze had never been so happy to see her family all together as she was at that moment. Jack immediately got up to offer Jewels a seat as he welcomed her and the girls each with a kiss on the cheek and vigorously shook the hands of Kush and Z. Kate joined them as the introductions began.

"You have a beautiful home," Jewels said to Kate.

"Why thank you," Kate said. "We just love it down here." "I'm very partial to this house, even more so than our home in Barbados." She added.

"Well as much as I love the islands," Jewels replied, "I, too, love being at the Jersey shore." The two women smiled in agreement making nice with one another mostly for the sake of their children. Kate introduced Jewels and her family to the other guests and took Jewels on a tour of her home. Jewels admired Kate's décor and she was most intrigued by the simplicity of her choices.

"I understand that you are quite a successful businesswoman," Kate said as they entered the living room.

"Well, it has taken a lot of time to build, but I enjoy what I do which makes it that much more rewarding." Jewels responded.

"Please have a seat." Kate motioned to Jewels as she sat on one of the chairs.

Not one to mince words, Kate immediately opened the dialogue between the two women.

"So, it seems that our children have developed a fondness for one another."

"Yes, it does seem that they have been spending quite a bit of time together," Jewels added.

"Are you comfortable with this arrangement?" Kate asked bluntly. Jewels looked directly at Kate before answering her.

"I don't think it matters whether I'm comfortable with it or not," Jewels stated.

"Blaze has always made sound decisions and I don't doubt that she has weighed this choice with ample consideration."

"Uhh—I don't think that matters of the heart are something that can be reasoned in one's mind—I think in this case the heart has taken charge," Kate added.

"So, you do at least think that my daughter genuinely cares for your son?" Jewels asked as she realized that Kate made it easy for her to support Blaze's position. Kate looked as if she had placed her foot into her regal mouth.

"Well, in any case, it's their decision to make and we can only hope that whatever they decide, it will be in the best interest of them both," Jewels smiled.

Kate had no rebuttal seeing that Jewels was as strong in her convictions as she was. She decided to save the battle for another time and for now join her family and friends for a pleasant afternoon. Standing up Kate motioned her hand in the direction of the patio.

"Shall we join the others? I'm sure they're wondering where we got off to."

"Yes, I'm sure that they have," Jewels agreed. "Kate, thank you for the tour. You have a lovely home and a lovely family as well. You're quite blessed," Jewels said walking out with Kate. Although the two women smiled at one another as they exited the living room, both had concerns on their minds after their conversation. Kate was still not convinced that Blaze would be a suitable match for her son, and Jewels just thought to herself how much of a bitch Kate Newman really was. When they arrived on the patio, all eyes were on them. Jack and Blaze especially were nervous as to the outcome of their meeting. When they appeared intact and smiling it put them both at ease. Jewels joined them as Kate mingled with her guests. Blaze whispered to Jewels with anticipation.

"So, how'd it go?" she asked her mother.

"Everything's just fine." Jewels lied.

"Wow! What a relief! I thought we were gonna have to call the police or something. What'd you guys talk about?" Blaze asked still whispering.

"I'll tell you all about it later. For now, let's try to enjoy ourselves. Shall we?" Blaze acquiescence and returned to the group where Jack and Kush were now discussing who was the favorite for the Eastern Conference Championship games and who would take the role of the most valuable player. Jack played football throughout high school and college another interesting fact Blaze learned about him from talking with his siblings. She was enjoying herself listening to all the stories about the Newman children's childhood when her eyes were diverted in Jack's direction. He was looking at her with that dimpled smile. He winked his eye to signify his pride in her before resuming his conversation with Kush and the other guys. Blaze felt a tingle of excitement run through her as she watched him from afar. He was so handsome and self-assured. Being in Jack's environment with his family gave Blaze another glimpse of the man she had grown to love. She blushed at the thought of his touch upon her body or the intimate things he promised when he whispered into her ear. A chill ran up her spine as she was jolted back to reality when Liz asked her if she wanted to do some shopping with her later in the week.

"Of course!" she replied, unsteady from the intrusion upon her private thoughts of Jack.

After another hour or so, everyone seemed to be enjoying themselves as the atmosphere was pleasant and festive. A few guests were dancing while others conversed near the pool when other guests arrived unexpectedly bearing gifts. To everyone's surprise, Parker Johnson entered the patio escorted by one of the servers. It seemed that he had come unannounced and uninvited. The look on Kate's face was one of surprise and disbelief. She was speaking with the other wives about their plans for the fall when she excused herself to investigate the new arrival. Thaddeus had long since retreated to the family room to play pool and smoke Cuban cigars, so Kate was left to deal with the intruder. Both Jack and Blaze were curious as to what Parker was doing there, but Z was the most surprised to see his colleague who had never mentioned an invitation to the event. As Kate walked towards him, Parker smiled holding out his hand to her.

"Mrs. Newman! What a pleasure to see you again." Kate looked at him quizzically.

"Mr. Johnson, is it? What brings you to our home and more importantly who invited you?" she asked with disdain.

"Well, I'm in town for a few days and I thought it would be a novel idea to visit you and Mr. Newman since I don't know anyone in town," he said smiling.

Kate didn't like the man and she wasn't buying his story.

"Well as you can see," she said looking around, "we are entertaining guests so this wouldn't be a good time for a visit as you call it."

Parks wasn't backing down and boldly brushed past Kate to look upon the festivities.

"Well, it looks like I chose an appropriate time for us to continue our conversation about our mutual interest," Parks whispered. Kate looked in the direction of Jack who was closely watching the exchange between the interloper and his mother. When he saw that Parks was entering the patio area, he became more curious as to what he was doing at his mother's brunch. Jack walked towards the two as Parks turned to Kate and whispered, "How is Mr. Thompson doing since you left him last night?" he asked between clenched teeth and a Cheshire cat smile. The hair on the back of Kate's neck stood up as she smiled nervously at Parks. When Jack approached them, Kate immediately grabbed Jack's arm.

"Jack, you remember Mr. Johnson from the firm that's handling your account. When we met at the barbecue, he mentioned he would be at the shore this week, so I invited him to stop by for brunch. Jack looked at Parks who was now extending him his hand.

"Jack, it's good to see again!" Jack accepted his handshake.

"So, Parks," Jack began, "you never mentioned that you had become acquainted with my mother when we last saw you at the Beaumont's.

"Well, it would have been rude not to accept your mother's gracious invitation."

"Parks was at the Beaumont's party last week," Jack said still looking Parks in the eye. Kate was still a bit uneasy at the intrusion and what Parks might have up his sleeve. She didn't want any drama while her guests were present which encouraged her to be tolerant of Jack's infatuation with Blaze Beaumont.

"Well, you're here now, so make yourself comfortable and enjoy the food and beverages."

"Thanks, Jack! That's very good of you. I think I'll go over and say hello to my colleagues."

Parks walked towards Z and Blaze. Jack turned to his mother who appeared to be a bit uneasy.

"What made you invite him to brunch?" Jack asked.

"Oh, you know me, Jack." She tried to seem as if the incident was insignificant. "The more, the merrier!"

"Mom, I do know you! Something about this just doesn't mesh!"

"Oh, don't be silly." Kate faked a smile. "It's nothing more than what it seems."

"That's exactly my point," Jack replied, "There's something about that guy that just doesn't sit right with me."

"Oh, don't be such a prude. Jack. Why don't you go back to your guests?" Kate commanded. "I'm going to see what your father is up to." Kate left Jack's side as she retreated into the house. Once inside, she didn't seek out Thaddeus like she said she was going to do but instead headed for her bedroom. She went inside and closed the door. She was shaken by the intrusion of this young man who made her skin crawl. There was something sinister about him and Kate felt that he was trouble. He simply could not be trusted. She picked up her cell phone and dialed Ed's number. He answered immediately.

"Hello."

"Oh, Ed darling, are you with Abby?" Kate asked.

"She's sleeping soundly now. I wanted to give it a few more minutes before heading out."

"Oh, that's good news," Kate replied relieved. "Ed, we may have a problem."

"What do you mean a problem?" he asked.

"It seems that someone may have seen me at your hotel room last night and he's here right now."

"What are you talking about Kate?" Ed asked alarmed.

"One of the employees of the firm that's working with Thad and Jack just mentioned you to me, but not in a very friendly way."

Ed hesitated for a moment before responding to her.

"I'll be there as soon as I can," Ed assured her before hanging up.

Kate felt better now that she knew Ed was on his way. She returned to her guests as they entertained themselves in conversation by the pool. Blaze was more than surprised to see Parks. She was annoyed at his presence. It seemed that lately, he managed to ingratiate himself everywhere she was. She didn't like it when he showed up unannounced at her mother's party, but to crash the Newman event was despicable. Although the Newmans were being quite gracious in welcoming Parks into their home, she felt responsible for him since he was part of the team representing the

Newman's campaign. As the lead on the account, she felt obliged to give him a piece of her mind, and so she approached him.

"Parks, could I have a word with you?" Blaze asked in her most gracious manner trying not to bring attention to either of them.

"Why, sure Blaze. What's up?"

"Please excuse us for a moment," she said as the two walked towards the path to the beach. As they exited the house and approached the beach, the sunset presented a glorious view of the horizon. This was one of Blaze's favorite times of the day when she was staying at the beach house. How tainted it all now seemed while walking on the beach with Parks. When they were far away from the party Blaze began questioning Parks.

"Parks, why are you here?" Blaze asked boldly.

Parks smiled and decided to brush off the offensive tone that she was delivering to him.

"I'm here as Mrs. Newman's guest."

"Do you realize how important the Newman account is to the firm?" she asked.

"Of course, I do. What does that have to do with me being here?" he asked pretending to be offended.

"You weren't invited, and this is the summer home of the owner and CEO of the company. You just don't drop in and crash their party like this was high school or something."

"Don't you think that you're overstepping your boundaries, Blaze?" Parks asked in return. "Why should you and Z be here and not the rest of the team who has worked equally as hard on the campaign?

"Because we were invited," Blaze retorted.

"Well, you may be playing house with Jack, but you're no Newman," Parks added with a snarl, "So don't get all high and mighty with me."

Blaze couldn't believe his attitude.

"What has gotten into you?" she asked.

"What's gotten into me? You're the one with delusions of grandeur my sweet. Don't think for one minute that you've arrived simply because you're sleeping with the client. I believe that there's something about that in the bylaws that strictly forbids any fraternization with clients, so don't force me to bring this to the board," he said smugly.

"You wouldn't dare!" Blaze said heatedly. "You'd only be biting off your nose to spite your face idiot. If you go to the board with such accusations, the whole account could be in jeopardy, and then nobody wins, not to mention we'd lose the account. I think it's best that you leave," Blaze suggested.

Parks grew angry and immediately lost control. He pulled Blaze by the arm pressing his wiry body against hers as he breathed into her face.

"Really? Well, maybe I'll just have to take my chances."

Blaze struggled to free herself from him.

"Get your hands off of me, Parks." She tried to smack his face. Parks was the stronger of the two and caught her hand in mid-air. He then continued to keep her in his grasp.

"You are sweet, I'll give you that," Parks said as he closed his beady eyes and inhaled her scent.

"You know I've been attracted to you for a long time, but you sashay your little ass around the office with your high and mighty attitude like I wasn't good enough for you or something. Well, baby, I'm gonna get mine no matter what, and the likes of you ain't gonna stop me." Parks pressed a sloppy kiss upon Blaze's lips grabbing her buttocks in his hand as she struggled to pull herself from him. When he was finished, he forcefully pushed her away almost knocking her down in the process. Blaze regained her balance and ceremoniously wiped the kiss from her mouth.

"You pig!"

She spat as she watched him walk away towards the house. She couldn't believe the audacity of the man, and she had no clue what to do about it. She didn't want to cause a scene by telling Jack for she knew what he'd do. He'd have Parks thrown out on his tail. She decided to say nothing to Jack, but she would warn Z of what happened between her and Parks. She made her way to the house and retreated to the powder room to regroup. As she was entering the house, a heavy-set, dark-skinned man was coming in the door. She had never met Ed Thompson, but she remembered seeing him at the barbecue. Little did she know that he knew of her and had run a background check on her for Kate. As they passed one another they exchanged greetings before Ed headed out to the patio and Blaze walked down the hallway and into the powder room.

| 54 |

Darkness

Pierre had been busy all afternoon making sure that Kate and her guests were having a great time. He took over coordinating every detail as he worked with Bert and the caterer to ensure everyone was comfortable and all needs were met. He didn't have time to socialize although he was welcome to do so at all of Kate's events. Things were finally underway, and his attention was not required in the kitchen, so he made his way out to the patio greeting guests he knew and making acquaintances with the few he didn't. As he made his way across the patio, he noticed a man conversing with Jack and his siblings. At first, he thought it was a friend of the Newmans and dismissed it as quickly as it caught his attention. But there was something oddly familiar about him that piqued Pierre's interest. As he approached, the group the man had his back to Pierre, but as he grew closer there was a familiar ring to the tone of the man's voice.

"Excuse me!" Pierre said clearing his throat. "Good afternoon, everyone. I just wanted to let you know that we have replenished the hot foods stations so please help yourself and enjoy." Just then, Parks turned around finding himself face-to-face with Pierre. The two looked as if they had seen a ghost with Pierre being by far more pleased with the surprise than Parks. The smile on Parks's face quickly disappeared and from his expression, Pierre immediately knew that he should probably refrain from letting on that the two had made an acquaintance on another occasion.

"You know, I think that I'm gonna refresh my drink," Parks said before turning to leave for the bar. He quickly walked away as if in a retreat of some horrible feat with all eyes upon him wondering about this abrupt exit. The group quickly returned to Pierre thanking him for the notice and then continuing their conversation. Pierre then made his exit towards the bar curious as to why Parks was at his employer's home. Parks ordered another Remy Martin as Pierre approached him.

"Well, Mr. Parks! This is a delightful surprise. Did you come all this way to see me?" Pierre asked batting his eyes.

"Don't be absurd," Parks spat back at him keeping his back towards the group.

"Well, what are you doing here?" Pierre asked baffled at Parks's tone and rudeness.

"Not now, Pierre," Parks stated trying to fake a smile through it all.

"If not now, when?" Pierre asked.

Parks spoke to Pierre in a whispered tone.

"Is there somewhere we can talk privately?" he asked.

"I have a room here."

"Absolutely not!" Parks stated.

"Okay! Okay! You don't have to be so rude about it."

"I know. There's an abandoned shack a few feet away from the lifeguard station on the beach."

"Fine. I'll meet you there soon," Parks said before leaving his drink and walking away. Pierre stood there smiling, "Well it looks like this just might be my lucky day after all."

Ed mingled with the guests as Kate made her way in his direction. She approached him as he was conversing with the Mitchells.

"Ed, how nice of you to come to brunch—but where's Abby?"

"She's not feeling well. Too much sun, I presume."

"Oh, what a shame! Please give her our regrets that she couldn't be with us," Kate continued.

"Well, let me escort you to the buffet. You must be famished and in need of a cocktail. You must catch up with the rest of us."

Kate said smiling as the Mitchells agreed. Kate placed her arm into Ed's as they walked over to the buffet.

"I'm so glad that you're here."

"It did take some doing," Ed replied. "What was all that about someone knowing about us?"

"It seems that I have a gate crasher on my hands, and he isn't someone I can just turn away."

"A gate crasher?" Ed repeated. "Who would have the nerve to crash one of your parties?"

"He's one of those dreadful people from the agency representing Thad's company and a colleague of that Blaze Beaumont."

"Ah yes! We ran into one another when I arrived."

"Well, unfortunately, she and her family are here as my guests. I thought it better to embrace her if I'm to have any success in getting her out of Jack's life. The boy is infatuated with her. It seems they've spent the last week in their love nest at Jack's suite in Atlantic City."

"I don't think we have room to criticize them. Now, do we?" Ed asked smiling.

"Ed, this is serious. This man is a threat to us and must be dealt with. I cannot take the chance of him speaking to Thad or Jack about this."

"Ok, let me see what I can find out about this," Ed replied.

"What'd ya say we rejoin the party? Your guest may begin to get suspicious if I continue to monopolize your time and we don't want that, do we?" Kate looked at Ed with adoring eyes.

"Of course, you're right, but before we do promise me, we'll meet again soon before this week is over."

"I promise!" Ed said as he took her arm and escorted her back to her guests. Although their little exchange did not present much interest to the festive partygoers, one person watched from afar. He, too, returned to the party armed with ammunition that would rival the most opulent Fourth of July fireworks display.

Although the invite was for brunch, many of Kate's guests lingered throughout the afternoon into the early evening. There was more than enough food and beverages to go around. Jewels Beaumont hadn't planned on staying more than an hour but found that she had been there for most of the afternoon enjoying the company and entertainment that the Newmans offered. Blaze just enjoyed the fact that she was with Jack, and he also seemed to relax after a while. If there was one thing for certain, it was that the Newmans knew how to throw a party. Even Parks's unannounced and uninvited appearance could not put a damper on the day.

The afternoon was ending as the sun began its descent in the Southern New Jersey skies. Blaze had a few glasses of champagne and was feeling elated and giddy. She was in a party mood as she danced with Kush and Z with her sisters joining in the revelry making a soul train line to the sounds of Philadelphia music. While everyone edged the group on, Pierre saw his chance to slip away anxious to rendezvous with Parks whom he thought would be waiting. The sun was nearly set as it cast a splendid glow against the skyline, while the waves rushed upon the beach in an ardent kiss on the sand pulling it out to sea repeatedly. The warm breeze promised a balmy and enchanting night as Pierre's thoughts swirled in his head anticipating his meeting. Pierre followed the worn path that led to the empty cottage on the Newman's property. Overgrown foliage was high around the entrance to the cottage and the perimeter of the building shielding it from the trail that led to the door of the structure. Walking barefoot with his expensive loafers in his hands, Pierre pushed open the cottage door. The rancor smell that permeated the room stifled Pierre as he covered his mouth and nose. He drew a book of matches from his pants pocket and pulled a single match striking it against the book. The flame ignited as a glower light filled the room. Pierre looked around as he searched for something that would provide more light. A candle sat upon the only table in the room as he touched the flame against the wick lighting the room with a warmer glow. He looked around at the meager trappings in the room with disgust.

"This place hasn't seen a good cleaning in years," he uttered. The only other piece of furniture was an overstuffed sofa that had seen better days. The smell of mildew stifled Pierre as he wished that Parks would be well on his way. Pierre heard a sound outside the door and his mood brightened with the thought that his little indiscretion was about to take place. As the door opened, a light shined brightly into Pierre's eyes, and he immediately shielded them with his arm.

"Must you shine that thing directly into my face?" he retorted.

The figure said nothing but quickly walked toward Pierre. Blinded by the light and unable to see, Pierre suddenly felt a thud against his temple, and everything went completely black.

| 55 |

Discovery

Z and Kush were having such a great time at the party. They decided that they would continue celebrating in Atlantic City and try their luck at the craps tables. Since Peyton and Sydney had their own plans for the evening, Jewels was left to her own devices which she loved since she would have the house to herself for the evening. As they prepared to leave the party, they said their goodbyes thanking the Newmans for a wonderful afternoon. Blaze walked the family to their cars promising Jewels that she would have dinner with the family next week. When they left, Blaze joined Jack on the patio coaxing him to take a walk with her on the beach.

"Haven't you had enough of the beach?" Jack asked as she pulled him along.

"I never get enough of the beach," she replied.

"I plan to retire in a place just like this one someday."

Jack smiled as he watched her picking up seashells and dipping her bare feet into the cold water. They walked along for a while holding hands and talking as lovers do. Blaze was being herself when she noticed a light in the distance.

"Where's that light coming from?" Blaze asked pointing in the direction of the cottage. Jack was surprised as he looked in the direction she pointed.

"Uhh, I don't know. That's strange. It's coming from the old cottage. Nobody goes down there anymore. We used to play in there as kids a long time ago." Jack stood there for a moment before he grabbed Blaze's hand and began walking in the direction of the cottage.

"Where we goin'?" Blaze asked trailing behind him.

"I just want to check this out," Jack replied.

Blaze didn't want to go to some old cottage that no one had been to for a long time. Something felt eerie about it, and she was uneasy as they approached the path that led to it. It was dark now and too quiet for Blazes' sake.

"There's a light on inside," Jack was more curious than before.

"I don't like this, Jack," Blaze said as she reluctantly followed him.

"Don't worry, baby. You're with me. There's nothing to be afraid of," Jack said pushing the door open. The musty stench of the cottage wafted out of the door choking Jack and Blaze as they entered. Jack walked in first with Blaze fast on his heels holding onto his shirt. They both looked around trying to focus through the gloomy light of the room when Jack stumbled and nearly tripped over something on the floor. He looked down at what he stumbled over.

"Oh shit!" he shouted while backing up and pushing Blaze back as he did. She peeped around him and looked down at the floor in front of Jack letting out a blood-curdling scream. A man was lying on the floor in a pool of blood around his head. He was lying face down on his side so they couldn't make out his face. Jack immediately took Blaze's hand dragging her out of the door and up the path to the beach. They swiftly walked back to the house, with neither of them uttering a single word. Blaze seemed to be in shock and Jack was a little thrown too. Jack led Blaze through the gate at the back of the house and locked it behind them. They walked around the path through the French doors that led to the living room.

"Stay here," Jack said. "I'm gonna get Pop and go back to the cottage."

"But Jack," Blaze protested. "I don't want to stay here."

Jack reached over and drew Blaze into his arms.

"Baby, I'll be right back. Just do as I say for once." He kissed her on the forehead and sat Blaze down on the sofa before he walked down the hallway to the family room. He went inside to find his father asleep in his chaise lounge.

"Pop! Pop, wake up." Jack shook Thaddeus hard. Thaddeus looked at Jack through red, glassy eyes trying to focus on his son's face.

"What's the matter?" he asked seeing the urgency in Jack's expression. Something happened at the cottage.

"The cottage! What are you going on about son?" Thaddeus asked, not understanding what Jack was saying.

"I just came from the cottage down the beach. You know the one we use to play in?"

"Yeah, what about it?"

"A man's lying on the floor in blood, and it looks like he's dead."

"Jack, this isn't funny!"

"Pop, I'm being serious. A man is in there and I think he's dead."

Thaddeus sat straight up in his chair and leaned down to slip into his shoes.

"Where's your mother?" he asked instinctively.

"She's out on the patio."

"Who else is here?" Thaddeus asked, now fully awake.

"Just the family. Oh, and Ed Thompson's still here."

Thaddeus quickly walked past Jack and headed towards the hallway with Jack following close behind. Blaze was still quite shaken as she sat on the edge of the sofa holding her arms close to her body.

She was clearly in shock as she had never seen anything like that before. Jack went into a hall closet and took out two flashlights as Thaddeus headed for his bedroom. He took a medium-sized metal box from the top of the closet and went to the armoire where he retrieved a key. He opened the box and took out a 44-magnum. He checked the clip in the gun. When he returned to the dining area, Jack handed him a flashlight, and the two men made their descent towards the French doors and around the path to the gates that led to the beach. They walked swiftly with Thaddeus asking questions along the way.

"When did you find this man?"

Jack went on to tell Thaddeus how he and Blaze were taking a walk along the beach when they saw a light coming from the cottage, so they took the path that led to the cottage and went in. That's when they discovered the man lying on the floor. Once they arrived at the cottage door which was left open by Jack and Blaze, Thaddeus walked in first shining his light into the room. He kneeled to check the man's pulse.

"Well, I'll be damned, It's Pierre!"

"What?" Jack asked.

"It's Pierre," Thaddeus repeated. "What in hell's name was he doing down here?"

"Pop, we better call the police."

"Yeah—but don't touch anything else," Thaddeus commanded as the two walked out of the cottage. "This is unbelievable. Your mother isn't gonna take this well. She gave the man a hard time, but he was her right hand and I know she depended on him a great deal." Thaddeus continued talking as they walked up the path that led to the beach.

"Let me handle this," Thaddeus said to Jack.

"You go and get your brothers and have Lizzy and Becca make sure they intercept Maria and Martha before they bring the children home. Have them use the back entrance when they bring the children in so that they will not be afraid. No need to get everyone upset. I'll call the police after I speak with your mother."

Jack agreed as the two men went in different directions, each preparing for the task at hand.

| 56 |

He's not here, Kate

Trouble was the furthest thing on Kate's mind. She was having too good of a time as she and Ed sat on the patio talking like old friends usually do. She knew that Thaddeus was sleeping in the family room, and he would remain so after having one too many glasses of his favorite whiskey. The Steinbergs and Mitchells had long since left for the evening, and all that remained were her children and their spouses. She didn't even care that Blaze was still among those present and that her son was enamored with this person that she was not fond of. The musicians had packed up their instruments and were now also gone leaving only the soft sounds of the stereo that filtered jazz music drifting through the back of the house, onto the patio, and out into the air across the beach. Thaddeus entered the patio area in a flurry of movement that startled Kate and put a frown on Ed's face. Kate was more than surprised and disappointed to see Thaddeus up and about. He strode over to the pair ignoring their closeness in his haste to reach Kate. She quickly went to her defenses but was stopped in her tracks when Thaddeus began to speak.

"Kate, I need to speak with you privately," Thaddeus said as he took his wife's hand and led her inside the house. Kate began to protest, but Thaddeus ignored her.

"What in the world has gotten into you, Thad?" She asked as he closed the doors behind them. Blaze was already in the room when they entered it. Kate looked at Blaze before speaking to her.

"Blaze, will you please excuse us for a moment?" Kate asked. "She can stay, Kate. She already knows what I'm about to tell you."

Kate immediately became agitated that Blaze would be privy to the family business.

"Sit down, Kate. I have something to tell you."

Kate looked at Thaddeus for the first time seeing the urgency on his face. She sat down as he took her hand.

"There's been an accident," he began. "Oh my God! The children. Are they alright? What happened?" She began to ask frantically.

"No, sweetheart. The children are fine."

"Thaddeus, you're scaring me," Kate replied.

"It's Pierre!"

"Pierre? What does he have to do with this?" she asked.

"He's dead," Thaddeus stated.

Kate looked at Thaddeus with disbelief.

"You must be mistaken, Thad. He just got here a few hours ago. He's probably in his room."

In a nervous voice, Kate began to call Pierre.

"Pierre? Pierre, will you come out here please?" Kate yelled as she got up to go to the back of the house. Thaddeus stopped her and placed his arms around her shoulder.

"He's not here, Kate. Jack and I found him down at the beach shack just some time ago."

"Thad, this can't be," Kate said as she slowly sat back down on the sofa. She stared at Thaddeus as if she were waiting for the punch line of some joke.

"What happened?" Kate asked.

Just then, Jack entered the room with Ed not far behind. He gathered his siblings and Ed as they all joined Kate, Thaddeus, and Blaze in the living room. Ed had connections with the local police, so he volunteered to place the call to them. Blaze joined the family who was asking questions all at the same time confused by what they heard. The police arrived within minutes since this was an affluent area that was frequently patrolled by a squad car as well as a private security patrol. Jack gave the police a statement as numerous police cars arrived in the area. The medical examiner was notified and arrived shortly after. It was Pierre alright, and it appeared that he had been bludgeoned to death.

All at once, everything became chaotic as the police asked that no one leave the premises until questioned. Kate was beside herself as she tried to maintain her composure. Thaddeus stayed nearby to make sure that his family, especially Kate, was okay. He gave his statement to a police detective assigned to the case.

Detective John Wilcox was the lead detective for Cape May County. He was a hard-nose burly black man who fashioned himself after Ezekiel Easy Rawlins from the fictional detective series written by author Walter Mosley. John grew up in a small town just South of Sea Isle City and knew the islands like the back of his hand. He was methodical in his manner when investigating a case and he was not that fond of the rich families who occupied the beach homes in the area. To say he was blunt and to the point was an understatement. Once the family had been questioned and the body removed from the cottage, the police left except for an additional patrol car assigned to the area. Elizabeth and Bradley left the house before the police arrived so that they could meet the children and their nannies in town. They stayed in town until Thaddeus called them to bring the children home. Everyone else gathered in the family room sitting in silence as the house was finally cleared of all police personnel. Ed had been involved in police investigations before and provided insight on the matter to both Jack and Thaddeus.

"I think it would be a good idea if you had a criminal attorney on retainer until this matter is settled," Ed stated.

"We don't know what happened to Pierre, but it happened on your property, so it wouldn't hurt to have legal counsel to advise you," he continued.

Thaddeus agreed and went to the study to place a call to his lawyer for a referral.

"What happens now?" Jack asked Ed.

"Well, forensics will dust for prints, take images and samples of the area, and then a pathologist will perform an autopsy to determine how Pierre died. Then, they will render an official cause of death. If the results determine that foul play was involved, an investigation will ensue. That's why it's important for your father to retain counsel should this be anything more than an accident."

"Thanks, Ed. You've been a big help to us. I'm glad you were here tonight," Jack said shaking Ed's hand.

"No need for thanks, Jack. I'd do anything to help the family. You know that." Ed looked across the room at Kate who looked back at him still distraught with tears streaming down her cheeks.

"Yes, Ed. Thank you so much. I think we are all pretty tired and should retire for the night," Kate added.

"Of course!" Ed replied.

"I'll be on my way then. I'll call tomorrow to see how everyone is doing."

"I'll walk you out," Jack said. Jack walked outside and thanked him again before Ed walked to his car and drove away. Jack stood there for a few minutes in disbelief at everything that had happened in the last two hours. He inhaled a deep breath of the night air before going back into the family room where Blaze was curled up on a chair. Bert made a pot of coffee and boiled water for tea. She was beside herself as well but kept a strong vigil for the family that she loved. She attended to everyone's needs including Blaze's. She made sure that the women were as comfortable as possible and brought throws from the hall closet for them as the night air grew cool. Thaddeus returned from the study after speaking with his lawyer and sat beside his wife enveloping her in his arms. Kate settled back into the warmth and strength of her husband's body relaxing a bit more now that he was near. James, Becca, and Michael retired to their respective bedrooms and Jack sat down beside a shivering Blaze taking her into his arms as she laid her head upon his shoulder. Both Thaddeus and Jack knew that this was the beginning of a long and arduous process to find out what happened to Pierre. Kate was clearly in shock and didn't say much at all.

"Darling, why don't you let me take you up to bed? You need your rest. This has been a busy day for all of us." Thaddeus stated. Kate just looked at her husband and nodded in the affirmative. Thaddeus stood up to help his wife to her feet. She reached out to him and leaned on him completely. As they were headed toward the stairs, Kate stopped and turned to her son.

"Jack, promise me you'll stay home tonight. I can't bear to think of you out there after the evening we've had."

"Mother I'll be alright. Besides, I have to make sure that Blaze is okay," Jack replied.

"He's right Kate. Jack will be fine. He's a grown man who can take care of himself," Thaddeus added. Kate wasn't happy that both her husband and son agreed about the matter, and she felt she couldn't win this argument.

"Well, goodnight then," she said reluctantly. Jack walked toward his parents and hugged his mother and patted his father on the shoulder as they walked into the foyer and up the stairs to the second floor. Blaze was still trembling as Jack walked to her and took her in his arms.

"Oh, Jack. How could something like this happen?" she asked.

"I don't know baby. Let's go back to the hotel and try and get some rest. The couple then gathered their things and headed out the door on their way back to Atlantic City.

| 57 |

Hands off!

Parks sat at the bar of the Park Place Hotel his hands trembling after downing his fifth glass of whiskey. He looked disheveled, a far cry from the well-groomed, smart-talking junior executive that just hours ago crashed the Newman gathering. He hadn't expected the evening to turn out the way it had. He came with a plan and was confident that all the balls were in his court. All he had to do was make sure that his target knew he meant business and he would proceed to make a small fortune by blackmailing the madam of the Newman clan. He had photos and receipts, and he was going to use every dirty little trick in the book to bring down his target. Things were set up and he was ready to make his move. That is until the unfortunate turn of events. The bartender looked at Parks.

"Hey, buddy. You alright?" he asked Parks. "I'm fine," Parks slurred his speech. "Just keep the drinks coming."

"No can do, man! I think you've reached your limit," the bartender flagged.

"I think I know when I've had enough. Just leave the bottle." Parks said as he threw a fifty-dollar bill on the counter. The bartender took the bill and gave Parks change. He then beckoned to a rather large man standing across the room. The bouncer headed for the bar where Parks was seated.

"Okay, sir. Time for you to get going. Would you like me to hail you a cab?" the bouncer asked.

"Hell no! I'm a guest here. Got a room upstairs. See?" Parks showed the man his room key.

"Okay, sir. Let us help you to your room then." The bouncer signaled another man to come over and assist. The men got on each side of Parks, and both grab him by the arm nearly picking him up off the stool.

"Get your damn hands off me. Do you know who I am?" Parks ranted. He tried to break free, but the bouncers were too strong for him. They carried him out of the lounge and headed for the elevator. They took Parks up to his room, sat him down on a chair, and left him there. Parks was drunk and couldn't control himself. He got up and went to the mini bar taking a bottle of liquor from the selection. He opened it and guzzled the small bottle. Staggering, he fell on the floor, mumbling as he crashed. That's when everything turned black, and he was out for the count.

The next day, Thaddeus stayed close to the house to keep an eye on things. He was seriously concerned about his wife and had never seen her in such a state. Losing Pierre was more devastating to her than anyone could have imagined. Kate stayed in bed for most of the day. She managed to get up and shower but remained in her bedroom having Bert and the rest of the family worried that she wouldn't eat. Bert made her famous homemade chicken soup, one that she reserved for the children when they would catch a cold or the stomach flu, but Kate would not even take a sip of the tasty rue. The family collectively decided that as soon as it was possible, they would all head back to the city. They had to wait for the police to allow them to head back home since they lived in Pennsylvania and the incident took place in New Jersey. The children were allowed to go out, but only as far as the back of the house and into the pool area. The beach was off-limits since the crime had been committed not far from there. Maria and Lydia kept the children occupied while everyone stayed close to the grounds awaiting information from the police department. Thaddeus had a security company send over a few men to patrol the area and two were assigned to the family's personal space. Although their presence was a constant reminder that their freedom was limited, they welcome the extra security. It was a somber time for the Newmans as time moved slowly ending what should have been a festive family holiday. Thaddeus sat in the kitchen talking to Bert as he had done many times before.

"What you think happen to him, mister Thad?" Bert blurted out suddenly.

Thad looked at her over his horned-rimmed glasses and exhaled deeply.

"I have no clue, Bert. He wasn't supposed to be here ya know. He was on vacation and Kate called him to come down and help her with the party. Poor guy shoulda stayed where he was." Bert sniffed and rubbed at one of her eyes.

"He was a real pain in the you know what, but I liked him. He was full of himself fo' sure, but he was loyal to her. He loved being her assistant. Told people all the time who he worked fo' and carried it like a badge of honor. What bout his kin folk? He got any you know bout?" Bert asked.

"No, he never once mentioned anyone. Maybe Kate knows about someone who might need to be called, but I don't want to upset her today. I have my assistant ready to make arrangements as soon as the police say we can proceed. I don't think it will be anytime soon though. These things take time."

"Ya think the killa is still round here?"

"That's hard to say, Bert. We don't know what happened to him and I hope that whoever did this is long gone. You know that you're safe here, right? If you need to go to the store just let the security team know and someone will go with you. I don't want you to be afraid Bert."

"You don't have to worry bout me, mister Thad. I's got my persuader under my pillow and if anything happens I ain't afraid to use it."

"Your what?" Thaddeus asked alarmed.

"Aw don't worry, mister Thad. It's just one of those billy clubs the police use to carry. My daddy gave it to me when I left home and I ain't neva been without it," Bert chuckled.

Thaddeus just laughed, shook his head, and continued to read his paper as Bert moved her rotund figure around the kitchen to continue preparing her meal.

| 58 |

Investigation

The forensic team acquired evidence from the shack where Pierre's body was found. The evidence included four sets of fingerprints that were viable and could be sampled. There was blood on the floor and walls that belonged to the victim. There was also sand from the beach in the shack, enough to lift a footprint that was not from the victim's shoe. The prints were distinctive, and the research that was conducted revealed a particularly expensive shoe made in Italy by a famous shoemaker. There were also fibers from a garment that was being analyzed for evidence as well. What initially didn't seem like much to go on, was plenty for the police to begin to put the pieces of the puzzle together.

Wilcox had been at the precinct for most of the night pondering over the names of the guest who had attended the Newman party. He wanted to get to know each of them personally—in his mind. He met the Newman family members, and all were accounted for. He also briefly spoke with the Beaumonts, the Mitchells, and a few other guests. There were quite a few people whose name was on the list that he hadn't met and wanted to interview as soon as possible.

It was his theory that details begin to fade, and stories change after the first twenty-four hours of an incident, so he was way off his mark for having all the statements. He was intrigued by two guests in particular—Ed Thompson, who met, and Parker Johnson, who was not at the Newman compound when he arrived. No one could tell him exactly when Johnson left the premises, so this piqued his interest in the man. After several attempts of reaching Johnson at his hotel room with no response, John decided he would pay him a visit.

Ed Thompson was up at the crack of dawn. He donned his running clothes and ran a few miles on the boardwalk. When he returned to his suite, he showered and then went over to the adjoining room to check on Abby. She was sound asleep so he didn't wake her and decided that he would head down to the café for a quick bite to eat. He chose a small table and read the paper drinking his third cup of coffee, black with no sugar. He checked his watch almost every minute, but time was moving slowly for him. He seemed anxious, which was the total opposite of his normal personality. He was always self-assured and didn't let things bother him, but the incident at the Newman's shook him up more than he realized. It was now eight-thirty in the morning so headed back upstairs. Ed entered his room and closed the door behind him.

In another part of the hotel, Parker lay on the floor asleep when a knock at the door woke him up. He tried to ignore the intruding sound, but it continued. Suddenly, he heard someone's voice calling his name.

"Mr. Johnson, this is detective Wilcox of the Atlantic County Police department. I have a few questions to ask you about last night."

Parker was wide awake now and sat up looking around the room. It took him a few minutes to gather himself, but the room was spinning and his head pounding.

"Mr. Johnson, I know that you're in there so kindly open the door."

"Hold on!" he shouted. "I'll be right there."

Parker managed to get to the door and open it. He peered out at Detective Wilcox who was smiling. He flashed his badge at Parks.

"Hello, Mr. Johnson. Sorry to bother you at such an early hour, but I need to ask you some questions about where you were last night."

Parker staggered back opening the door for Wilcox to enter.

"Thank you, Mr. Johnson. I hope this isn't too much of an inconvenience." Wilcox looked around the room.

"No, no. It's fine." Parks slurred trying to fix his disheveled appearance. "Please have a seat."

"Well thank you, Mr. Johnson. That's mighty nice of you," Wilcox said as he sat on the armchair. Stuffing his shirt in his pants Parker asked, "So what's this all about?"

"Where were you last night, Mr. Johnson?"

"At last night? Well, um I was at the Newman's house. They had a party and well I was there," Parks said.

"What time did you arrive?"

"Um, I guess a little after seven maybe." Parks did not sound sure of the time.

"Did you come with someone or alone?"

"I was alone."

"And were you an invited guest?"

"Well, no I wasn't exactly invited, but I work with some of the guests, so I dropped in."

"Are you in the habit of dropping into private parties without an invitation, Mr. Johnson?"

"No. I just stopped by is all. What's with all the questions anyway?"

"Mr. Johnson do you know Pierre DuBois?"

Parks froze saying nothing and staring at the detective.

"Is there something wrong, Mr. Johnson?" Wilcox asked.

"Ah no, I'm a little foggy this morning. Late night and I'm hung over."

"Well sorry to hear that but please answer the question. Do you know Pierre DuBois?"

"I know of him. I believe he's Mrs. Newman's personal assistant."

"Yes, that's correct. How well do you know him?"

"Ah, not well at all! I've only seen him at the Newman's barbecue, and I think he was at the Newman gathering last night."

"And this is the only contact that you've had with him?"

"Why, yes. I don't know him personally or anything," Parks answered. "I'm not sure why you're asking me about the man. Has something happened?"

"What makes you ask that?" Wilcox asked suspiciously.

"You come to my hotel room early in the morning and start asking me all these questions, so I think I have every right to ask why."

"Where were you, Mr. Johnson between the hours of eight-thirty and ten last night?"

"I was at the party. I had a few cocktails and was mingling with the guests."

"And what time did you leave the Newman's house?"

"I think it was around nine," Parks answered.

"Ok, Mr. Johnson. I think that's all the questions I have for you now."

"Well, wait a minute. Can you at least tell me what happened?" Parks asked nervously.

"I'm not at liberty to divulge any details at this time, Mr. Johnson. Are you planning an extended stay in this area?"

"Well, no. I was planning on leaving today," Parks said.

"Mr. Johnson we are asking everyone who attended the party last night to stay in the area until we can safely say it's alright for you to leave."

"Well, how long do you expect that to be? I have to get back to the office."

"I suggest that you call your office and let them know what is going on and tell them you may not be back as soon as you expected. We will try and wrap this up as soon as we possibly can. Good day, Mr. Johnson."

"Yeah, good day to you too, Detective Wilcox," Parks said.

Once Wilcox was gone Parks exhaled deeply. He sat down on the armchair and held his aching head in his hands. His memory was fuzzy since he had been drinking most of the night. He couldn't remember what happened between the time that he arrived at the Newman's and waking up this morning. He started drinking well into the afternoon so by the time he arrived at the party he had already consumed quite a bit of whiskey.

"What the hell happened last night?" he asked out loud.

After several minutes, Parks got up and went into the bathroom to take a shower. He was unsure of what would happen next, but he had a feeling that it wasn't going to be anything good.

When Wilcox got back to the precinct he went directly to his office and sat down. He began to cross-reference some of the statements from the guest at the party. He knew that he needed to speak in depth with Kate Newman who would probably have the most insight into Pierre's character. It just so happened that Pierre DuBois was not the victim's name at all. Rather, he was born Peter Brown from North Carolina. He had a record of shoplifting and petty theft, but no major crimes were listed. He arrived in Philadelphia somewhere around the 1990s, but it was unclear to the exact date and time. He moved frequently from rooming houses around the city and never too long in one place. There was an uncle who lived in Youngsville, North Carolina but had long since passed on. There wasn't much to go on about Mr. Pierre DuBois other than the fact that he liked bar hopping and frequently picked up younger men. Wilcox had been in touch with the Philadelphia Police Department who cooperated in providing information, addresses, and photos. There were several bars that DuBois frequented but one more often than the others. The name of the place was the Trade Winds Club and Wilcox, and his partner, Shields, were on their way to check out the place. They needed to see what they could find out about Pierre. Before they left, they notified the Newman family as well as the others on their list that it was okay for them to leave the area and go back home. This was indeed comforting news for Thaddeus and Kate as the family began their descent back home to the Philadelphia area.

Later that day Wilcox checked in with the 35th Police District before making his way to the Trade Winds Club. There wasn't much to go on and the staff that was interviewed had little to say about Pierre's personal life. They only mentioned that he was a frequent patron and that he spent a lot of money there. One of the barmaids named Peaches told them about a thin dark-skinned man named Parks who was seen at the bar with Pierre. She remembered that he called her one day and asked questions about Pierre. She seemed to think that the man knew him. Wilcox and Shields also went to Pierre's room which he kept in the city but didn't find anything significant or suspicious. The police had already been there and made inquiries so when Wilcox asked the rooming house manager questions about Pierre, he could only say that he paid his rent on time and sometimes months in advance. He was a quiet tenant and stayed to himself except for a few times he had seen him return to his room during the early hours of the morning with different men. The manager remarked that Pierre was kind of snobby but never made any trouble, so he didn't notice anything peculiar about him. Wilcox and Shields felt that they had reached a dead end with the case except for the description that the barmaid Peaches gave them of the man last seen with Pierre at the bar a few weeks ago. They agreed that this might prove to be a good lead and Wilcox was sure he might know who the unidentified man might be. As the two headed out of Pierre's rooming house a shadow of a man appeared from the back corridor where the fire escape was located. As soon as they left, he went into Pierre's room and closed the door.

| 59 |

Person of Interest

The Newmans arrived home around four o'clock in the after-noon. Bert immediately set up shop in the kitchen, while the rest of the family settled in and made themselves comfortable. The screen-ing room was set up for streaming movies and the popcorn machine was ready to go. Soft drinks and other beverages were on hand and the pool was uncovered and prepped for anyone who wanted to swim. Thaddeus was hard-pressed to get Kate to participate in any of the activities. He tried to get her to relax by the pool. He challenged her to a game of backgammon, but she wasn't interested in any of those things. She just wanted to know what happened to her assistant and confidante Pierre. Thaddeus made Kate a martini and took it to her bedroom. She sat in the chaise lounge staring out of the window onto the grounds.

"Have you heard anything yet?" she asked Thaddeus.

"No, nothing yet. These things take time darling. You may not hear anything for a while. It's best that you try and put your mind to something else if you can."

Thaddeus sat beside Kate and wrapped her in his arms. She nestled her face into his chest as he sat back holding his wife. They sat there for what seemed like forever when Becca called for Thaddeus to come downstairs.

"Pop, there's someone here to see you," she yelled.

"I'll be right down," he answered.

"You'll be alright till I get back?" he asked Kate before getting up.

She nodded as he placed a cashmere throw across her legs. Detective Wilcox and Shields were standing in the foyer waiting for Thaddeus.

"Good afternoon, gentlemen," he said.

"Good afternoon, Mr. Newman. So sorry to bother you at home, but we have a few more questions that we would like to ask Mrs. Newman."

"I'm afraid that's not possible. My wife has retired for the evening."

"This is very important, Mr. Newman or I wouldn't have bothered you folks at home. I was trying to avoid having to ask Mrs. Newman to come into the precinct."

"Why would she have to come into the precinct? Is she a suspect or something? Do I need to have my lawyer contact you?" Thaddeus asked annoyed.

"Oh, no sir, nothing like that. It's just that we have a few more questions about Mr. DuBois and since he was Mrs. Newman's assistant, we thought it best that we ask her about his character. You know, things like that," Wilcox said smiling.

"Give me just one minute and let me see if she's okay to come down."

"That won't be necessary, Thad. I'm right here." Kate said as she walked down the staircase.

"Are you sure, dear? You don't have to do this now if you don't want to."

"It's fine, Thad. What do you want to ask me, detective?"

"Well, do you know if Mr. Dubois was involved with anyone exclusively?"

"Detective, I don't make it a habit to pry into my employees' personal lives. I have no idea what Pierre did when he wasn't here. He spent a great deal of time with me, and he often would stay on the grounds if he were working here very late."

"Oh. Where would that be?

"There's a small office behind the kitchen that he used, which also has an adjoining room where he would often sleep."

"May we take a look?" Wilcox asked.

"Of course. Right this way."

Kate led the detectives to the back of the house. They all entered the kitchen both detectives, Kate, and Thaddeus. Wilcox and Shields looked around the office and the small bedroom.

"Everything looks to be in order in here. Nothing looks out of place or disheveled," Shields added.

"Pierre was very neat and organized. He was a very efficient assistant, and I grew very fond of him," Kate said with tears welling up in her eyes.

"Okay, gentlemen. I think that's quite enough for tonight. We just arrived home and we're all very tired from the trip and the series of events that have taken place. If you need to speak to my wife any further, you may do so through our lawyer, Thomas Finch. I'll give you his information on the way out," Thaddeus said motioning to the door of the room.

"Thank you, Mr. Newman. Sorry for the inconvenience. Oh, by the way. One more question. How well do you know Parker Johnson?" Wilcox asked.

Kate's eyes widened at the name. Wilcox noticed her reaction to the name.

"We don't know him very well at all," Thaddeus replied.

"I was speaking to Mrs. Newman," Wilcox replied.

Kate looked at Wilcox with a peculiar expression.

"I'm afraid I don't know the man either. He crashed our party at the shore and before that, he showed up at the annual barbecue, but I don't remember him being on the guest list," Kate replied.

"Ok gentlemen. I must insist that you leave now. My wife is tired, and quite frankly, I'm tired of the inquisition, so I'll show you to the door."

"Thank you, Mrs. Newman. We'll be in touch," Wilcox added before turning to leave.

Thaddeus walked the men out of the house.

"I have to ask detective, why do you have an interest in Johnson?"

"I'm not at liberty to discuss this with you but what I will say is Mr. Johnson is a person of interest. Good night, Mr. Newman."

"Good night, gentlemen."

Thaddeus turned and walked back to the house and closed the door bolting it behind him.

| 60 |

Confession

Ed Thompson was in his room when he heard a knock at the door. Abby's car arrived promptly at ten o'clock, so Ed walked her down to the lobby to see her off. He had to stay in the area a little longer until the police notified him that he could leave. He tried to reach detective Wilcox, but he was in the field. He went to the precinct to try and get some information but there were no updates. He called the Newman compound only to find that the family left for home earlier that afternoon, so he checked out of his suite and drove home.

Once he was back in the city, he made some calls to the local police departments making inquiries about the case. Although the incident took place in New Jersey he was certain that Wilcox contacted the Philly police since that's where Pierre lived. He found out that Wilcox and his partner were in town. He was well known at the Philadelphia police headquarters in downtown Philly, so he went there as he did from time to time just to keep up appearances and maintain his relationship with some of the detectives that worked in the precinct. When he arrived, he made light conversation with some of the guys on duty. When he had the chance, he made his way to a back office where there was an available computer. He was able to access the information he was looking for by using a bogus username and password. Once into the system, he accessed everything he needed to know about Pierre DuBois, originally Peter Brown. He had a record of petty crime as a juvenile and had some minor traffic violations, but nothing that would suggest anything sinister. He needed more information, so he took Pierre's address and headed uptown to take a look around. When Ed arrived at Pierre's rooming house, he nearly collided with Wilcox and Shields. He was coming up the steps as they were about to leave the premises, so he detoured around the corridor before he was seen. Once Wilcox and Shields left the building, Ed came out of the shadows and approached Pierre's room. It didn't take much to enter since the door had only a single lock on it that was easy to pick. Ed began to go through Pierre's belongings and rambled through his drawers looking for clues to what might have prompted the man to be killed. There were no photos, no letters, nothing, just a few bills on the table. Ed surmised that the police had taken anything that might have some significance to the case. Ed headed towards the door when he saw something out of the corner of his eyes; a piece of paper lying on the floor in the corner. He bent down to pick it up to find it was only the end that had been torn off somehow. When he looked closer at the floor, he could see a sliver of light coming through the worn floorboards. He took out his cell phone and held the light closer to the floor. He stepped down on the floorboard as it squeaked beneath the weight of his body. He bent down to further investigate and found that the board was loose. He looked around for something to pry the board out and found a butter knife in one of the drawers near the sink. He jammed the knife into the crack and began to push against it as the board lifted. There was a long box laying in a crevice beneath the floor. Ed lifted the box and placed it on the kitchen table. The box had a key lock on it, but Ed was able to pry the lock open with the knife. Inside were several papers including a certificate of life insurance, a certificate of stock for a start-up technology company, and a flash drive neatly tucked away in a manila envelope. Ed took the papers and stuffed them into his jacket and the flash drive into his pants pocket. He was eager to see what was on the drive, but Pierre didn't have a computer, or at least there was no computer in his room. That didn't mean that the police hadn't confiscated it during the initial sweep of the room. Ed took the box and placed it back under the floorboard and replaced the board to cover it. He turned out the lights and carefully looked out into the hall to make sure he wasn't seen. When he was sure it was clear, he took the stairs two at a time and walked out of the building unnoticed into the night. He headed straight for his home office so that he could view the contents on the flash drive.

When Jack and Blaze arrived back in town, they went straight to Jack's apartment. Jack was determined to keep her as close to him as possible while the investigation into Pierre's death was being conducted. Blaze drew a bath and prepared to turn in early. The last few days had been quite eventful, and the couple was exhausted. When she was finished, she curled up in the big bed waiting for Jack to join her. Just as he was about to go to bed, the phone rang. At first, Jack ignored the call and let it ring. A few minutes later, his cell phone went off. It was a call from Thaddeus, so he immediately picked up the phone.

"Hello, Pop?" he asked.

"No, I'm sorry my friend. This isn't your daddy."

"Who is this?" Jack asked.

"This is someone you know, and if you know what's good for you, your mom and dad, and that pretty girlfriend of yours, you'll head out here and find out."

Jack froze not knowing what to say.

"Hey look, who is this? Is this some kind of joke?" Jack asked.

"I can assure you Jack as much as I enjoy a good laugh this isn't one of those times. So, if you know what's good for you, you'll stop with the questions and get yourself out here to Blue Bell or else."

"Are you threatening me?" Jack asked.

"No, Jack. But I am threatening your mother and father. Say something to your son, lovely."

"Jack! Jack! He's got a gun. Please don't come…."

The caller snatched the phone away from Kate's mouth.

"Okay, Jack! So, this is how it's gonna go. You get your high and mighty ass out here. Bring your girlfriend and don't even think about calling the cops or your parents are dead. Do you understand?"

"Yes! Yes, I understand! Just leave them alone. I'll be there."

"That's good Jack. Don't keep me waiting." Then the caller hung up.

Jack sat on the bed next to Blaze whose eyes were wide as saucers.

"What the hell was that about?" she asked.

"I don't know but I think someone has my mom and dad. He said I should come to the house and bring you with me."

"What are you talkin about?" Blaze asked.

"Get dressed. We're going to Blue Bell."

Jack frantically started to get dressed as Blaze jumped out of the bed and grabbed a pair of jeans and a tee shirt. She threw her clothes on not bothering to wear underwear. She grabbed her purse and followed Jack out of the door and down to the garage where he kept his cars. They took the Porsche since it would be faster. Jack got on the highway and was there in record time. He turned onto the road where his parent's house was located. It was very dark and isolated. He drove up the driveway and turned onto the circle leading to the front door. Jack parked the car as both he and Blaze got out of the vehicle. The house looked larger and more ominous to Blaze than it did the last time she was there. No lights were on in the house except for one coming from the library. Jack grabbed Blaze's hand and led her up to the front door. The door was unlocked as they made their way through the foyer and into the grand hallway. Jack called out as they entered the open area.

"Mom? Pop? Where are you?" Suddenly a voice bellowed from the library.

"Hello, Jack. Glad you could make it. Now, make your way in here slowly and don't do anything that would make me pull this trigger."

Jack walked towards the library with Blaze close behind him. They walked through the door to see Thaddeus and Kate tied up in chairs across from one another. They couldn't see who the man was as the lighting was dim and he was hiding in the shadows. Jack briskly walked over to his parents, but the man stepped out of the shadows between Blaze and Jack pushing Jack to the floor. Blaze screamed as Jack fell and the man grabbed her and dragged her away from where Jack was laying. Jack attempted to get up, but the man warned him to stay where he was.

"Don't make any sudden moves Jack ole boy or I'll put a bullet right in her pretty little head." Jack knew the voice but didn't realize who he was until he looked at him as he held Blaze by her throat with the gun pointed at her head. It was Parks who was barely recognizable. His clothes were tattered, and he had a crazed look in his eyes like a mad man. Blaze was terrified and tried to break free from his grasp but was no match for his strength.

"Hold still girl before I smack you," he yelled at Blaze.

"You better not hurt her, man," Jack said furiously.

"Oh yeah? What you gonna do, man? You gonna stop a bullet 'cause if you make one move, I will put a cap in yo behind," Parks screamed.

Blaze through tears pleaded.

"Jack, no! Please just stay there I'm alright."

"Listen to her man. I'm in no mood. Like I was tellin ya folks here. I need a few things and then I can be on my way."

"Oh yeah? And what would that be?" Jack asked.

"Well, first I need cash, and a vehicle that I can use to get me across state lines. Once I get to New York I'll hop a plane and be on my way, but not before your momma and daddy hooks me up with enough money to keep me going.

"Man, this is crazy. Why you doing this, Parks? Why do you think my folks should help you?"

"Well, because I got the goods on yo momma there and it ain't pretty. I know they don't want this to get out. I'm thinking they want to keep it quiet and it's gonna cost."

"What the hell are you talkin about Parks?"

"Do you want to tell him, momma, or should I?" Parks asked Kate.

Parks was still holding Blaze with the gun to her head. He began to rant again which revealed his motives.

"You see, Newman, I've wanted to make partner at Brickhouse, Becker, and Shuman for as long as I've been with the firm. I had big plans when I came aboard, and I think things might have gone well had it not been for miss high and mighty Blaze Beaumont here. Every time an important account was brought to the firm Miss Beaumont was elected lead on the account and I was always the second on her team. It pissed me off that I had to report to her since she treated me like trash and always seemed to be given the praise when the accolades were given out. I vowed to get even with her so when she hooked up with you, I knew that was my opportunity to blow her out of the water with the information I gathered about you two. That's right! I followed you two around a bit. I saw you together at your apartment in the city. I was gonna use that information to discredit her and take my rightful place as the next in line for partnership, but it didn't work out that way, so I had to devise another plan. That's when I stumbled upon some interesting information about your lovely mother and what she had been up to all these years. Pierre ran off his mouth when he had too much to drink. All it took was a couple of shots and a few nights at a motel to get the information out of him. He was a willing participant. I even followed Mrs. Newman to a hotel in Atlantic City where she spent some time with Mr. Thompson right before that little party she threw down there. Isn't that right Kate?" Parks asked. He was still holding onto Blaze.

"Oh sorry! I forgot to take the gag outta your mouth," Parks pushed Blaze down on the sofa.

"Don't you move, Miss thang." He then walked over to Kate and removed the gag in her mouth. Tears were running down her cheeks as she began to yell.

"Jack, don't listen to him. He's lying and will do anything for money."

Parks slapped Kate across her face and Jack quickly reacted trying to get up to protect his mother from Parks, but he turned the gun on him saying.

"Go ahead hero. Try me! I dare you."

Jack slowly sat back down angry at what was happening to his family. With fury in his eyes Thaddeus tried hard to loosen the ropes around his hands but they were tied too tightly. He struggled as he watched his son and wife tormented by Parks.

"Okay so you want me to do the honors and tell your son and your husband what you been up to all these years?"

"No! No, please don't," Kate cried out.

Kate looked at Jack and then Thaddeus with tears in her eyes. She pleaded with Parks not to say anything, but Parks was out for revenge since Kate treated him with contempt whenever he was in her presence.

394 – TANYA BECKWITH

"Yeah, look at you now. Begging me—Parks, to keep quiet. All your kind is alike. You and miss high and mighty Beaumont here all uppity and thinkin' yall better than me. Well, whose got the upper hand now?"

"What's this all about Parks? If you need money, we'll give it to you. Name your price. I'm sure we can come to an agreement," Jack said.

"This ain't one of your business acquisitions, Newman. You can't negotiate your way outta this, so shut up. This between me and yo momma. She knows what's at stake."

"Then let me in on it, Parks. Maybe I can help. Just name the amount and we'll make it happen."

"Oh, is that so? You willing to pay me to keep this secret too? I know your mother is."

If it hadn't been for that fairy, Pierre, none of this would've been necessary. He had to develop a liking for me as if I would ever consider that freak. Well, ya see what happened to him. I didn't want to hurt the guy I just wanted some information from him. But he started making demands on my time and I couldn't have that. I didn't mean to kill him. It was an accident!"

Kate gasped in horror at Parks's admittance to Pierre's murder, while Jack stared at the man in disbelief. They all sat in horror as the murderer confessed to his crimes.

Thaddeus did you know your loving wife has been having an affair with her long-time lover, Ed? Yeah, that's right. They've been at it for years right under your noses and no one was the wiser. Thompson has been whipped ever since college when the two were sweethearts and they continued the affair right through your marriage and the birth of all your children. You might want to get a few paternity tests just to make sure they all yours, Thad."

Thaddeus growled like an animal that had been injured and tried again to get up from the chair, but the ropes were secured tightly, and he could only sit there looking at his wife with pain in his eyes. Jack was angry too and lunged at Parks only to be face to face with the barrel of the gun.

Parks let out a loud boisterous laugh as Kate tried to deny what he said.

"Don't listen to him. He's a liar. He'll say anything to get what he wants," she replied.

Blaze was horrified by Parks's confession. Tears streaming down her face blurred her vision. While Parks confessed to being Pierre's killer, Blaze saw someone else in the house. It was a man, a tall broad-shouldered man. The flash of light was coming from his gold watch. He was watching from the bathroom that was connected to the library. The door was cracked enough where he couldn't be seen by Parks, but Blaze could see him from where she was sitting. Blaze became more frightened than before but tried to stay calm. The man stood back close to the door so no one else could see him. Jack couldn't believe what Parks was saying about his mother. Kate was horrified that Parks knew about her affair with Ed. Thaddeus was unable to react at all. They were engrossed in what was happening and didn't see that someone else was in the room.

"Okay folks I'm growing tired of this charade, so it's time to wrap things up!" Parks began ranting and raving about how he was entitled to the Newman money and what he was going to do with it. He was waving the gun in the air and not making much sense. Jack looked at Blaze and motion with his head towards the doorway. Blaze frantically shook her head no and looked towards the bathroom door trying to get Jack to look and see the man there. Kate was sobbing quietly so not to annoy Parks. At the first chance he had of not being noticed, the lone figure slowly entered the room. Parks back was turned towards the man, so he didn't see him emerge from the bathroom. Both Jack and Blaze saw him as he leaped and wrestled Parks to the floor.

"Get down," Jack yelled out. Blaze dived onto the floor as Jack ran toward Kate to shield her from the melee. The two men were fighting for control of the gun with Parks being overwhelmed by the huge figure that emerged from the shadows. With his mouth gagged and hands tied all Thaddeus could do was look in horror at the two men struggling for control. Kate looked in horror as she realized the man was Ed Thompson.

"Oh no! Ed! Ed!" she screamed out. A shot rang out loudly echoing through the room. Blaze covered her ears and screamed as Jack crawled across the floor to her. There was silence as the two men slumped onto the floor with neither moving. Then Ed's hand moved as he pushed Parks off him. Parks had blood oozing out of his shoulder. The shot wasn't fatal but was enough to stop the frantic murderer from killing again. Ed quickly got up from the floor with the gun still in his hand. He looked around and spotted Kate and hurried over to her.

"Are you alright?" he asked. Kate nodded. After Jack made sure that Blaze was okay, he went to his dad and removed the gag from his mouth and untied him. Kate brushed past Ed towards Thaddeus as he rubbed his wrist. She flung her arms around his neck sobbing.

"Oh, Thad. Are you okay?" she asked.

"I'm fine, Kate. Did he hurt you?"

"No." she sighed. "I'm okay."

"Good!" Thaddeus said.

"Thad, let me explain."

"There's no need Kate. I think I understand everything now," Thaddeus said walking away from his wife.

"Pop, you can't believe what that maniac said. He'd say anything to get revenge and money."

"Jack, stay outta this. This is between me and your mother," Thaddeus said as he went to the liquor cabinet and poured himself a drink."

Kate walked towards her husband.

"Can we please talk about this?"

"No, Kate, we can't. Did you really think I didn't know what's been going on all this time? What kind of fool do you take me for?" Thaddeus asked.

Kate was shocked. She stood there trembling more out of fear for what her husband knew than what had just transpired in their home.

"Shouldn't we call the police?" Blaze asked.

"They're on their way," Ed answered. "I called them before I arrived. I knew that Parks would pull something like this. I found evidence that he was Pierre's killer."

"What do you mean you knew he'd pull something like this?" Jack asked.

"I began to look into Pierre's murder, so I went to his rooming house to see if there were any clues the police overlooked. Pierre kept a box under the floorboard in his room in the city. Inside was a photo of him and Parks at the Trade Winds Club, a flash drive, and a couple receipts for a motel room in town. Pierre recorded his conversation with Parks. Seems he was smarter than Parks gave him credit for. It seems that Parks was leading a double life and he used Pierre for what he thought would be a big payday."

"So, Parks really did kill Pierre. But why?" Blaze asked.

"My guess is that Pierre threatened to reveal Parks's plan, so he panicked and killed him. Poor Pierre never saw it coming and Parks was as surprised as anyone. Once the deed was done, Parks knew he was in deep, so he came after your parents with a not so very well thought out scheme; one that backfired," Ed stated.

Just then the police arrived in full force banging on the front door. Several patrol cars were parked on the property with Wilcox and Shields leading the charge. They entered the library where everything had just taken place.

"Everyone alright in here?" Wilcox asked.

"As well as can be," Thaddeus said.

"Well, Parks, looks like your plan didn't work out so good," Wilcox said.

Parks was coherent but still on the floor bleeding out.

Wilcox spoke to one of the policemen.

"Get the paramedics in here and patch this guy up so we can take him in."

Parks never said a word as the paramedics began to take his vitals and place a temporary bandage on his wound.

"We need to get this guy to the hospital," one of the paramedics said.

"Okay, but I want two armed officers with him at all times. I'm not taking any chances with this guy. He's a cold-blooded murderer," Wilcox stated.

"I know you folks have been through quite an ordeal, but I'll need your statements so please everyone stay put."

The police were at the Newman's for the next three hours. The local news outlets were on the scene trying to get the scoop on what happened. Kate and Thaddeus were questioned first, while Blaze and Jack sat in the kitchen awaiting their turn. Blaze called Jewels to let her know what happened and to assure her that everything was okay in case she heard anything on the news.

The rest of the Newman clan showed up to garner support for their parents and brother. Ed Thompson was questioned and then released and told not to leave the city. He tried to get a few minutes with Kate, but Thaddeus made sure that after he was questioned that he was escorted out of his home. The night seemed to never end, and it was dawn before the family was left alone. Reporters hung around the property but were told to keep a distance from the house. Kate followed Thaddeus upstairs to their bedroom where she found her husband packing an overnight bag.

"Thad, we should talk!" she said.

"Not now, Kate. I'm exhausted."

"Well, why don't you let me get you something to eat. You can take a shower and then go to bed."

"No, I think I'll stay in the city for a few days," Thaddeus replied. "I need some time to process all of this."

"Of course, you do darling, but we need to do this together," she pleaded.

"No, Kate. We don't. Maybe you should call, Ed. I'm sure he'll be happy to comfort you.

I, too, have someone to help me through this," Thaddeus said as he took his bag and left the bedroom and his home. Kate sat on her bed and wept.

James and Michael decided to stay with their mother. So, after things began to settle down, Jack drove Blaze back to his apartment in the city.

"This has been a hell of a couple of days. You alright baby?" Jack pulled Blaze closer into his arms.

"I'm not sure," she answered honestly.

Jack was in shock.

"I'm still trying to process my mother with Ed. I knew he had a thing for her. Hell, everybody did. But an affair? For over thirty years? That's just unimaginable."

"I'm sorry, Jack." Blaze looked into his eyes. "What do think will happen with your parents now?"

"I don't know. My dad is probably crushed and my mother—well I don't know who to support on this. I can't think about it now."

Jack pulled Blaze to him and kissed her hard and long.

"If you ever do that to me..."

"Shh don't say that." Blaze whispered placing her fingers on his lips. "I love you Jack and I want to be with you and only you for as long as you want me."

"Then you better plan on forever cause that's how long it's gonna be, Ace."

"Make love to me, Jack," Blaze requested as she kissed him.

Jack drew her to him in a longing and passionate embrace. They stayed in bed for the next three days making plans for their future, and of course, making love!

The End.

TANYA BECKWITH

Tanya Beckwith lives in Pennsylvania with her husband and her favorite feline, Cali. Beckwith's background includes writing for media, public and community relations, sound design and engineering, news writing for radio and television, and hosting a weekly music program.

She has an extensive background in communications. During and after college, she was awarded the opportunity to lend her services in the Office of The Provost at the University of Pennsylvania, the Office of the Chief of Staff for the Mayor's Office of the City of Philadelphia, and the Philadelphia Housing Authority's Office of the Executive Director.

Her passions include her two children and grandchildren, music of all genres, films, dancing, and of course, reading and writing different forms of literature.

uct-compliance